"Dale Suderman was a remarkable character. His essays and journals will enlighten conventional insider Mennonites about the possibilities of outsider identity."
—JAMES JUHNKE,
professor emeritus of history, Bethel College

"*Coffee with Dale Suderman* might have been an alternative title for this absorbing, wide-ranging reader. People who had the good fortune of meeting Dale will hear the voice of a supremely gifted conversationalist jump off the pages as he reflects on topics that extend from being a Mennonite soldier in Vietnam to male identity, to homelessness, addiction, and the challenges facing the Christian church."
—MURRAY HIEBERT,
author of *Under Beijing's Shadow: Southeast Asia's China Challenge*

"*The Essential Dale Suderman Reader* offers a much-needed distillation of the life and mind of one of the great underground intellectuals to emerge from the American Anabaptist tradition. The writings and interpretations gathered here serve as the nearest approximation of what it was like to sit for hours with Dale in some greasy spoon, his agora, engaged in the co-construction of his two favorite things: deep conversation and abiding friendship."
—ADAM SCHRAG,
senior lecturer of communication, University of Minnesota

"In some ways, Dale Suderman lived against the grain of his traditional Mennonite upbringing: he served as an American soldier in Vietnam; he was a gay man; he struggled and overcame an addiction to alcohol; he smoked incessantly. But *The Essential Dale Suderman Reader* reveals how deeply and profoundly Suderman manifested Anabaptist values of nonconformity, hospitality, empathy, peacemaking, and loving God by loving others. Those who knew Suderman through his words will be enriched by this volume, as will those encountering him here for the very first time."
—MELANIE SPRINGER MOCK,
professor of English, George Fox University

"Daniel Born has assembled an intriguing and varied collection of texts that allows access to an astute and candid observer of history and culture. Dale Suderman's writings present, and then undercut, an easy reading of his world, highlighting the primacy of the observer—in this case a nomadic, questioning, and evolving Mennonite Kansas farm boy—as he attempts to make sense of inscrutable political, theological, and cultural realities. This 'most subjective reminiscence' is certainly worthy of attention."
—CHRISTOPHER M. DICK,
professor of English, Tabor College

THE ESSENTIAL DALE SUDERMAN READER

The Essential Dale Suderman Reader

Journals, Essays, Letters, Interpretations

edited and with a foreword by
DANIEL BORN

RESOURCE *Publications* · Eugene, Oregon

THE ESSENTIAL DALE SUDERMAN READER
Journals, Essays, Letters, Interpretations

Copyright © 2024 Daniel Born. All rights reserved. Except for brief quotations in critical publications or reviews, no part of this book may be reproduced in any manner without prior written permission from the publisher. Write: Permissions, Wipf and Stock Publishers, 199 W. 8th Ave., Suite 3, Eugene, OR 97401.

Resource Publications
An Imprint of Wipf and Stock Publishers
199 W. 8th Ave., Suite 3
Eugene, OR 97401

www.wipfandstock.com

PAPERBACK ISBN: 979-8-3852-1765-6
HARDCOVER ISBN: 979-8-3852-1766-3
EBOOK ISBN: 979-8-3852-1767-0

05/13/24

To all the friends of Dale, far and near.

Contents

Foreword | xi

Acknowledgments | xvii

From Ebenfeld to Vietnam, 1944–1968: Letters and Journals | 1

Beginnings: Looking at a Picture | 1

Gay and Mennonite Brethren | 2

In the Army: Letters Home, 1966–1968 | 3

Letters to Keith Harder, 1968 | 20

Undated Draft of an Article for Mennonite Publication | 28

Soldier Home: Writing Against War: Letters, Journals, Journalism, 1969–1997 | 30

Moratorium Day Speech | 30

Letter Sent to President Richard M. Nixon from Dale Suderman and Daryl Schmidt | 36

Letter to Reverend Dick | 40

One Week in Saigon | 43

Will You Be Our Son? | 45

A Failure of Liberalism | 46

Of Cocks, Contras, and the Cubs | 53

The Vietnam Veterans Against the War March in Chicago | 54

Ginsberg (1926–1997) | 58

Sweet Home Chicago to the World: Selected Essays, 1996–2008 | 61

On This Winter Solstice | 61

9/11 | 63

New and Cosmic Billboards | 65
Nice | 66
The World Is Already All Around Us | 68
Want More People? Be "Interesting" | 70
Pushing for a Tax on the Poor and Stupid May Have Merit | 72
Figuring Out the Male Condition at the O'Hare Ramada Inn | 74
Thinking About the Men's Movement | 80
Euphoria and Banality: The Quest for Getting High | 90
First Amendment Is a Broad Freedom | 98
"Dumb Bomb" Fallout Still Evident | 100
Raking Leaves Was Hard Work to Avoid | 102
Goat Gland Brinkley | 104
The Groenings, the Simpsons, and the Mennonites | 106
You Know You Are a Criminal If: | 109
Galileo's Heresy Predates Darwin's | 110
Osage Orange Trees Deserve Respect | 112
A Meditation on Carl Jung | 114
The Age of Abundance | 131
Moody, the Media, and the Birth of Modern Evangelism: A Cautionary Tale | 139
Grumpy Old Men | 143
McDonald's Goes Bust | 144
On Reading Paul Fussell | 146
Exposing the Demons of War | 152
Superman | 157
When the Bible Divided the Land | 158
All Strauss's Children | 163
Notes on Manliness | 170
Chinese Whorehouse Case Note, or How I Was Taken to a Chinese Whorehouse in Gary, Indiana and What I Learned On the Way Back to Chicago | 171
Thinking About Andrea Dworkin and John Stoltenberg | 173
Islamic Profiles | 175

Why Vietnam Is Vacation Location | 181

Cynicism as Therapy: Seeing the Log in Our Own Eye | 183

The God Who Provides Parking Places | 194

Interpretations | 198

Remembering Dale Suderman, by Keith Harder | 198

"Little Brother" Comes Home Sooner Than Anyone Planned, by Elva Suderman | 201

Dale Suderman: Seer of Friendship, by John Kampen | 204

The Arc of a Restless Mind, by Ben Hartley | 210

Dale Suderman: Edge Worker, by Tim Nafziger | 215

Shock and Awe, by Ruth Harder | 221

Letter to Dale Suderman, by Clint Stucky | 223

Insatiable Drive, Profound Passion, by Delbert Wiens | 226

Contributors | 231

Foreword

BY ALMOST ANY STANDARD, Dale Suderman led a life so protean and unconventional that to attempt an account of his career, his multiple personae, and his range of intellectual interests is to risk cognitive whiplash. William Blake tells us in *The Marriage of Heaven and Hell* that "Without Contraries is no progression." Dale carried multiple contraries within his complicated self. This collection of Dale's writing affords a glimpse of a man who explored his own contradictions with unceasing curiosity. And he was happy to talk them through—usually over a cup of black coffee and cheap cigarettes.

The entry for Dale in The Global Anabaptist Mennonite Encyclopedia Online (GAMEO) describes him as an "administrator, businessman, and denominational critic." Those are good places for a biographer to start an investigation, although to his closest familiars, Dale could also be described as a prophet, prankster, listener, skeptic, and the best of friends. Some of us thought of him as a kind of shaman, long before that term had been debased by New Age woo-woo, not to mention political chaos monkeys. Dale's journey into sobriety through Alcoholics Anonymous made possible his practice as an addictions counselor, and his immersion in Jungian thinking suggests that the "wounded healer," a central trope in shamanic practice, influenced the way he thought about himself and others.

The writings collected here, both by and about him, explore the terrain of his restless mind. This is not an exhaustive collection of Dale's writings but a representative and essential one. The selections provide a means of seeing the arc of his experience that began in rural Kansas and extended through a formative Army tour of duty in Vietnam, and subsequently life in the American Midwest, including three decades in Chicago—before he returned to Kansas after suffering a stroke in 2008. That event silenced his pen, though he retained a measure of his conversational brilliance and continued to read voraciously. The brain hemorrhage struck him when he was not quite sixty-four years old. He would survive another twelve years which, to borrow a phrase from John Keats, might best be considered a "posthumous existence."

Adding to his gifts as a writer, Dale excelled in the art of conversation. He was an entertaining talker, whether one-on-one or in front of a college crowd. He could be charming and he did not mind basking in the glow of a well-turned phrase. His skill as a friend and as a mental health counselor had much to do with his ability to make others *feel listened to*. He treated conversation with fellow human beings as a sacred institution. This gift, combined with his stamina, resulted in the multitudes of case histories he scribbled over the years in his journal or on the backs of napkins in late night restaurant sessions. Like Studs Terkel, perhaps Chicago's most famous journalist and raconteur, Dale knew both how to tell a tale and how to listen for the life stories that fill many of his notebooks. Dale's conversation could soar. He was also content listening to people talk. He believed that personal narratives are more than the sum of their entertainment value—though he would let you know when his attention began to drift. For Dale, these accounts taken in the aggregate are the stuff of which history is made.

He delighted in exposing cant. He loved the writing of Jonathan Swift and was quite proud of his own riff on *A Modest Proposal*. In Dale's version, the rule for warfare going forward is that you are allowed to kill only as many people as you can eat. He liked to shock his listeners with harsh, sometimes flagrantly dirty talk. In this way he emulated Allen Ginsberg, the Beat poet he first heard at a live performance in Wichita in 1966. He could go deadpan after drily uttering some outrage, either to test his audience's IQ or take the measure of their Emily Post index of squeamishness. Or else, after a punch line, he would flash his perverse grin, displaying his mouthful of crooked teeth in all their splendor. In this way he signaled that it was safe for you to laugh or applaud. Like comedians in the vein of Larry David, he was not afraid to demonstrate delight in his own wit.

The best analogy for Dale's verbal skills has to be Oscar Wilde. "I have nothing to declare except my genius," Oscar once said. The words apply to Dale, who typically dropped sayings like this: "One of my . . . principles with clients is Rule Number 9: After age seventeen, you are not allowed to use the word *hypocrite* unless you are actually Jesus." If he was going to put the verbal knife in and twist it, he preferred to do so with his barracuda smile. One of Dale's friends, the Dead Sea Scrolls scholar and professor John Kampen, said at Dale's funeral: "I never had a boring conversation. There were conversations that I wished would end because I was mentally and emotionally exhausted, but I was never bored."

I met Dale in 1975, while I was a freshman at Tabor College in central Kansas. We met in the town of Newton, where he served as an administrator for the General Conference Mennonite Church's alternative service program. In those years, Dale projected charisma, experience, and wily strength. In his passport picture from 1975 he evokes both Che Guevara and Lord Byron but with none of the dandy and more than a touch of the bookish nerd to offset the brooding thinker. He spent most evenings, often late into the night, at Leonida's twenty-four-hour restaurant inside Newton's aging brick train station, where he went to read, smoke, drink coffee, and find new audiences for his conversational addiction. Like other college students who frequented Leonida's for late-night study sessions, I was intrigued by the mystique of Dale. This was a nice Mennonite boy from the rural community of Ebenfeld who had ditched his pacifist heritage and actually enlisted in the Army, gone to the war, seen the Tet offensive, and then returned Stateside to double down as a hardcore peace activist and complete a master's degree in theology at Anabaptist Mennonite Biblical Seminary in Elkhart, Indiana.

In those years he alluded cryptically to his alternative sexuality, and not until he moved to Chicago in the late 1970s and bought a bookstore on Clark Street in Lincoln Park, did he come out of the closet. I moved to Chicago in 1980, when my wife Mary took a position as social worker on the stroke unit at Illinois Masonic Hospital in the Lake View neighborhood. Only then did I begin to understand more about Dale's jagged, complex self. He hired me at his bookstore, and from him I learned the basics of the business, not to mention rambling tours of Boystown's bars and bookstores several blocks north on Clark and Broadway.

Dale cultivated a vast network of friends and customers, all attesting to his myriad interests as well as insatiable hunger for conversation and companionship. There were the radical nuns at the Cenacle Retreat House on Fullerton, who came in to buy dozens of copies of works by Dorothy Day and Thomas Merton; there was evangelical author Phil Yancey and church historian Donald Dayton; there was Chicago news anchorman Bill Curtis, and *Windy City Times* journalist and gay activist Jon-Henri Damski. There was nationally syndicated film critic Roger Ebert—who would eventually become Dale's sponsor in Alcoholics Anonymous. Through the front door came the lost boys from Moody Bible Institute and Wheaton, ostensibly looking to purchase obscure titles by C. S. Lewis and the rest of the Inklings, but actually more interested in moral guidance and a father figure they could trust. There were cruise ship song-and-dance entertainers who had second careers as drag queens. There were eccentric Lincoln Park millionaires who, in their ragged, unkempt appearance, did not look very different from the homeless drifters and winos who traversed Clark and Lincoln. Sixty-year-old bag ladies shopped in the store, ready to argue that animal rights were more important than human rights. At the center of this circus was the ringmaster, Dale.

Bookstore customers inevitably asked for Dale. If he was around, and in the mood, he'd take them out for coffee at the Medina diner on the corner of Clark and Fullerton, sit in one of the red Naugahyde booths with them, and talk. He was making friends and collecting life stories.

When the bookstore closed, Dale segued into his final career as a mental health counselor for the Salvation Army. By this time, he had achieved sobriety for a number of years, and he did individual and group therapy with men struggling with addictions. They spanned the entire American class system, all the way from West Side destitution to North Shore inherited money and corporate boardrooms. Some of them had just been released from jail. The life stories of his clients as well as the budding men's movement in American culture gave new direction for Dale's increasingly ambitious writing about male identity and development, sexual identity and gender, and about Jungian thinking in general. He talked convincingly about the shadow self because he was so transparent about his own shadows. For many of us who counted ourselves his friends, he became a crucial architect of our own mental categories.

Dale was most comfortable in the role of outsider—of the maverick prophet, of the gonzo journalist. But perhaps the most important statement he had to make was as a sinner coming to the Episcopal communion rail for grace. This occurred as many of his friends, myself included, drifted in and out of various states of agnostic doubt. His voice does not echo from the groves of academe or learned ecclesiastical councils. He understood power and he knew how to wield it, but he had no interest in becoming its representative or its tool. He hated bullshit, whether it came from the mouths of church leaders or Chicago aldermen or even liberal-left activists with whom he frequently associated, whether they were singing the righteousness of *sandinismo* or the ethical free-trade, shade-grown coffee from El Salvador.

He eventually understood his sexuality and became comfortable with who he was. This process took years of searching, reading, and talking. (I hesitate to say sexual *identity,* for even though Dale embraced being gay, he often spoke of himself in language that anticipated "fluidity" at least two decades before the term went mainstream.) Dale's knowledge of the field of addictions counseling was vast. He came by it honestly in terms of hard experience, encyclopedic reading, and hundreds of clients. That knowledge runs through much of Dale's writing, and a couple of pieces here, "Euphoria and Banality" and "Chinese Whorehouse Case Note," demonstrate that whether in a college convocation lecture or a case history scribbled at night, Dale was trying to make sense of the path to sobriety he had taken—and was helping others to take.

This selection of Dale's writing suggests the breadth of Dale's mind and the polymath quality of his reading. The contents include previously published and unpublished essays, while all the letters and journal entries are seeing print for the very first time. Whether writing about the history of twentieth-century warfare or evangelist D. L. Moody's relationship to Gilded Age tycoons, Dale imagined an audience of thinking people, and he delivered in a voice that was granular, plainspoken, and direct. You didn't need to have a graduate degree to keep up with him, but you had to pay attention.

And if he was no narrow academic specialist, let it also be said that Dale could do different voices. The collection contains some of Dale's "View from Afar" columns that regularly appeared in the *Hillsboro Free Press*, a Kansas newspaper, for more than a decade. In these essays Dale laid down his wisdom as a small-town insider who spoke the vernacular but also provided the perspective of a cosmopolitan world citizen. In his last active years, he traveled to Paris, London, Vietnam, the Mediterranean coast of France, Colombia, and various other locales from his home base in metropolitan Chicago, where he liked to sit on his roof deck porch on Huron Street. In the best of the many editorial features he wrote for his hometown newspaper, Dale summoned a distinctive voice best described as an amalgam of legendary Kansas editor William Allen White, American humorist Will Rogers, and Chicago newspaperman Mike Royko.

Which brings to mind one evening in the mid-1990s, when I sat with Dale at the counter of Chicago's Billy Goat Tavern on Lower Wacker Drive. Who should appear but Mike Royko himself, bursting into the joint with the manic energy of a marching band field commander and trailing a posse of at least fifteen people, most of them thirty to forty years his junior. Royko sported a wrinkled suit that matched the topography of his beaten, late-career face. The Billy Goat staff started pulling together tables in an adjacent room for the posse to gather around.

Royko, always eager for adulation and love, spotted Dale and me as he crossed the room to hold court with his salon. We waved. What else could we do? This must have bathed his ego in a warm flood of admiration, because he acknowledged us. There was that moment of electricity when you feel transfigured by a celebrity's presence.

Looking back on that event now from the distance of thirty years, I realize that the great man was actually sitting next to me. Dale, like Royko, I've come to realize, had the ability to make sociability a transcendent experience. The essays collected here don't stand as an exhaustive record of Dale Suderman's voice and wisdom, but they represent a step toward greater comprehension of him in his time, and in all his timeless, uncouth glory.

Dale was complicated, yet like Walt Whitman, who claimed to "sound" his "barbaric yawp over the roofs of the world," he knew how to distill his voice to the raw truth of the moment. In this way, like Whitman, he was "untranslatable." He consistently wrestled with the question of how to live with himself and others. He exhibited relentless self-awareness. These writings comprise their own rationale for preserving Dale's vision. Perhaps they will bring smiles of recognition to those who knew him. I hope they will also appeal to those who never met the man but can recognize a kindred spirit, one who understood the challenges of negotiating life's restless journey at the margin of many different worlds.

Daniel Born
Chicago, Illinois
2024

Acknowledgments

THE FOLLOWING ESSAYS FIRST appeared in Dale Suderman's regular column, "View from Afar," in the *Hillsboro Free Press*: "On This Winter Solstice"; "9/11"; "New and Cosmic Billboards"; "Nice"; "The World Is Already All Around Us"; "Want More People? Be 'Interesting'"; "Pushing for a Tax on the Poor and Stupid May Have Merit"; "First Amendment Is a Broad Freedom"; "'Dumb Bomb' Fallout Still Evident"; "Raking Leaves Was Hard Work to Avoid"; "Goat Gland Brinkley"; "Galileo's Heresy Predates Darwin's"; "Osage Orange Trees Deserve Respect"; "Grumpy Old Men"; "McDonald's Goes Bust"; "Superman"; "Why Vietnam is Vacation Location."

"One Week in Saigon" was originally published in *The Mennonite* magazine.

"Will You Be Our Son?" originally appeared in *Fellowship* magazine.

"A Failure of Liberalism" originally appeared in *The Post-American* magazine, Oct./Nov. 1975. Reprinted with permission from *Sojourners*, (800) 714-7474, www.sojo.net.

Several essays were originally published in *The Common Review*, the quarterly magazine of the Great Books Foundation: "Exposing the Demons of War"; "When the Bible Divided the Land"; "All Strauss's Children"; "Islam in America."

"Moody, the Media, and the Birth of Evangelism" was originally published in *Books & Culture*.

"The Simpsons and the Mennonites" was originally published in the *Hillsboro Free Press* in 2007. Subsequent versions of it appeared in periodicals including *The Mennonite* (now *Anabaptist World*), *Mennonite World Review*, and *Roots and Branches*, the periodical of the Mennonite Historical Society of British Columbia.

"Thinking About the Men's Movement" was originally presented as a lecture at Marietta College, Marietta, Ohio in 1996.

"Euphoria and Banality" was originally presented as a lecture at Bethel College, North Newton, Kansas in 2001.

"Cynicism as Therapy: Seeing the Log in Our Own Eye," a conference presentation made by Dale Suderman in Evanston, Illinois in 2008, was first published in *Cynicism and Hope: Reclaiming Discipleship in a Postdemocratic Society*, ed. Meg E. Cox (Cascade Books, 2009): pp. 41–51.

The selections in section one under the heading, *From Ebenfeld to Vietnam*, are published here for the first time, as are the following selections under the heading *Soldier Home: Writing Against War*: "Moratorium Day," "Letter to Richard M. Nixon," "Of Cocks, Contras, and the Cubs," "Vietnam Vets Against the War March," and "Ginsberg." Other essays seeing print for the first time include: "Figuring Out the Male Condition at the O'Hare Ramada Inn"; "You Know You Are a Criminal If"; "Notes on Carl Jung"; "The Age of Abundance"; "On Reading Paul Fussell"; "Notes on Manliness"; "Chinese Whorehouse Case Note"; "Thinking About Andrea Dworkin and John Stoltenberg"; "The God Who Provides Parking Spaces."

Special thanks to John D. Thiesen, Co-Director of Libraries and Archivist at Bethel College, North Newton, Kansas, which houses the Literary Estate of John Dale Suderman, including the collected essays, books, journals, and correspondence.

John Kampen was an invaluable source of encouragement and critical reflection for this collection of writing. Many thanks as well to Keith Harder, Ben Hartley, and Tim Nafziger, who provided feedback, suggestions, and wisdom in thinking about Dale's life and career.

From Ebenfeld to Vietnam, 1944–1968
Letters and Journals

BEGINNINGS: LOOKING AT A PICTURE

Journals, 21 September 1997

Cleaning up Dad's stuff, I found and reproduced an aerial photo of the farm where I was raised. Many flashbacks. First, I think everybody in the family hated that farm. Dad and Mom bought this farm in the late 1930s. Its location was eccentric—located exactly midpoint in a section (square mile of land) and thus a half mile from even a vaguely improved road. The house was small and the outbuildings probably decrepit already when they purchased it. The farm lay in a sort of cultural no man's land. It was on the edge of the Ridge School District—probably a pathetic one-room school even by one-room school standards of the time. It was exactly halfway between Hillsboro (German Mennonite) and Peabody (old line English/German), two towns in conflict since World War I over the issue of military support for the American cause. It was outside the traditional land use pattern of the Ebenfeld Church where our family had attended since its founding in 1876. This meant the farm was low status by Ebenfeld cultural standards. Dad bought this, his first farm, from Mr. Eberle, probably an Irish Catholic farmer, wealthy, with one spinster daughter. Eberle was Dad's mentor at the time—and he held the mortgage.

The farm was nowhere. A few trees, but no stream, no landscape feature defined it. It was as though a few unpainted buildings had simply been abandoned there.

I was born there, and, a year later, my brother Ron followed. Here I came to consciousness. Growing up between age three and seven,

I remember Kansas in one of its periodic "wet" cycles—with record rainfall and floods in nearby towns. Life was playing in the mud in the flat yard in front of the house. Then the "dry" years began, five or six years of record drought. Wells dried up and cattle were sold since there was no water or grass for them. Farmers survived on winter wheat, which could survive on a few spring rains, but corn and milo were exercises in futility.

GAY AND MENNONITE BRETHREN

Journals, 31 May 1995

When I was twelve, I went to the Mennonite Brethren District youth camp. A very popular coach at the church college led a class for boys about sex. One story stands out vividly. While he advocated nonresistance, he did say that an exception could be made if one was approached by a homosexual. I remember going on a walk by myself, very confused and frightened. As a young follower of Jesus, I could not kill communists or Nazis. But I was so evil that I deserved to be killed because of what I had already done and continued to feel about other boys.

The next summer when there was a class on dealing with the draft, I brazenly announced that I would never be a CO (conscientious objector). My reasoning was shallow but my emotions ran very deep.

In recent years I have recontacted two male sexual partners from my high school and college years, partially to make amends for my involvement with them. Curiously, both are pastors now in evangelical churches. X, who had taught me the joys of sex with another boy as a teenager, remembered his anger that we had another sexual encounter while in college at my initiation. I offered an apology.

"You were a scary person to most of us guys. You were soft, while we were trying to learn how to be macho and tough. We were afraid of you too because you were smart. Today as a pastor I have to learn to be soft and gentle to be really a compassionate pastor, and smart like you were. I do see the irony of that." We parted, as friends again, realizing we were now in very different worlds.

I was even more anxious when I contacted the other pastor. We had not had even secondhand contact for many decades. I did not recognize him when we first met in a restaurant. He was middle-aged and paunchy, not the shy sensitive college freshman I once knew. When I delicately brought up our past relationship in college, he laughed.

"Why would you apologize for that?" he said. "I was a totally emotionally suppressed teenager when we were students together. That was the first time another person ever cared about me." He went on to report having a great family and moderately successful pastoral career. I walked away relieved but a bit confused by his reaction.

IN THE ARMY: LETTERS HOME, 1966–1968

Dale writes in a journal entry dated 17 October 1999: "These are excerpts from correspondence to my parents and other persons while I was in the Army from 1966 to 1968, age twenty-two to twenty-four. Keep in mind, during this time my mother was first experiencing the beginnings of a long-term illness which eventually took her life, and my brother Ron was in the Pacific with the U.S. Navy. For that reason, I kept the letters to family deliberately safe and superficial. Before I went into the Army, I took my first tour of America. Drove a car from Kansas to Chicago, to Elkhart, Indiana, then New York City and Washington, D.C. This was my first time east of the Mississippi and I had no agenda. Following are parts of a letter from Elkhart where there was free housing at a seminary conference. I had never heard of the seminary but somehow knew about the conference. Plus, I needed a shower."

1966, Elkhart, Indiana

Dear Dad and Mom,

Well, here I am in Elkhart, Indiana. I was driving through Missouri when I decided to go to Chicago. On Sunday I went to the Woodlawn Mennonite Church which is the major Mennonite Church in Chicago. About two-thirds of the membership is Black and the church is located in the worst slums of Chicago. Fascinating service that moved me very deeply. In the afternoon I toured the Chicago Museum of Natural History, the Aquarium, took a boat ride on Lake

Michigan ($1.00) and just walked around downtown. Monday, I toured Chicago's Chinatown, drove by the stockyards, and some of the downtown area. The entire core area of the city is predominantly Black. The overwhelming thing is the crowded conditions that most people face. Still, I love Chicago and would like to live there someday. It has everything. A few miles out of town it's like you're in Marion County. Lake Michigan is as nice as an ocean. Many of the residential areas are fabulous. So the city has everything. I'm real proud of my ability to handle Chicago traffic but actually it's easier to drive in than Elkhart or Wichita. At least streets are marked and drivers know their business.

1966, Fort Leonard Wood, Missouri (End of basic training)

Dear Mom and Dad,

Got my medal for rifle proficiency. Not much of an honor as everyone gets one. The slow-moving Texan that seemed to be able to talk only about farming and cows got his orders this week. He is to study Chinese and become a security agent. Found out he spent two years in Vietnam where his father directed highway construction and he has almost a master's in modern literature. Funny guy never mentioned it.

In a journal entry of 17 October 1999, Dale comments on his time at Fort Leonard Wood: "I had rejected Officer Candidate School, had no orders, and was stuck in a holding company doing odd jobs on base."

January 14, 1966

Ft. Leonard Wood

Dear Dad and Mom,

So what have I been doing? Finished the two paperbacks I bought in Newton, then read a book by Hans Küng that L. J. Franz raved about for a whole hour after he read it. Küng is a German Catholic theologian and critic of the church. Also reading *Catholic, Protestant, Jew*, a classic study done in 1958 . . .

Writing in 1999, Dale would preface the following letter home with this comment: "UH HUBRIS, give me a break, I was twenty-two."

1966, Fort Rucker, Alabama

Dear Dad and Mom,

The additional work I took over has pretty well straightened itself out. This is the third time that I've been asked to straighten out a mess in an office and it gets easier all the time and more enjoyable. The first time was in the public relations office at Tabor, the second time in the off-campus housing situation at Wichita, and now the Army. Disorganized as I generally am, for some reason I find setting other people's affairs straight and setting up an orderly system so it is not too difficult for me. I still think that some day—a long time from now—I could end up in college administration—maybe as a dean.

1967, Fort Rucker, Alabama

Dear Dad and Mom,

On Sunday morning Darrell left for Wichita and I went to the most unusual church service of my life. The church was simply a group of people who met in a private home. Several were ministers who had been kicked out of their churches for civil rights activities. For the first hour we sat in the kitchen and drank coffee while the children had Sunday school in the living room. Then we had church in the living room. It was mainly testimonies and silence (Quaker style). Afterwards we had lunch together. All have suffered tremendous hardship because of their beliefs—several have spent time in prison. They ranged from age twenty-four to seventy-five. Yet none of them were bitter and they were tremendously open and warm people—laughing all the time. I have to admit they made a tremendous impression on me. I didn't get a chance to talk to Vincent Harding. Called him and he said he had sent his wife and kids out and was refusing to see anyone because he was finishing some writing that was on a deadline . . .

Going back to that Sunday morning service. I think it was the nearest thing to a New Testament church out of the book of Acts which I have seen. The people were from all levels of society—farmers and college profs. All were outcasts in some form and had suffered for their beliefs. The services are not held at any one place. The last Sunday they had met in a mountain cabin with friends from Tennessee, who may be going to jail because the Tennessee legislature is trying to get the records from their social work center to find out who is supporting the integrated school up in the mountains. They won't give up the records for fear of reprisal. (The legislature of Tennessee claims they are communists.) They never plan ahead more than a week for service and never know who will come. They have no name and no leader—only a common spirit. Extraordinary thing—really.

1967, Fort Rucker, Alabama

Dear Mom and Dad,

Well, it looks like I'm going to be doing some traveling while I'm in the Army after all. Although it's not completely certain, it looks like I will be going to Vietnam in the Saigon region for about eight months. My tour will begin the last week of January. The type of work is still uncertain but will be some type of clerical work. Needless to say, my first reaction was not entirely positive to this news. But then again, I've had things pretty good so far, and most certainly my good fortune will continue. Went to the Peanut Festival in Dothan, Alabama Saturday afternoon with some friends. Did you know that 50 percent of the peanuts grown in the U.S. are from this area?

Got to run now—am writing this over my noon hour. Like I say—nothing is 100 percent certain about this little trip—where or when or what but will let you now as the picture clears up. Do hope this doesn't upset you—because things will work out very well—they always do.

Love,
Dale

1 February 1968

Fort Buckner Army Base, Okinawa, Japan

Dear Mom and Dad,

Greetings from the South Pacific. The last days have been very interesting—to say the least. We left Oakland at about 3:30 and went to Travis Air Force Base by bus and then 165 of us boarded a Boeing 707 jet, Flying Tiger Airlines. Flew to Anchorage, Alaska and then to Okinawa. Anyway, now we're stranded in Okinawa because of the attack on the airports in Vietnam. Now the word is that we leave at six a.m. tomorrow. Finally got some sleep last night. Hope to be at Bien Hoa Air Base by lunch tomorrow...

Love,
Dale

In his journal entry for 17 October 1999, Dale commented on the previous letter: "This ... was a bit disingenuous. The Tet Offensive had happened [launched by the Vietcong on January 30, 1968]. I was aware it was a disaster for U.S. forces and that the airport was nearly overrun by VC, but hoped my parents had not noticed."

4 February 1968, Sunday

Bien Hoa, Vietnam

Dear Family,
We arrived safely and happily here about one a.m. this morning. Our transportation was a flying box car. We traveled about ten miles from the airport to the 90th Replacement battalion by bus. The weather is very dry and hot. The country looks like Kansas in August during a dry spell—with banana trees added. Spent the morning cleaning latrines so church was out. My prayers and thoughts are with you today, however in a particular way. I suspect that the news from Nam was rather alarming for the past few days, 30 January to 4 February. Let me assure you that there are no problems here and we are all doing fine. I feel like a newcomer here. Everybody else has a good tan and looks healthy as a horse.

In his journal entry from 17 October 1999, Dale comments on the previous letter: "I cringe reading this. I was scared to death, cannon fire all night long a few yards from our tent, and everybody in country was dirty, unshaven, and scared too."

5 February 1968

Monday, Saigon

Dear Mom and Dad,

I have my unit orders. They are too good to be true. We're living in a hotel on the port of Saigon. The four-story, once very elegant structure is located in a large slum along the river. This is a dream assignment. I can't emphasize that enough. So much happens here that it's hard to believe that I've only been gone a week, from Oakland that is. I've already traveled further and seen more new sights than in the past years. For this I must be very, very grateful. Don't be alarmed if my letters are spaced out a little over a week apart. Seems we're a little shorthanded and so one does office work all day and works on the docks all night . . .

Note by Dale, 17 October 1999: "This is either diplomacy or a lie. Cholon and parts of Saigon were still in flames, sniper fire, high alert. We took a convoy with M60 machine guns to travel the two blocks to the port. I think I believed that Mom and Dad wouldn't read the papers or watch the news and therefore not notice Tet. I wrote daily because mail service was so uncertain. It was also my first time living in a big city."

9 February 1968

Saigon

Dear Little Sister [Elva Suderman],

This is indeed an historic occasion. The water pressure is up on the third floor. I may wash myself today. As my friend Gil said as we watched the red sun set tonight, "When I get back to the States and hear a kid bitch about what he's got, I'm gonna kick his teeth in." He meant of course that the slum and the waterfront bothered him. We took a really wild ride to the finance office in Tan Son Nhut. You ain't lived till you gone forty miles per hour into a solid bank of oncoming traffic and watched them split to each side of you—pedicabs, motor scooters, little cars. We travel in steel helmets with rifles loaded—look like something out of the TV show *Combat!* Note that last letter was for my files . . . I may give up trying to describe this city—words fail to convey the sound, smell, feel of this place. But I am learning more about it every day—old-timers here know me as the kid full of questions: "Who is that? Why that? What is that?"

Love,
Dale

Writing in October 1997, Dale noted that the recipient of the following two letters, Ken Kornelson, was his debate coach at Tabor College who had moved to California to teach.

28 February 1968

Saigon

Dear Mr. Kornelson,

Today is, I think, Tuesday. If I hear the Protestant Hour on Armed Forces radio, I will know it's Sunday and start keeping track all over again. For the past month I have been a supply clerk in Saigon at the Army Port Terminal. The job is a bore and tedious—twelve-hour days, seven days a week. We live in a once-nice hotel that very often has running water.

Because of the "restrictions" from Tet, no GIs are allowed to walk anyplace. So far, I have only seen Saigon as a guard in the alley in front of the hotel, and riding shotgun on jeeps, trucks, and an occasional gas truck. In this first month I've still managed to see and feel a great deal.

In the evenings, for entertainment, we go up to the fifth-floor terrace and watch the war. The mortar and heavy artillery fire starts at about sunset and is fairly constant all night. There are usually about five to fifteen flares in the air at all times, lighting perimeters. During the first week we could watch Cholon burning every evening—in fires that reminded me of prairie fires back home. One GI commented, "Gee, I sure hope they don't get the PX—I got a forty-dollar watch in repair there." Fortunately, damage to the PX was minimal—it was primarily homes we saw burning.

One does not forget a lot of little scenes. The flicker of embarrassment when I frisk the interpreter at the hotel entrance after he has gone out for cigarettes. We search the maids' handbags as they leave and discover that they have collected all the little packets of sugar and coffee that we throw away from C-rations. Waitresses at the snack bar hide bread slices in a paper sack behind the trash can. The people at the market fight over the trash we empty into the street. Riding through downtown Saigon, we force our way through traffic and scream obscenities at every woman under forty. There is the sight of six little kids trying to sleep in one chair in the alley with one sheet between them—it was cold that night. The little girl in the same alley explained to me that she could go to sleep at five a.m. but until then had to wait in the alley for people to leave for work. She was cold and trying to keep warm, with one towel draped over her head and shoulders—looking like an oriental Madonna in a grotesque sort of way. She was too small and ugly to be a prostitute so she was a masseuse at the brothel across the alley. Because of the restrictions there was no work and no food. The prostitutes never seem to sleep. I was on guard duty in that alley for four days and they were always there. They are not attractive and at times act their age—fourteen to seventeen. Back home girls would be wandering about going steady. These girls can make sailors blush.

It is difficult to get any accurate news. Last night I found a recent edition of *Newsweek* and it filled in all sorts of mysterious gaps in military news. Nobody believes the body count during Tet; certain actions reported as victories here were defeats. That explains the interview with the "survivors" of Lang Vei—which I read in *The Saigon Post*. The *Post*, the government newspaper published in English, rates somewhat below *Pravda* and the *Beijing Review* for journalistic integrity.

Vietnam is 67 percent secure. Then who shoots sniper rounds at the hotel? Let E. Bunker travel across the street without an armed escort and then make that statement. The Embassy announced that the number of civilians killed and kidnapped by the VC had nearly precisely doubled in the past year. This shows their "increased desperation." It also effectively demonstrates our inability to protect the people in our 67 percent secure country.

Please don't ask me for options. I don't know any. A few days ago, I asked five noncommissioned officers in a bull session if any of them had seen any progress in the war during the several years they had been here. They emphatically agreed they had not. When asked for alternatives I heard simplified versions of everything from the enclave system of Galbraith and McCarthy to proposals for nuclear warfare.

While on leave I made contact with a group of professional people who call themselves Kansans Concerned About Vietnam. I would like to work with this group and hope that Jerry Kliewer might be persuaded to do the same. Are you by any chance receiving Jerry's letters? His Christmas letter was a powerful and persuasive indictment of our present position here.

The tremendous tragedy of the antiwar movement in the States is that it demands a freedom it is unwilling to give others. Darryl Smith and I decided about 4:30 a.m. New Year's morning that the new fascists in America are on the left and not the right. These people have made rational opposition to, or even discussion of, the war almost impossible. I suspect that you know this, living in California, about as much as anybody.

Assorted footnotes:

Pot: Well, John Steinbeck, Jr. exaggerated but then the American mother is kidding herself. Approximately one-third of the prisoners in the stockade at Long Bien are serving three-to-four-month sentences for possession. At our hotel it sells for four dollars a pack. These are filter-tipped joints very neatly packed in discarded Kool cigarette packs. Perhaps one effect of the war will be increased pressure from veterans of all socioeconomic backgrounds for legalization of marijuana.

Atrocities: Not being in the field I'm only getting secondary information. I discount any story unless the informant can swear he saw it personally. This eliminates most stories. Those that survive are not pleasant and I fear that we may have a generation of men with bad dreams. Last night's story came from an extraordinarily informed and reliable source about armored personnel carriers (light tanks) being driven over the bodies of dead VC in order to see them squoosh. It made both the source and me a little ill.

The GI battle uniform: the GI wears jungle fatigues, jungle boots, either a bush hat or a steel pot with camouflage material. He carries an M-16, wears a pistol belt with first aid packet, two ammo pouches and canteen attached. In his various pockets and in his belt are several extra clips of ammo. On one shoulder strap he has his Kodak camera.

He is usually drinking a can of Seven Up. Altogether he is the most extraordinary soldier in world history.

I am aware that this letter is rather premature. If I see and experience events which change my opinions, I hope for the grace to do so as publicly as I have expressed these.

Sincerely,
Dale

P.S. You will note that this is a very subjective reaction and not a prima facie case for anything. It is also a very badly written subjective reaction and for that I cannot apologize.

$1 billion a month for this damn war and not a ballpoint pen in any supply room for the last thirty days.

13 July 1968

Saigon, Vietnam

Dear Mr. Kornelson,

Kindly cease flagellating yourself for the frequency of your correspondence. Truthfully, I've written to you a couple of times as I have to other people and ended up throwing the letters away because of a certain (newfound) hesitancy to say anything. Right now, my wall locker is a jumble of unfinished letters and unanswered correspondence.

The longer one is in Saigon, the more difficult it is to say anything about it. My timid explorations of the city have been rewarding to me but always leave a sense of frustration at the language, cultural, and most of all time barriers that block a really careful study of the area. The million or so military restrictions since Tet haven't helped a great deal either.

Jerry Kliewer has been flying into Saigon almost every month since I've been here and he has been a wonderful guide. He speaks Vietnamese very well and really appreciates this country. This is probably a major factor in his extending here for another year. He spent a few days up here last week waiting for a plane to Bangkok for the beginning of a six-week vacation. Officially he is only going to Bangkok but he will go to Cambodia and Laos also, as he has done previously.

Howard Jost writes from Calcutta that he will try to take a few days . . . at the end of this month and visit Saigon. I had hoped that Jerry could be here also for the most offbeat Pi Kappa Delta reunion in history but this won't happen. Howard will be doing graduate work at the University of Chicago in the area of religion.

While I'm gossiping about old Tabor College people, you may have heard that Roger Harms was among the eight faculty members purged at Southeast Missouri State this spring. The administration got rid of its radical element among mass student protests. Roger's sin was being SDS [Students for a Democratic Society] faculty sponsor. He plans to stay on at Cape Girardeau so that Ann can teach and he will commute to Carbondale for doctoral studies. As a matter of fact, I feel increasingly illiterate as many old friends are in various stages of completing their doctorates. Pete Enns is in Texas, Jim Nickel is virtually finished at KU, J. Dean Schroeder is finishing at Oklahoma University, etc., etc.

Another minor footnote on this. I asked Jerry if he had experienced "culture shock" at the beginning of his tour here. He said no, "not as much as the culture shock involved in going from Tabor to Wichita State after graduation." Ahem! . . .

Dale wrote the following letter to Howard Jost, who, he noted in his journal entry of October 1999, was then in Bangladesh with Mennonite Central Committee. Jost was a friend from high school and college.

18 March 1968

Saigon, Monday afternoon

Dear Howard,

It's a sleepy and relaxing Monday. Am on duty but have no intention of doing anything today. Maybe tomorrow or next week . . . Life here is mellow—or I feel mellow today. The restriction is still on so we continue as 210 men in a hotel—almost like a ship at sea. The restriction has been lifted enough to put Mama Sans in the hotel alley on limits so it is now legal to get a short time with the whores without doing anything illegal. But mostly we just drink and talk. There was a phenobarbital kick in the hotel last week and it got out of hand. The experienced avoid them and the inexperienced get hurt when they use them. About 40–50 percent of the men use "M" and the chaplain gave us a little lecture last week. For all the world it was reminiscent of a chapel talk on smoking at Tabor College. Almost made me homesick. The chaplain's talk had about as much effect as a Roy Just lecture. I enjoyed it because I was drunk at the time . . .

"fighting for freedom"
Dale

The following undated fragment was stapled to the letter above. Dale referred to it in 1999 simply as "Of Cabbages." He remarked that it "was probably a letter to Darryl Smith in the U.S. Army language school in the [Monterey] Presidio, partially written in code because of his high security clearance." Furthermore, writing in October 1997, Dale notes that the "year with Dr. Vogt" was "an allusion to a psychiatrist in Wichita whom I had seen once for depression and to be 'cured of homosexuality' before service. Today I would say some Higher Power protected me from my aspirations to do therapy with this man."

of cabbages:

Remember your missing the students. As intimated, I've lightly touched the same thing. However, after two weeks of drinking and long introspective conversations, I dried out for four days and then last night remembered the 36 in the best yet. In great moderation but for real. I await your letter concerning mail and security before going into detail. It was not what I expected and very mellow.

Of a truth I am becoming a flower child. The old ambitions and even tensions are less than ever before. Service is fulfilling its mission of allowing a time of unwinding and putting the pieces together. A year with Dr. Vogt and perhaps that self that has been dormant for some time will emerge. Words like "grace," "forgiveness," and even "peace" are starting to mean new and powerful things. And perhaps with this I am more of an agnostic than you. Or at least theologically unsound . . .

I plan to see you in 198 days. If you are in California—good. Elsewhere—will still see you. You don't usually have weekend duty, do you? When the hell do you make PFC? Jerry Kliewer is supposed to show up today or this week. If so, I'll write a long letter. Do write but don't apologize when you can't.

Sincerely
Dale

Letter to parents

Saigon, undated

Little Scenes from Saigon: A beggar woman and infant sitting on the sidewalk in front of the office selling mutual funds to rich Americans. The cyclo driver whose motor always conks out about one block from your destination. You just jump out and give him twenty cents and walk while he frantically tries to fix the one-cylinder engine. Vietnamese boys who look about thirteen lined up in civilian clothes in front of the ministry getting drafted . . .

The family who moved in by the alley built a house smaller than our outhouse from scrap lumber and paper . . . about five or more very small children. They sleep in the back of a pickup that is parked there without any covering at all. In the morning they are huddled together looking for all the world like little naked field mice. It is difficult to figure out which people belong to a family unit here. Everybody just sort of hangs out around the alley together.

Last week was National Library Week. In the library I saw a soldier just in from the field looking intently for a book in the card catalog with his rifle still strapped on his back—live and learn? There was a big free chicken barbecue last Sunday afternoon with both Vietnamese and GIs from the company invited . . . two serving lines—one for Vietnamese, one for Americans. This was done at the orders of Captain Timmons . . . he is a Negro . . . I wonder if he remembers?

Talking the other night about things we miss from home. The thing we all missed was a peanut butter and jelly sandwich. Carner said he found some peanut butter and went to the Plaza restaurant and ordered two slices of bread and some jelly and made his own, to the bewilderment of the management.

The word "absurd" means we want to laugh and cry at the same time. I made four cents matching pennies with a Vietnamese kid one night here. I felt bad because they usually win. Three questions the Vietnamese will ask you no matter how little English he speaks: "How old are you?" "Where did you live in the United States?" "Is very rich, yes?" I can't get over the fascination these people have with Sears Roebuck catalogs. They sell them in all the sidewalk bookshops. Birth defects and eye diseases are very common here. Many people are hideously deformed. Saigon is absurd.

14 April 1968

Saigon

Dear Elva,

This letter is written out of boredom. The situation is that it's about 10:30 in the evening and I've been shooting the breeze with an idiot in the office until now. The guy is trying to persuade me that America needs a new Adolf Hitler to lead the white people against the colored people. He's an eighth-grade dropout from Kentucky so you can imagine how impressed I am with his argument. Anyway, I can't do any work because there isn't a ballpoint pen in the entire office or anyplace else so I'm stuck with doing nothing.

This morning I went to my first Easter sunrise service and probably to the most unusual one I will ever attend. The service was held on the ship *Robin Trent* on the very top deck, about three floors up. About seventy-five men attended. The view was breathtaking as the sun came up in a cloudy sky shining over the broad Saigon River and throwing eerie shadows from the warehouses and little houses of Saigon. The sermon was not particularly well done but the point of the possibility of resurrection now for human lives was interesting. During the closing hymn a flock of helicopters came in from strafing missions, flying low over the rice paddies with that peculiar sound that only a large number of helicopters can make. It was funny and sad because their engine noises were in perfect pitch with the hymn.

21 April 1968

Dear Elva,

Well, here it is 7:30 in the evening and I'm done working already. Got to work at six, unlocked the door, read *Stars and Stripes* and anything else that came in today, listened to the news and part of the Lutheran hour, locked up and went to supper (chili and rice, ice cream and pie) and here I am back. Around one a.m., I'm going to try to get some sleep and get up at five and work till six when the day crew comes on and finds me slaving at the desk. How long I can keep this deception about being busy is doubtful and I expect to be back on day shift in a few weeks but really don't give a d——.

Funny, but the longer I am here the less I feel I know about this country and this war. When I get home, I won't be quite as outspoken as when I left but in some ways my feelings will be more intense.

My buddy Clayton was just by. He supervises loading the trucks at night and right now they're unloading a refrigerator ship. Got to go by and pick up some oranges later on. Last night they had eggs and were having a ball throwing them at people. Said only a case was stolen—the Vietnamese workers eat them raw—slurp. Also eat onions raw. Anytime a case of anything is broken they devour the contents. Clayton says he almost gets trampled to death in the mob sometimes. Of course, occasionally a forklift driver just happens to drop a case of something valuable and then unavoidable shortages occur.

THE SUPPLY SCENE:

PFC Sherd: "I want a mirror for the Colonel's jeep."

Supply: "Sure, go to the good ship *Anna Belle* and steal a case of steak."

Sherd: "Then give it to you?"

Supply: No, give it to Navy Supply and get some twelve-volt batteries."

Sherd: "Give them to you?"

Supply: "No, stupid. Give the batteries to the Philco Ford contractors and get some jeep tires."

Sherd: "I wanted a mirror."

Supply: "Shut up and listen. You take the tires to Camp Davis and give them to the motor pool supervisor. He gives you a case of staples and a staple gun and you take them to 4th TC Supply Office and they give you the mirrors."

Sherd: "But the 4th TC Supply handles office supplies."

Supply: "This is the Army, ain't it?"

FINIS

19 April 1968

8:00 p.m. Saigon

Dear Dad and Mom,

    The death of Martin Luther King was a terrible shock to me and the Negro servicemen in particular. As one sergeant said, "Why am I fighting over here when my wife and kids have to live through that back home?" Dr. King was a Christian with rare courage, determination, and incredible love. There is now no one to replace him unless we all pitch in and do our small part.

    Easter is coming soon and may be past by the time you get this letter. My thoughts this week have been about Easter meaning new life. The entire meaning of the word life is too often something I have taken for granted. One angry GI wrote in a letter recently, "The death of Martin Luther King was the crucifixion all over again." But he missed part of the point there because Dr. King lived for a new life for Black people and was inspired to do so because of his unshaken faith possible because of the crucifixion. His tombstone will be inscribed with an old Negro spiritual, "I'm free, I'm free, Lord, I'm really free." Dr. King's death should inspire us all to new dedication and to remembering what being a Christian can really mean.

Commenting years later, Dale wrote in 1997, "There are numerous subtexts in this letter. This was a fairly daring confrontation with my right-wing parents. The Negro sergeant who was upset got drunk and punched out a white NCO the next morning. I got the word when reporting to duty at ten p.m. from a Southern NCO who said, 'they got the nigger.' I took a long walk along the Saigon River and cried privately. At the same time, re-reading this now, it feels didactic and pedantic . . ."

Letter to Delbert Wiens

4 July 1968

2:00 a.m. Saigon

Guard Post #2

Dear Delbert,

Did you really cry when you saw the Statue of Liberty? Good, then I can feel safe in admitting that I also have learned to cry. Sometimes from the thrill, the shock, and even the joy of self-realization—but that is another story. I was on this same post when I heard of the shooting of Senator Kennedy. I did not cry when I heard that he was dead—in the same way that one does not cry at Greek plays.

When Armed Forces radio presented the CBS tribute to Dr. King on the day he died, I was working night shift. At the end of the "I Have a Dream" speech, I bolted from the room and cried like a baby. Though no one knew until the next night, Sergeant Hagewood talked to me for four hours about his experiences in a segregated society. This quiet man revealed a pool of anger so deep I couldn't fathom it. Last week he was fined $200 for assaulting a private with a switchblade after the private said "nigger." Crying for a dead prophet really isn't doing very much, is it?

Excuse the unevenness of this writing but it's too dark almost to read the words. There will be no official observance of Independence Day in the Republic of Vietnam, according to official sources. There are fireworks though. I can see them very clearly right now. Funny we take away inch-and-a-half firecrackers from sixteen-year-olds and give five-hundred-pound bombs to our eighteen-year-olds.

Perhaps this year nobody should celebrate Independence Day. Perhaps a national day of thinking should be set aside for Americans to ask if they want independence, and if so, what is it they wish to be free from? But I think it might be too risky. We as Americans are losing our nerve. I am not certain we could so boldly ring bells and read declarations as we once did. We still observe all the rites, we rattle our escalations, chant our commissions, and pray nationwide, but the bogey man still refuses to go away. And because we are a dynamic people, we do the same old things faster and faster. Only, doing nothing faster and faster is still a nothing.

What hope there is, is in small events. Orlando Harms prints brave and blunt articles [in the *Christian Leader*] and says he will not be silenced, a friend writes from Long Bien that he has grown to be a man, some scattered Tabor rebels sign their letters to each other "love" because they don't care and do, Ann Harms writes after Roger is fired, "In spite of all this I still work in the garden every day and the flowers are doing well," and I think about some day soon being reconciled with Roy Just and of "making opening" at Ebenfeld Church for my last time and talking a little bit about people loving each other and how I have not done it.

And now the light really is so bad that I must close.

Dale

Reflecting on the preceding letter in 1997, Dale observed: "Delbert was a philosophy instructor at Tabor College and a Mennonite Central Committee worker in Vietnam during the 1950s. He recently retired as a professor from Fresno Pacific University. Most important, he has been a friend, correspondent, and often the mentor and depositor of my secrets for decades. My best guess is this letter was never mailed.

"Guard Post #2 was on the roof. Flares and strafing from helicopter gunships were visible on all horizons."

LETTERS TO KEITH HARDER, 1968

In a journal entry of April 2006, Suderman notes, "Letters to Keith Harder—cousin and friend. Some of these may have never been mailed from Vietnam." Harder was at Harvard Divinity School at the time.
Dear Keith,

Good to hear from you that school is going so well. I'm counting the days until I can join you again as a fellow student. So the draft deferment is bothering you? Well at least you're thinking about the question, which is a lot more than most guys are . . . at least thinking seriously.

A lot of people have been curious about why I joined the Army. "After all," they say, "You're a Mennonite and they don't join the Army."

And in looking back I have to admit my reasons are a little unclear, even to myself.

I had done some reading about the idea of rejecting military service before I was drafted.

Most of the arguments against military service that I heard as a child did not then and do not now make a lot of sense. And I think it was the absurdity of the positions I heard that caused me to react and join the Army.

I can still get angry thinking about some of the high school discussions we had about being "conscientious objectors." The very term would usually cause some smart aleck (usually me) in the back row to pipe up, "Yes, I'm a conscientious objector, I object to anything conscientious." Well, the program would usually include some former I-W worker who would mumble a few words about Christian witness and then show us some slides from Germany, if he was over thirty, or from the States usually in a big city, if he were twenty-five to thirty. And that was it.

After the formal program was over and we adjourned to the city cafe or whatever teen hangout was in fashion that year, the real discussion would start:

"Well, I asked for a 1-0 classification because my folks said I had to. Maybe when I'm older I can change it."

"My brother said he had a real great time in Denver and got his convertible paid for."

"Yeah, I had a good buddy who joined the Army and he said it was pretty rough. You have to get up early and do a lot of running and can't talk back or anything."

"Besides, how could I leave my girl behind? You never know where you'll go in the Army."

"Yeah, and a lot of those overseas assignments are pretty soft and you can travel and everything and just have a lot of fun."

"Besides, all the guys from my hometown are going alternative service."

THE OLDERS:

"You are a Mennonite. You will not join the Army and associate with a lot of rough, dirty people. We never have and never will!"

"But, son, you could get killed!"

"I think I-W service was one of the greatest opportunities of my life. Why, I traveled and saw new places, and met the girl who is now my wife."

"Do as we say. You're only eighteen and too young to make up your mind."

Dear Keith,
Your letter received yesterday which again leads me to believe in premonitions since I was about to write another epistle to you. I am unable to respond directly to your discussion of the draft and the peace position since it seems to me that you have presented yourself with an insoluble dilemma. Christian ethics are sufficiently in conflict with the norms that society sets up for itself, in that the decision is between two worlds—not participation in both. It simply is not possible for a nation to pursue a "Christian" foreign or domestic policy as such. Instead, the actions of nations must be measured vis-à-vis the actions of nations. Under these circumstances the United States still doesn't win any morality contests, of course.

Howard Jost is going to be in Saigon next Monday afternoon for a three-day layover on his way back to the States. I am looking forward to his visit with unusual interest as it has been a long time since I've seen him. Meeting in Saigon does have its bizarre aspects also.

Harvard students. I do hope you don't react to the Ivy League (my God, you ARE Ivy League, what am I saying?) the way I always have . . . with extreme disdain for their very real and imagined superiority. But then my contacts have always been with the draftees from the Ivy League—perhaps they are a unique minority.

I'm going to Japan early in September for a seven-day R and R. Have considered going to Hiroshima and renouncing my membership in Western Civilization but doubt this is possible—train schedules and all.

Enclosed find various clippings and articles . . . that may or may not amuse you. Be so good as to return the first draft of "voices" as it is still in process. There may or may not be another letter to you in this envelope which is a first draft of an article for "With," a new intra (inter) Mennonite "youth" publication. The bit was solicited by somebody named J. Lorne Peachey (pretentious name) who was advised of my existence by somebody-or-other Thiessen via Bob Suderman.

I'm cutting off the drug scene after my last two "highs" produced nothing more than total sensual disorientation. Not certain of the precise cause, although the suppliers have apparently been mixing in larger and larger quantities of opium and perhaps a more potent type of grass. In addition, I suspect that there is a principle of diminishing returns on experiences of this sort. Still, it was an interesting experience which I was happy to have undergone.

Stars and Stripes gave us the happy headlines that the VC units were withdrawing from around Saigon and that the danger of a substantial third wave was abating. Which is rather good although I had hoped that Howard would be able to appreciate the sound of "incoming." Ah, well, perhaps Charlie will schedule something for the Democratic Convention. Can't you see it now? The VC flag flies from the Presidential Palace for about forty-eight hours until airborne units can clear the city. Senator McCarthy very calmly assails the administration for their failure to prepare for this contingency and even while mourning the destruction of the South Vietnamese establishment, points out that it gives an unparalleled opportunity for a new coalition government. His calm and control so impress the delegates and the nation that he wins the nomination on the first ballot. Presented the idea to a few friends here and one replied, "Look, I said I'd die for Gene, but I didn't mean in Saigon."

Couple more GIs got killed coming out of a whorehouse the other day. Past few weeks have sort of plodded by and are unworthy of comment...

The fact that President Thieu asked Houng to return from self-imposed seclusion to accept the position of Premier is an acknowledgment of defeat on his part, particularly on the security of Saigon. Another point to consider is that the offensive against Saigon is very reasonable strategy on the part of the NLF [National Liberation Front]. There is very little local autonomy in Vietnam. If Saigon could be held for only a day or two by the VC the war would be over—even though the American military would not have been defeated.

The attitudes of Americans in Vietnam run through the same spectrum as they do in the States. There was an incredible amount of Kennedy-McCarthy support among the *enlisted* men. There is a growing antiwar movement among about 20–30 percent of the EM I know here. Out in the field it may be higher. I understand that "dove tags" (dog tags with the SANE peace symbol) are selling like hotcakes. Most officers are still true believers, of course. I've been eating at a little restaurant in the old American Embassy a few blocks away and have been able to strike up conversations with about thirty to forty different embassy officials and civilian contractors. On one point, however, without exception, there is agreement. Nobody believes we are winning or even making any substantial progress in Vietnam.

Most GIs hate "gooks" with a terrible passion. Charlie is respected as a fellow soldier and as a matter of fact he is cussed a great deal less than our coworkers. This attitude will inevitably build up enough anti-Americanism to prevent Vietnam from ever being an ally, no matter how long we stay or how much money we spend. Lenny Bruce said we created a generation of anti-American Europeans because they remember us screwing their mothers for chocolate bars. Here daughters support families by going down for C-rations. This is rough language but the reality is even rougher.

Over on Tu Do Street there is an American stockbroker selling mutual funds to Americans. He has the Wall Street closing prices posted on a board out front. Sitting in its shade is a woman and her infant son begging alms from passersby. Incongruous scenes like this occur all over the city. The tragedy is that I take them for granted after being here only five months.

In spite of working a seventy-five-hour week and having guard duty one night a week, I still have found time to do a great deal of reading and thinking. The USO has a good collection of free paperbacks and I've been able to catch up on current fiction, Mailer, etc., as well as a great many of the classics. Today I'm finishing *The Aims of Education* by Whitehead, which is rather good. One line cracked me up. "Great readers who exclude other activities are not distinguished by subtlety of brain. They tend to be timid conventional thinkers. No doubt this is partly due to their excessive knowledge outrunning their power of thought" (p. 61). Throw that at the next bookworm you meet . . . (like me).

Plans for the future are a little vague. I become a civilian around 28 September in Oakland. After that I would like to get a job with the *Wichita Eagle* but if this falls through, I may spend a few weeks in California to see the America of the next decade. Other plans include more graduate school and maybe hitchhike around the world or something. If I get anywhere near your home this fall, I shall call you and would like a chance to visit with you. Thank you for your letter and please overlook the egocentricity of this epistle. I shall not apologize for the spelling or form as time does not permit second drafts and this was written among a thousand interruptions.

Sincerely, Dale

Dear Keith,

This is the second or third effort at writing a letter to you. At least one effort was made prior to receipt of your epistle. This is not to say that you are a difficult person to write to (watch the preposition boy) but instead is a small indication of the difficulty I presently feel in communicating with anybody back in the States (the world?).

Howard Jost is going to be in Saigon Friday evening for a brief visit on his return to the States. I am hoping that he can spend at least one night at our hotel and have arranged a day and a half off while he is here . . .

In attempting to meet Howard I went to MCC Vietnam Christian service headquarters today at lunch and had my first cordial reception there since arriving in country. Prior to today I had not identified myself as a "Mennonite" and was received about as cordially as a roast ham at a bar mitzvah. Or at least I thought this was the case until I realized that Mennonites do not display their cordiality as do most people and are very distant with strangers. So once again I realized that it was in part my fault that no communication has been built up here since I failed to be cognizant of this. Anyway, today I had lunch with a couple of pax men [Pax Christi]—among them Gayle Preheim from Bluffton, who was a high school friend of Darryl Smith. The conversation was pretty open although I still felt a bit like exhibit A at an anthropologists' convention.

The war continues but at a slower pace. Sweeps are netting only three or four VC per day and large arms and supply caches but not much else. The third-wave attack on Saigon has not come off and there are strong rumors of a pullback of the X number of VC battalions that surround the city.

Had sort of a bad night on guard last Friday when an intelligence report was called in that said there would be an attack that night by three or four NVA battalions armed with tanks and armed personnel carriers and ground forces accompanied by another attempt at overrunning Tan Son Nhut Air Force Base across town. As usual nothing at all happened anyplace that night. Someone once said that "military intelligence" is a contradiction in terms.

Had an interesting conversation with the chaplain on Sunday while riding shotgun for him in a jeep taking him back to his billets after curfew. He's rather a liberal for a military chaplain in that he concedes the possibility of a peace position for certain eccentric or supersensitive persons. Sort of a strange place for a conversation riding through the darkened streets of Cholon with clips in our rifles, talking about the idea of being a pacifist.

In thinking about your letter, I agree we must get together for a fairly prolonged dialogue some day in order to make ourselves clear and to understand each other better. My own position is still not one of alienation from at least the less demanding requirements of existing institutions but one of participation in them. I recognize the dangers of such a position (it is usually a way of selling out and attempting to maintain self-respect) but still I am unwilling and unable to "drop out," as it seems in part would be the conclusion that you would have to reach.

Have had some interesting conversations with a nine-year career man who's getting out in January to finish college and go into juvenile delinquency work with the LA police department. He's a former semi-pro football player and Black. Sergeant Harris has achieved a sort of secular Christianity even though he's a nominal Presbyterian. His big pitch is that we must become persons prior to seeing ourselves in various roles—for him, "big wheel Negro," or even "Christian." Then our responsibility is to assist others in becoming persons also. He describes gang leaders, for example, as being less than their potential because they are still only able to see themselves as gang leaders. Once they are separated from their role or are at least aware that the role is only one manifestation of their personhood is there the possibility of change. This has interesting implications to me. For example, what would happen if I were able to achieve this type of awareness?

Last night I borrowed a copy of *The Atlantic* (June 1968 issue) with the feature article on the four Navy deserters in Sweden. If you have read it, let me say that it is a fairly accurate picture of a small minority of people in Saigon also. My best friend here has a couple of years left (he's ex-ASA) and talks occasionally of cutting out as a protestor but like most conversations of this type the romantic element is drowned out by "reality."

I've been writing a bit of poetry lately which my friends here contend is pretty ghastly but since I find the act of writing a tremendous release of tension, I continue writing undeterred. Lately I've been experimenting with the sounds of words without concern for their meaning. Plan to take this a step further next month by purchasing a transistor cartridge tape recorder and making tapes in which all the words are unintelligible but still convey the meaning of a scene, e.g., the murmured small talk of restaurants, the belligerence of intoxicated people, the hesitating sharpness of honest dialogue, etc.

The local Armed Forces Radio station has been playing a new jazz LP entitled *Soul of the City*, which is an effort to describe specific scenes and events in a big city using only jazz and certain minimal sound effects such as sirens. Fascinating project and rather successful, I thought.

Highlight of the week's *Stars and Stripes*:

> East St. Louis, Ill. (UPI)—Emmett Ross, 31, was shot to death during an argument with a friend over the wording of a passage in the Bible.

End of article. Enclosed find another article from the *Army Times*, which is a semi-official military publication with pretty close Department of Defense connections. I found this to be one of the most blunt statements yet on what is happening here among the "Allied Forces." Most of the Koreans take a 300–400 percent increase in salary since they are paid on the same pay scale as American troops. In addition, most "Allied" troops are in secure areas doing handling work. Everybody knows that the minute any of them take any large casualties, their governments would call them home. Yet we continue to tell the American people that at least some Pacific countries support our position. Bullshit. If you ever run across a source giving the total casualties for allied forces in Vietnam, please jot them down as evidence of the above contention that they are showpiece troops only. Standing joke here is the amount of ammunition expended by the Koreans who blast empty jungle is used as evidence of having been in combat.

Once again I suspect the attention we are giving Vietnam is blinding us to other significant world events. This fall, Japan will achieve the third-largest GNP in the world. The possibility of a neutralization of Europe up to the Urals is no longer just a pipe dream. The U.S. is simply not free to respond to these significant events so long as we are tied down here. This could turn out to be a large part of the tragedy of Vietnam.

I'm going to Japan early in September. Will be in California by 26 or 27 September and a free man. If I don't have employment waiting for me in Wichita, will spend a large part of October in California, prior to returning. My best to you and Judy.

Dale

UNDATED DRAFT OF AN ARTICLE FOR MENNONITE PUBLICATION

Dale wrote in 1997, "Possibly a draft of an article for a Mennonite youth magazine on alternative forms of responding to the draft. I am uncertain if this was ever mailed or published in any form."

Now that my two-year hitch is almost completed, I see the entire thing a little differently. First of all, let me say with few exceptions this has been one of the most enjoyable experiences of my life. Probably never again will I have the chance to be friends with people from all over America. My service buddies come from the ghettos of New York and the farms of Iowa. They include musicians from California and teachers from Hawaii. They are Protestants, Catholics, Jews, unbelievers. They are graduate students and grade-school dropouts. I've gained a new sense of responsibility and in my own ability to take care of myself. In Vietnam I have had my first chance to see and work with people of a different culture. And in a small way I have watched the writing of a small tragic footnote in the history of the world . . .

Postscript, October 1997: I don't recall how this story ended—or maybe if it has ended at all. I remember the silence on the plane flying back to Oakland Air Force Base in California. I remember getting separated from my best friend Don Sherman on the same flight out processing at Oakland AFB and not seeing him again for several years. He joined the anti-war protests while in service, later spent two years in Attica prison for bombing something or other as part of the violent underground. I think I saw my uncle and aunt in Fresno. I think I hitchhiked to Oregon and somehow flew to Wichita. I do recall my mother and sister picking me up at the airport there. We drove to where my father was planting wheat and I walked across the autumn landscape to ride with him on the tractor.

"So you're back?" he said.

I pondered his low-key response for thirty years. I often felt resentful that he didn't show more emotion. Today I realize he greeted me more as he would another man and an equal—not the little boy he had known.

Two months later I marched in my first anti-war protest in Kansas City where I had found a job as a social worker.

Soldier Home

Writing Against War

Letters, Journals, Journalism, 1969–1997

MORATORIUM DAY SPEECH

(October 15, 1969, Goshen College)

Speech delivered at Goshen College at an antiwar moratorium event. Writing in April 2006, Dale commented: "I had just started attending Associated Mennonite Biblical Seminaries [now Anabaptist Mennonite Biblical Seminary]. Jonathan Lind was a former Mennonite Central Committee person who knew me from Saigon and got me the opportunity to speak."

Today we and millions of Americans have a chance to once again discuss the longest, the most illegal, the most deceptive, and the most evil war in American history. Already billions of dollars have been spent on senseless destruction; a great country is nearly hopelessly divided, a small country is nearly destroyed, and more than a million men, women, and children are dead. More than 44,000 of them were Americans. I doubt if too many of you have not known at least one casualty of this war. And yet I find it impossible to comprehend the horror of this war and I feel that most Americans have become numbed to its reality. Frankly I'm sick of talking about this war, thinking about it, hearing about it, reading about it, arguing about it. Most of you share my feelings. Yet neither can any of us forget about it. And before you get too blasé about the whole mess, remember that unless we change the policy of this country, the statistical odds are that some of you in this room will die because of the war that bores you so much.

I can only talk about this war as an ex-GI and a Vietnam veteran. Speaking to you today I feel that at least I am fulfilling a vow that some of us took in Vietnam. A few of us agreed that when we got back, we would give as much time as possible to oppose this war. I notice by the press that some Americans, among them the Vice President and a few Congressmen, seem to feel that our discussions and protest represent some sort of treason or aid to the enemy. "Well, let me be perfectly clear about that." My argument this afternoon is identical with the position of the Veteran of Foreign War bumper sticker you have probably seen: "Support our boys in Vietnam." Because the kind of support they need and many of them want is to demand that the President bring them home, now . . .

Many of you, perhaps most of you, do not expect to ever become cogs in the military machine. You expect to remain in college—until the war ends, or you don't know you won't pass the physical, or you will do alternative service. You don't feel the military involves you very much.

The GI was not so fortunate. He often was the wrong color to remain in college indefinitely. He was the wrong religion to become a conscientious objector. He lacked the football injuries and the legal advice to circumvent the military system. I would estimate that 80–90 percent of the enlisted men in the Army do not know that they have any legal alternative to military service. They have heard of Canada and Sweden and refusing induction, but to expect an eighteen- or nineteen-year-old to make that decision alone and totally out of step with his culture and society is expecting a great deal. For many servicemen the military was an escape from worse alternatives. Juvenile judges still present the military as an alternative to prison or reform school, many are in service to escape intolerable home or community situations. This is the type of society in which military service represents a way to move up on the socioeconomic ladder—their one way out. And there are those for whom service is a family tradition, or those who join the Army to avenge the death of a brother or buddy killed in Vietnam. These are a minority—a very small minority.

The enlisted man is a tool, a pawn in the largest military establishment in the world. He is totally overwhelmed and engulfed by a system that shapes his life twenty-four hours a day. He cannot participate in political decision-making beyond voting—if he's old enough.

He can be court-martialed and imprisoned for dissenting or even questioning too loudly the policies of his country. As a matter of fact, he is legally and constantly faced with double jeopardy, that is, he can be tried once by civilian courts and then by military courts for the same offense.

Now I know that you may have a different picture of the serviceman. I know the scene—you come swaggering back to your hometown with your shiny buttons and phony hero's medals telling the local yokels how you run forty miles and wrestle a wildcat before breakfast. And then you go overseas—maybe to Vietnam, and you come back with stories that make the show *Combat!* pale by comparison. I must say that I can speak about my experiences in Vietnam because I am not a combat veteran in the precise sense of the word. My theory of war stories is this: in most cases, the amount of blood and gore you talk about often varies inversely to the amount of combat you saw. So beware the Vietnam vet who tells you how he won the war—he was probably a bartender at the officers club in Saigon. And beware the American Legionnaire—patriotic, pot-bellied drunks (I say this as a member of the Legion) whose heroism and 100 percent Americanism varies proportionately with the amount of beer they've just consumed and inversely with their mentality.

After two years of being a GI and listening to hundreds of their life stories, I found them to be rather ordinary people, frequently very young, very innocent, and naïve. I have seen them cry with homesickness, totally bewildered by the system that engulfs them. I never heard a USO show in Vietnam that didn't close with the entire audience singing, "I wanna go home, oh how I wanna go home." It is a mournful sound.

The primary secret of morale in Vietnam is the twelve-month tour of duty. For twelve months your primary mission is not to win the war, not to become a hero, but to stay alive. You run the gauntlet of boredom, loneliness, fatigue, and Charlie, and if you are successful, you get to go home—a certified patriotic American. Now GIs sometimes say that they volunteered for Nam for "a chance for a promotion and an extra $100 per month and a chance at some good and inexpensive pot." And to a degree this is true. But I have not seen too many GIs who could keep that façade up when they made that phone call to their wife or girlfriend or parents to tell them that they got their orders for "Southeast Asia." The military knows you want to stay alive for 365 days and capitalizes fairly cynically on it. For example, if you're in a company that's seeing a lot of action and taking a lot of casualties, you don't just go to see your friendly company commander and say you want to transfer to a nice relatively safe outfit at Lang Bien or Bien Hoa. Instead, you say, "Gee, sir, I like the Army. I'd like to re-enlist and I'll do so if you transfer me to Lang Bien." GIs do this regularly and the press is told stories for the civilians back home about how GIs re-enlist and extend their tour of duty in Vietnam because they believe in the war. Bullshit.

The GI isn't too much different from you. We want our worlds to make sense—we want a sense of wholeness and unity about ourselves. And we engage in all kinds of self-deception and fantasy to allow ourselves to live with our world. And we've got to account for our actions in Vietnam so that we can live with them. The stories you will hear about Vietnam are almost as varied as the people who go there—so I won't be at all upset if some of you come up and say that what you saw in Vietnam or what your brother or buddy saw doesn't correspond at all with what I'm reporting. First, because nobody has seen all of Vietnam, and second, because we all have different worlds of reality into which we fit our experiences.

I remember Vietnam as absurdity and even now as I think about it, there is an air of unreality about it . . . I was astounded to find a fairly general cynicism about the war, among enlisted men and noncommissioned officers. Particularly from those career sergeants doing their second and third tours in Vietnam, I heard stories not of progress in the military campaign but of actual regression. Roads that were once secure could now be traveled only in armed convoys, and villages were increasingly unsafe. I don't recall a single military official who could, with a straight face, tell GIs about "progress" in liberating Vietnam.

There are a lot of scenes I won't forget: waitresses in the military restaurant hiding my food scraps in a paper sack behind the garbage can; GIs searching women leaving the port and finding little bags of rice—feed baby san, maybe feed VC husband; families living in cardboard boxes—squatters that reminded me of naked field mice; a dozen kids trying to sleep in a chair.

There are enough American civilian contractors getting rich in Vietnam that Saigon has a branch of a Wall Street mutual funds office on Le Loi Street. On the easel out front they post the closing share prices daily. A beggar woman and her infant son sleep in the shadow of that sign.

Anyone who wants to see can tell these stories all day long. I saw suffering, I saw and felt absurdity. But then one day it begins to dawn on me that I am a part of that suffering, I can't just ache and sympathize for these people while I'm part of the very system that is creating their anguish.

Wars are actually pretty funny—some of the best humor I've ever seen. Officers used to say, "Don't knock it—it's the only war we got." And they're right. If you're going to be a career officer you simply have to have combat experience and hero's medals to get certain promotions.

Our unit had a presidential citation for increasing the efficiency of the port of Saigon and relieving a serious logistical bottleneck. A GI compiled the figures—kept refiguring them until the curve looked like a hero medal for everybody. The colonel was happy, the Pentagon was happy, the GIs were happy and laughing.

The ultimate story I've heard but can't confirm is about an Army officer in Saigon who was barefoot at a cocktail party. Some VC rockets started coming in and while heading for a bunker he dropped and stepped on his cocktail glass and got his Purple Heart.

You've probably been hearing some of the allegations presented to a congressional investigative committee about corruption in the clubs in Vietnam. Now they are just allegations so far . . . but most of us recall seeing easy money in Nam. Examples: A roommate made up to ten thousand dollars, he claimed, by selling jeeps and other stuff. He was a seventh-grade dropout from West Virginia. A black sergeant obtained a truckload of boots, sold them first to my friends, second to companies along the way, and third to ARVN and associates. "But, sir, I don't know anything about this, I'm just a truck driver." The sergeant also traded in TV sets and Chivas Regal whiskey.

Doug probably told you this morning about how the Vietnamese saw us. Bluntly, in looking back, I can't believe we were Ugly Americans, nor is the term nation of sheep appropriate. We found ourselves to be a nation of barbarians and savages.

Practically any female between the ages of twelve and fifty, unless she was a nun, was treated as a prostitute. I can recall riding in convoys yelling obscenities at school girls in their starched uniforms returning from class. Many Vietnamese girls could make a sailor blush because they learned their English from American GIs. There were stories without end with the phrase, "win the hearts and minds of the people." One day we would tip the cab driver five bucks, the next day we'd refuse to pay. In bars, customers threw grenades because of jealousy over girlfriends and wives.

So, what happened to the naïve, lost, childlike GI I was defending earlier? Well, I suppose there are several explanations, all of them partly true. First, we as Americans extend our ethical system only to those creatures we consider human. Now the average GI is no anthropologist. And when for the first time in his life he finds somebody who speaks no English, and lives in a very different culture, he usually decides that they aren't exactly human. So the same GI who can be the picture of uprightness can still be a barbarian to a Vietnamese.

Then of course as you may have heard, war is hell. If you accept the idea that hell is beyond grace and therefore there are no ethics in hell, anything goes.

Last, the average GIs picture of the Vietnamese is that of the prostitute and bar girl who roll him, the pickpocket who robs him, the merchant who cheats him. The laborer who runs and hides every chance he gets (no matter that malnutrition limits him, he may have been up all night in a police raid, or he may be working two jobs). The ARVN soldier who is incompetent or simply a Vietnamese avoiding service. The coworker who steals everything, the cleaning lady who doesn't starch his uniform correctly and loses his socks. And from his perspective, the GI is partly correct because the Vietnamese seem to think the big, rich, loud-mouthed foreigners who can't speak their language are beyond the pale of their own ethical system.

And so the war continues.

Now I know that some of you still think you're part of the peace movement because you're going to do alternative service. Well, General Hershey has slept well for years because he could let Mennonites and a few others avoid wearing a uniform. He always knew he was liberal and tolerant—he had forced nobody to violate their conscience. You can continue to be PAX men and hospital workers for another one hundred years and you still will have nothing to stop this war except to personally avoid its implications and guilt. The ending of this war is the beginning. The president asked for a moratorium on thought—not for a moratorium on killing. But that should be first: a moratorium on killing. Then . . .

Bring the boys home, now.

Put the money where it belongs.

Free America from the grip of militarism.

Declare total amnesty for all exiled people and prisoners because of this war.

Stop the Selective Service system now.

Get ROTC off the campus.

Get this country moving again.

Don't delude yourself. America is tired of this war, but America is just plain tired—of everything, race, poverty, developing countries. We are a nation of sprinters, not long-distance runners. Our job does not end when we stop this war—our job is to demand that this American eagle continue to fly right, for once.

LETTER SENT TO PRESIDENT RICHARD M. NIXON FROM DALE SUDERMAN AND DARYL SCHMIDT

(February 4, 1970)

Writing in April 2006, Dale described, in a journal entry titled "A Minor Footnote on AMBS [Associated Mennonite Biblical Seminaries] History," a letter that he and fellow student Daryl Schmidt sent to Richard Nixon in February 1970. In Dale's telling, "It was a Friday afternoon at seminary. For some reason Daryl Schmidt and I were talking about the letter President Nixon had sent to MCC thanking them and MDS [Mennonite Disaster Service]. We presumed this was a political effort to court the ethnic and religious vote.

"We drafted a letter to the President. Then we casually asked students to sign it and went and knocked on faculty doors and asked them to sign the letter. (In those days, everybody signed petitions and letters of protest.)

"*Where we went too far was to type up the signatures and make it a press release to every Mennonite publication. It was front-page news in* Mennonite Weekly Review *as I recall. The Republican donors to the seminary hit the fan.*

"*A community meeting was called. Daryl and I went and were astonished to see William Snyder, head of MCC, and other important folks there for the meeting. Fortunately, John Howard Yoder was in the audience. After admitting that Daryl and I violated protocol by not telling faculty that we intended to make their signatures public, he then chewed out Snyder for his suck-up letter to Nixon thanking him profusely for Nixon's letter. Basically, he pointed out that Snyder didn't get clearance for his letter either.*

"*Apparently, this little innocent stunt cost the seminary a good deal of donor money. These are the original copies.*"

Associated Mennonite Biblical Seminaries
3003 Benham Avenue
Elkhart, Indiana 46514
February 4, 1970

The President
The White House
Washington, D.C. 20500

My Dear Mr. President,
Sincere thanks for your letter of January 21, 1970 expressing appreciation for the work of Mennonites in the clean-up operations after the Hurricane Camille disaster.

We seem to have mislaid your previous letter expressing appreciation for the 350 or more volunteers who were in Washington on November 15–16, 1969 expressing outrage at your allowing the continued murder of American and Vietnamese in Vietnam because of your foreign policy. The only response was a statement by your Attorney General about the lawlessness of that assembly.

We are also waiting for your letter of appreciation to those Mennonite men who have "performed magnificent service" for the conscience of this country by returning their draft cards or refusing to register for the draft. Perhaps you could have your Justice Department forward your thanks to them.

Perhaps you could also respond to those Mennonites who have warned you about the folly of your escalation of the arms race through appropriations for the ABM [anti-ballistic missile] system. Certainly it would be reasonable for you to "commend them for their excellent work and for the example they set for their fellow citizens."

Sincerely,

Dale Suderman	Eleanor Loewen	Lauren Friesen
Frank Soher	Denny Weaver	Walter Hochstetler
Del Epp	Edwin M. Yoder	Ardean L. Goertzen
David Janzen	Bruce Harvey	Don Lind

DS:mf

cc: The Mennonite

The Christian Herald

Christian Leader

The Canadian Mennonite

Mennonite Central Committee

Mennonite Denominational Offices

All Mennonite Student Publications

The signatures in the letter above were hand-signed. What follows is the press release that Suderman and Schmidt sent to Mennonite publications and MCC. It contains a typed list of signatures by faculty, administration, and students. Presumably the actual signatures of the persons listed below are somewhere in archives.

Dear Sir:

The enclosed letter was written in response to the letter of President Nixon to MCC. That letter is being distributed to Mennonite publications and churches by MCC. The enclosed letter was signed by the following students and faculty of the Associated Mennonite Biblical Seminaries:

Erland Walter, President, Mennonite Biblical Seminary

Ross T. Bender, Dean

John H. Yoder, Prof. of Theology
Clarence Bauman, Prof. of Theology and Ethics
C. J. Dyck, Prof. of Historical Theology
Howard H. Charles, Prof. of New Testament
Millard Lind, Prof. of Old Testament
Paul Miller, Prof. of Pastoral Counseling
David Habegger, Admissions Counsellor

Daryl Schmidt, Parker, S. Dak.
Denny Weaver, Kansas City, Ks.
Dale Suderman, Hillsboro, Ks.
Walter Hochstetler, Goshen, In.

Don Lind, Goshen, In.
Ardean Goertzen, Henderson, Neb.
Noah Kolb, Goshen, In.

Ray Gingerich, Goshen, In.
Henry Shank, Harrisonburg, Va.

Wesley Mast, Morgantown, Pa.
Noah Hochstetler, Goshen, In.
Bruce Harvey, Malvers, Pa.
Amzie Yoder, Goshen, In.
Keith Harder, Elkhart, In.
Don Klassen, Newton, Ks.
Gary Harder, Niagara, Ontario, Can.
John Kampen, Fiske, Sask., Can.
Bob McKelvey, Des Moines, Ia.
Keith and Gretchen Kingsley, Elkhart, In.

Kenneth Schrag, Elkhart, In.
Paul M. Gingrich, Goshen, In.
Moses Beachy, Goshen, In.
Norman Lundaker, Nappanee, In.

David Janzen, Hillsboro, Ks.
James Derstine
Lorne and Marie Friesen, Winnipeg, Man., Can.

Lyle Preheim, Freeman, S. Dak.
Eleanor Loewen, Abbotsford, B.C., Can.

Ruth Bixler, Kidron, Ohio
Frank Sohar, Kidron, Ohio
Jacob Dyck, Elkhart, In.

Ronald E. Brunk, Elkhart, In.

The letter below from Dale Suderman and Daryl Schmidt appeared in The Mennonite, *March 10, 1970, p. 172, under the headline "Not an official statement." It explained the letter they had written to President Richard Nixon and subsequently cc'd to major Mennonite publications.*

Dear Editor:

You recently received a copy of the letter sent by students and faculty members of the Associated Mennonite Biblical Seminaries to President Nixon. [Letters, Mar. 3, p. 158]. Some additional information is apparently needed to clarify the origin of the letter.

The concept and draft of the letter to the President were totally the result of student initiative. As you will note, the cover letter was signed by the two of us, who originated and drafted the original letter to President Nixon. The signatures attached, as typed on the cover letter, were arranged for clarity into groupings of faculty and students. It was never intended that the letter would represent an official statement by AMBS and faculty titles were listed only for identification. Indeed, the letter was not, and could not be, an official statement, since the entire community was not involved and a majority of them did not sign the letter.

We are hopeful that the letter will produce dialogue and open brotherly discussion of the issues concerned. We trust this background will help facilitate that end.

Daryl Schmidt and Dale Suderman, 3003 Benham Ave., Elkhart, Ind.

LETTER TO REVEREND DICK

Dale commented on this in April 2006: "I don't think I ever mailed this letter to Rev. Dick . . . related to the letter to President Nixon incident. But it is a good summary of my thinking at Elkhart and reflections on Vietnam.

Dear Rev. Dick,

This is a personal response to your letter sent to three faculty members at AMBS regarding the letter that we as students prepared for President Nixon. I am taking the liberty of writing you as a brother. Until about a year ago I was a member of the Mennonite Brethren Church at Ebenfeld near Hillsboro, Kansas. My search for a viable Christian faith has been a long and at times difficult one, involving four years at Tabor College and finally two years in the U.S. Army including a tour in Vietnam. It is that latter experience that continues to trouble me. The Church has constantly been co-opted by government and very often has not been in the vanguard of the new life that Jesus asked his disciples to proclaim. In Vietnam I cannot forget the chaplain saying that "This is a *holy* war, because we are fighting communism." Even the most pagan GI knows that this is simply a lie. Our involvement there is incredibly brutal, dehumanizing, and in violation of every constitutional, international, or even just war standard of conduct. The Mennonite Brethren conference, which still vaguely holds a peace position, said nothing about this. While in Vietnam I received a clipping that indicated a part of the Canadian Mennonite Brethren conference was refusing to assist Americans who took refuge in Canada. My experience in Vietnam gave me a determination along with several fallen GIs to tell the truth about this war and about our American society when we were free. I have tried to fulfill this promise through moratorium activities both here and in Washington. A close friend is attempting to do this while still in the military and has been jailed and received other forms of harassment.

While working in the ghettos of Kansas City I transferred my membership to the Rainbow Boulevard Mennonite Church, not out of bitterness but sadness.

I am aware that there are MBs attempting to develop an awareness that the Good News of Jesus Christ is not limited to personal piety but involves a new way of living in the world and a new way of looking at the structures of the world, be they economic, political, military, or cultural. The Christian must always be giving an earnest plea for justice to be completely faithful to Jesus. To do so will at times seem foolish or impudent but these are the charges of the world.

Now this must seem terribly irrelevant to the issue about a letter to President Nixon. You could easily have added to your letter that the open letter was futile, would only cause needless controversy, would be misunderstood by some of the Church. Perhaps I would agree on these points.

I am troubled that the Mennonites have been found worthy of praise by a government that shows itself insensitive to justice in so many ways. Maybe our grandfathers and great-grandfathers had more wisdom than we thought. They passed resolutions forbidding participation even in Fourth of July celebrations, not just because they were riotous affairs but perhaps because they feared the nationalism that so often blinds men and causes them to misunderstand history. We as Mennonites have several ways of looking at history. One way is to say that God has led us out of Europe and Russia to a new land and here we shall enjoy plenty. If so, we are justified in our quiescence in that land. But is it not also possible that God led the Mennonites here and preserved them so that they might be a witness and even a stumbling block to their neighbors?

We have often felt guilty that we did not participate in the defense of this continent in the two great wars, and uneasy that we were different from our neighbors. I know this feeling well. It was a major factor in my doing military service. But is it not possible that this is a snare which diverts our attention from our real mission of proclaiming Jesus and the New Life that he brings? Our standards cannot be set by government nor is their praise any mark of accomplishment.

But I would go further and say that, ironically, by our unceasing, often futile, always difficult and unrelenting pleas for justice in this country, in the long run we will ourselves to be not only faithful to Jesus but better citizens.

I agree that it is easy to make mistakes both in strategy and in being faithful to this vision. The guidance of the Holy Spirit and the brotherhood is constantly required. But in these desperate, turbulent times can we not presume that acts of acquiescence, of remaining silent, or of wanting to be accepted more than to be faithful are always wrong? I feel certain that you will agree to this and that your dissent is only to a particular incident. I hope that you will give this matter further consideration.

ONE WEEK IN SAIGON

(May 12, 1970, *The Mennonite*)

Prefacing this article was the magazine editor's note: "This was written while the writer was a member of the United States Army stationed in Saigon in 1968. At present, he is a student at Mennonite Biblical Seminary, Elkhart, Ind."

"Tis a strange, strange world we live in, Master Jack."

So goes a popular ballad on Armed Forces Radio, here in Saigon. I can't argue with the singer, either, for I am in a strange, strange world—the world of fighting a war. The military gives me many explanations of what I'm doing here.

You are defending the freedom of the Vietnamese people. Last week in Saigon, the Vietnamese Government sentenced a former presidential candidate to five years in jail after a farce of a trial. A five-year sentence was also given to the editor of the university student newspaper. Their crime? They stated too boldly the need for peace in Vietnam. But I'm defending a free people.

You are stopping communism. Everybody knows that if we don't stop the commies in South East Asia we'll soon be fighting them in Southern California. That fact is what makes it right and good (even holy according to some chaplains) that we kill women and children, that we destroy a culture, that we waste and destroy the human and material resources of America and Vietnam. Last week in Saigon, we killed almost as many Vietnamese civilians with our American trucks as we did Vietcong in combat.

You dare to say the communists commit atrocities on war. Listen, tonight I can take you by the hand and lead you to half a dozen combat veterans who will tell you that we can match the enemy atrocity for atrocity. Some of them will tell their stories with voices suddenly gruff, "That night, I and a couple of others . . ." If we are stopping communism, and fewer people here believe that than most Americans think, we are doing it by using their tactics of force and terror.

You are bringing peace—you are part of a peacemaking organization—the United States Army. Last week in Saigon, there was a press statement by some American leader stating that Americans must turn from domestic violence and learn to live together. The same newspaper story assured us that more guns and ammunition were coming to Vietnam for purposes of international violence. I sit on my guard post, holding my rifle, and hear that Martin Luther King has been shot and I am certain that only a madman could commit such a crime. Then I look at my rifle and wonder if, in some small way, I am also part of that society of violence.

You are helping a nation to remain independent and a people to determine its own destiny. Last week in Saigon, our Vietnamese secretary wished, out loud, that Vietnam weren't such a crummy country. Like too many Vietnamese who have associated with us for too long, he has lost all confidence and faith in his own culture.

Last week in Saigon and the week before and the month before that and today, I walk the streets and I see kids who should be in school, kids that should be bathed and fed and taken home. I see a box not more than three feet high and I look inside and there is a family living in it. There is an old half-crazed beggar woman with terribly crossed eyes who sits on the hot sidewalk and mutters incantations and aimlessly waves her alms hat.

I go to the military restaurant and see the Vietnamese waitress hide the bread crusts from my plate in a paper sack behind the garbage barrel. At night, she will take them home to her family. I feel revulsion. I feel pity so intense I almost cry. And I stop short and realize that all my sympathy and all my concern aren't worth spit, because I am not doing or able to do one thing to help these people. My mission as a member of the military is to defend their freedom to suffer. The Africans say that when elephants fight the grass is trampled. Last week and every week in Saigon, I see the grass we are trampling.

I recall a conversation very late one night last week in Saigon. Three Black GIs talked candidly about how they did not want to die fighting in Vietnam because that would be a waste of their lives. They wanted to die in the streets of their hometown, bringing America to its knees in terror.

I protested a bit, "After all, things are changing?"

"No, not fast enough. Doesn't history show that all change comes through force? Look, man, you think nonviolence is so great why don't all of you that believe that way join hands and sing 'we shall overcome' to win in Vietnam?"

I was at a rare loss for words until I recalled to them the story of a people called Mennonite who in Europe and Russia and Canada and America had rejected violence as an answer for their problems. I would have liked to speak further about the source of their vision being a man from Galilee who came only to bring life and how He had also rejected violence as a means of change. I would have liked to stay and point out that His kingdom had no armed guards.

I said none of these things. My little audience was impressed with the story about Mennonites and I left quickly before they could ask questions. I was afraid they would ask if these people really wanted peace for yellow people. I was afraid they would ask if their young men rejected military service only to bring peace or if they had other motives. I was afraid they would ask if these people really loved people different from themselves. I was afraid they would ask me how I knew so much about these people and their vision.

Dale Suderman, 3003 Benham Ave., Elkhart, Ind. 46514.

WILL YOU BE OUR SON?

(March 1975, vol. 41, no. 3, *Fellowship*)

Only after he trusted us a little, that night, would he tell us about the war. Sitting in the restaurant, he was a friend of a friend who had joined us at our table for lengthy discussions about almost everything. He seemed young to have spent a year in Vietnam. His hair was starting to grow out from the military trim, and his hands trembled a great deal.

A friend of his, while on patrol in the jungle, had killed a Vietcong. This American GI was an orphan, drafted into a war he cared nothing about. He had been overcome with remorse as he looked at the body. In the dead enemy's wallet he found an address. The interpreter said it was a North Vietnamese address, probably his parents'. The GI wrote a letter to the parents, and the scout translated it. He said, "I killed your son. I did not want to do it, but I was drafted. Can you forgive me?"

Many months later he got a response written in bad English. "We can forgive you for killing our son. Will you be our son?"

His hands were trembling so that he could barely hold the cigarette in them. All of us looked away from each other. I wonder how many recognized a parable of the incarnation when they heard it.

A FAILURE OF LIBERALISM

(Oct.–Nov. 1975: 22–25, *The Post-American*)

The end credit notes, "Dale Suderman is on staff of the Mennonite Volunteer Service of the General Conference Mennonite Church in Newton, Kan." The Post-American *changed its name to* Sojourners *in 1976.*

An old country editor once said that while a just God would condemn all editors to hell, he believed that a merciful God would not condemn them to reread all their editorials once they were there.

The editorial stance of *Christianity Today* on Vietnam is well-known (see John Oliver's May 1975 *Post-American* article, "A Failure of Evangelical Conscience"). Less well examined is the response of the house organ of protestant liberalism, the *Christian Century*. While humbly recognizing that few of us had prophetic vision on the subject, it is appropriate to review how the religious media responded to the challenge.

The *Christian Century* recognized Vietnam as an unjust war no sooner than did secular liberal publications. Its attempt to see the world through a theological perspective made it no more prophetic than the *New Republic*, *The Nation*, the *Progressive* or even the *New York Times* editorial department.

Until early in 1963 the "dirty little war" was only a small cloud on *Christian Century*'s bright international horizon. In spring of 1963 it noted that "China is also the source of subversion in South Vietnam, where American soldiers are helping an unpopular ruler maintain the country's independence against communist imperialism." While maintaining a wall against communism in South Vietnam might be essential, it would be necessary for the Diem regime to stop political and religious discrimination. Thus a petition of American churchmen was wrong in calling for withdrawal because "the administration has our support. South Vietnam can be saved." Ironically the *Century* noted with approval the visit of General Maxwell D. Taylor to Saigon as a positive step in improving a situation in which Vietnam was in "grave danger of becoming a victim of communist aggression." Ten years later it would be officially revealed, as it was known unofficially much earlier, that this visit was a key stage in the Saigon generals' overthrow of the Diem regime. The *Century* was naturally shocked at the coup and concluded that "our costly effort in South Vietnam is reduced simply to preventing the communists from taking over there so they cannot take over elsewhere in South East Asia."

Until late in 1964 the *Century* followed a policy of basic support for JFK's objectives in Vietnam with a few reservations about the means. The war was not the central issue for the *Century*. Civil rights was the central editorial theme. It endlessly called for more action by the federal government. Perhaps it seemed contradictory to oppose the administration on a minor, distant conflict when administration support was so strongly desired on domestic issues.

Commenting on the war as a 1964 campaign issue, the *Century* noted General De Gaulle's opposition to United States policy and said that it "encouraged the Viet Cong to fight harder and has discouraged the war weary Vietnamese in their resistance to communist aggression . . . Our efforts to keep Southeast Asia from falling under the control of communism, which in that area is controlled by the Red Chinese, are not succeeding, but we dare not let them fail."

The *Century* endorsed Lyndon Johnson for President in 1964 (and lost tax-exempt status for several years as a consequence) as much for his civil rights policy as his foreign policy. It was troubled by the Gulf of Tonkin resolution but decided that it was LBJ's way of showing toughness in the face of Republican attacks.

The *Century* ended 1964 with a review of the Vietnam situation. It felt the United States should not escalate the war for fear of starting a major war. But neither should the U.S. leave and lose prestige in Asia. Since the present escalation was not working, the U.S. must find a way to achieve a ceasefire in Vietnam. No explanation of how this was to be accomplished was given.

At the end of 1964 editor Harold Fey retired. The effect of this on editorial policy cannot be determined. Fey continued as a contributing editor and in 1966 wrote in the *Century* that the U.S. must not abandon its commitment in Vietnam at "this late date."

In 1965 a steady stream of editorials against the war began to appear in the *Century*, now edited by Kyle Haseldon. The goal was a negotiated peace, self-determination for South Vietnam, and compelling Red China to stay out. Few clues were given how the *Century* expected the U.S. to achieve these objectives. But somehow the President must do it.

In 1965 the *Century* began to print the litany of protests by denominational and church leaders. Its international correspondents gave detailed reports of overseas reaction to U.S. policy in Southeast Asia. It supported the 1965 March on Washington as a "good deed in a bad time."

But certain forms of protests were strongly condemned. In November 1965 it editorialized: "To lie to escape the draft, to destroy draft cards as a gesture of contempt for social involvements and responsibility, to urge emotionally immature young men to commit irreversible acts against the state—these are morally and legally reprehensible acts." However, the *Century* argued that the government was overreacting to the protestors and thus itself jeopardizing the social order.

Two eloquent statements were printed in 1965 by *Christian Century*. Dr. Vincent Harding, a civil rights leader, wrote of the irony of Americans being outraged at the deaths in Selma while remaining silent on Vietnam and said the same federal troops which protected civil rights workers would oppose them when they someday marched to oppose the war. The second was a letter by Norman Thomas who asked by what right the Church of Christ accepted the cruel war in Vietnam.

In 1966 the *Century* shifted to a more militant opposition to the war. It also shifted its viewpoint on China. Whereas for the previous five years the *Century* saw the war as a means of stopping Chinese aggression, it was not the U.S. which was using the war as part of a U.S. attack on China. The U.S. was moving into a war which would engulf the world. Somehow the U.S. must obtain a ceasefire in Vietnam and at the same time stop being a world policeman. How these two goals were to be obtained simultaneously was never clarified.

By the end of 1965 the *Christian Century* was firmly in the antiwar camp. Yet it maintained a curious neutrality in terms of breaking with national institutions. It was neutral about military chaplains, except in 1966 to oppose lowered educational standards for the chaplaincy (by implication it seemed to fear this would admit too many fundamentalists.) When Clergy and Laity Concerned suggested that Air Force chaplains counsel airmen about the morality of bombing and perhaps encourage them to refuse to do it, the *Century* felt it was wrong to counsel others to disobey. The ethical position involved here is difficult to determine. The *Century* by this time had unfurled all the banners of unjust war and "inhumane slaughter." Yet it argued it was wrong to suggest that someone not obey unjust orders. At the same time the *Century* endorsed the conviction of Lieutenant Calley [in the investigation of the My Lai massacre] as an effort to uphold some "standard of personal accountability" and warned against a "surrender to an orgy of national recrimination over the responsibility of higher authorities." Yet the *Century* beginning around 1971 also stated repeatedly that the war was the responsibility of a few men such as LBJ, W. W. Rostow, and other leaders.

A continued *Century* editorial policy has been its hopes for a policy permitting selective conscientious objection. Pacifists were helpful but selective objection was the ethic for the politics of realism. From the *Century*'s vantage point, "there is no greater moral gain arising from the Vietnam war than the emergence of selective conscientious objection ... Even apologists for the war should celebrate that victory for it may mean that the American system of freedom and justice is still worthy of loyalty and sacrifice." In other words, any country with provisions for selective objection is worth fighting for.

It is fascinating to attempt to understand the ethical position in the *Century*'s call for an end to seminary deferments. It reasoned that those seminarians who registered as conscientious objectors would lend "new moral power" to the antiwar movement. But, also, those who joined the military would be "able to identify more meaningfully with their fellows in the military ... In every case the church's moral position will be clarified and the vocation will assume a dignity now denied to it." Even though Vietnam was an unjust war, the church would still gain dignity by joining the military—or rejecting it. Perhaps one of the joys of liberalism is that it sees a little truth everywhere.

The *Century* never understood the depth of rage and anguish involved in those who broke with the mainstream of American politics because of Vietnam. The protests of the New Left were never taken seriously. The *Century* was impressed by the protests of clergymen and veterans who had paid their dues of participation in mainstream society. But it viewed with distaste those who would interrupt a church service or burn draft cards. "America is sick" it editorialized in 1967, but it never recognized that the end of the war might not restore health.

The *Century* remained fascinated with the Presidency as the institution symbolizing the national covenant. In a rage it compared LBJ to Pharoah and accused him of leading America into World War III. Yet it saw his resignation as a sign of strength in the system and after he left office, wrote that "Mr. Johnson, it is clear, is the *major casualty of the war in Vietnam*." How the retirement of a politician exceeds the deaths of hundreds of thousands of men, women, and children is not clarified.

The *Century* concluded its coverage of Vietnam subdued but unchanged in its support of the American covenant. If anything, it was more political in the traditional sense. It concluded that the McGovern moralistic arguments against the war were impractical. "The moral approach to politics will not work unless there is general agreement that something is morally wrong and needs correction . . . By suggesting that the war in Vietnam was immoral, religious leaders may have helped shorten the war, but they left a residue of bitterness among many Americans."

The politics of American realism operate best in a "well" society and not one undergoing convulsive social change. The politics of realism is essentially reformist, liberal, system-modifying politics. In it, Christians speak as good loyal citizens to reasonable men who hold power. The dialogue is carried on in mutual respect by both parties, but during the Vietnam war, and perhaps in any international conflict in which the power of national leaders is at stake, neither side appears reasonable to the other. When Christians enter into covenants of loyalty with the political power structure, they may dissent from the direction the covenant is taking but only with great difficulty can they say no. Thus *Christian Century* saw, as a primary goal, the replacement of Lyndon Johnson as a means to ending the war. When he was replaced by Richard Nixon, they made valiant and absurd attempts to see hope in this. There had to be a way in which the national system could again become reasonable—there had to be a way to solve Vietnam within the national covenant.

The prophetic voices of the sixties were not the liberals but those who broke with the politics of realism by stepping outside the national covenant. *Christian Century* could never understand the protestors who applied for a permit to levitate the Pentagon one hundred feet in the air and turn it upside down or the Chicago Seven who refused to take the courts seriously, or a Morrison and LaPorte who immolated themselves to protest the war. Nor could it understand students who joined SDS [Students for a Democratic Society], even in the early years when that organization itself was barely free of traditional liberal values. For all of these acts had in common the end of the politics of realism and the national covenant. No matter that some forms of withdrawal from the national covenant might have greater merit than others for Christians—none of them were acceptable to Christian political realists.

The question of draft legislation exemplifies this. *Christian Century* consistently advocated that Congress recognize the rights of selective objectors—the right of the individual to say that some wars were wrong and to have the state excuse him from these wars without undue penalty. Now the possibility of a state fighting a war in which its essential national interests are not at stake, or its very survival (and twentieth-century wars always involve only essential interests as defined by the state) and yet admitting that for some citizens this particular war might not be valid, is extremely remote. The *Century* urged Christians to take absolute pacifists seriously as one form of Christian witness—a special subgrouping of people akin to Trappist monks or celibates—but never that their position might have validity for other Christians.

The *Century* spent far more energy and time attempting to make the ship of state ride smoothly through rough and troubled waters than it did interpreting to the church how it was to ride when the ship of state had gone aground in foul weather. It never asked Christians to get off the ship, to enter into a new vessel of covenant apart from the nation. By its reasoning this would not have righted the ship of state; no matter that it might have righted some portion of the church.

Just as in sixteenth-century Europe the radical reformation broke the back of the existing religious consensus, so in the 1960s the political consensus that America represented began to deteriorate. The civil rights movement shifted from Black people asking for passage on the ship of state to the Black Power movement demanding and building its own vessel. Young people attempted to develop a culture of their own rather than struggling to fit into mainstream society. Political activists, at times, seemed more interested in telling this society what its government might be like than in gaining control of the existing structures. In a society that prided itself on religious pluralism and religious freedom, an underground church appeared, seeking sanctuary from the covert bounds of ecclesiastical and social structures that struggled to maintain consensus. As groups dissociated themselves from the ship of state, nearly all eyed the old structure so recently left and wondered if there was merit in taking over the vessel. Talk of revolution filled the air.

Christian political realism rests on the hope that the patient will live so that it can be healed. To its credit, the *Century* did not deny the gravity of its patient's illness, but it could not become involved with the children being born in the next room. It wished to save the Democratic Party, not nurture the New Left; it wished to unite the Christian community through NCC [National Council of Churches] and COCU [Consultation on Church Union], not nurture the free form renewal groups emerging; it paid more attention to reforming draft laws to make dissent cheaper than it did to the people who paid a high price without waiting for legal reform and who perhaps did more to hasten the demise of the conscription system than did the reformers.

If the *Christian Century* took the position of self-appointed advisor to the captains of the ship of state, *Christianity Today* was the captains' subordinate and uneasy passenger. Whatever course the ship of state took was correct so long as other passengers behaved themselves. If the passengers misbehaved, it was because the captain took insufficient steps to maintain order among them. Since he did not, they appointed themselves to this task.

Although both had totally divergent viewpoints on the war in Vietnam, they shared the same sense of national covenant, the same sense that the war issue was an effort to save America. As mainstream Protestants, they both failed to produce a vision of how the church of Jesus Christ might take a direction other than saving the nation-state.

OF COCKS, CONTRAS, AND THE CUBS

(Early 1980s, undated unpublished journal entry)

What does fasting mean? Probably to go without something normally a part of one's life in the belief that something will take its place—both internally and externally.

For the next days, I want to "fast" from people. To be passive, withdrawn, instead of addicted and searching for them. Frankly, I doubt if I can work without food. Let my fasting be private, quiet, and prayerful. Let it be a silent, naïve way of identifying with Friar Miguel D'Escoto in Nicaragua [D'Escoto was a Maryknoll priest who actively supported the Sandinista revolution that overthrew the Somoza family]. Let it be a way of identifying with him as a person as well as political and public figure. To attempt to share his doubts and fears, as well as hopes and dreams. To be silent for the dead, to develop a true sense of the terror that is and will be in Central America.

Privately, I do not see the people of Nicaragua as brave or heroic. I suspect they are ordinary people forced to act bravely. To sacrifice and to work together because there is no other option left. Somehow that makes it the more urgent to support them, knowing this. When circumstances have made people brave, it is even more important to stand with them.

(Not sure I believe above paragraph.) Maybe just a long way of saying I want to identify with them as people, not as abstract political symbols. That's easier for people like Lauren who've been there. I only know Vietnam—and that only a little.

***

... It also means an obsession with self. At times that disgusts me as much as it bores other people.

While I worry about relationships and my cock, contras kill people in Nicaragua and planes bomb villages in El Salvador.

Why do issues like Central America, South Africa, poverty or oppression seem like hackneyed clichés and dealing with my cock seems so sensitive and important? Literally because I can hold the one in my hand. Because in this society, neither is regarded as appropriate for discussion. One is too insignificant and "personal." The other is too large and impossible. What is appropriate? The Cubs, the new GM plant, VCRs, movies, new restaurants. Personal economics and mass entertainment are the appropriate "small talk" of the culture. Is there a way in which these things are the "bread and circuses" which entertained and dominated the Roman Empire?

Is there a chance that we are lulled into small talk so that we will not talk about our cocks or about contras? And is there a sense in which both things are dominating our lives, while we regard one as too introspective and personal and the other too abstract, impossible, and complex for appropriate thought and action?

The personal is the political. Sexuality and spirituality are one. To be unwilling to be dominated by mass culture is to be thought mad. And often to think that of oneself. It is an act of faith to believe that God cares more about cocks and contras than he/she does about the Cubs. A faith that runs close to madness—hopefully divine.

THE VIETNAM VETERANS AGAINST THE WAR MARCH IN CHICAGO

(June 13, 1986, unpublished journal entry)

In April 2006, Suderman observed, "This journal entry was written when I was involved with CISPES [Committee in Solidarity with the People of El Salvador] in the fight against aid to the Contras in 1986. Vietnam Veterans Against the War initially had John Kerry as a member, then was taken over by a Maoist cult and continues to this day as a few Viet Vets in Chicago." The Chicago Tribune *described the parade as the Chicago Veterans Welcome Home Parade, with an estimated 200,000 veterans of the war marching, and an estimated 500,000 spectators.*

Pardon the Xerox© but I wanted to tell you about the Vietnam Veterans Day parade today.

Basically 200,000 people marched, and 300,000 watched, according to the last press reports. Anyway, a lot of people were out there. So was I.

Never thought I'd march in a parade led by General William Westmoreland. He led the parade, surrounded and protected by a cadre of double amputee wheelchair victims, plus one incredible guy walking on his hands, the bottom of his torso a strange burlap pad. All day I felt surrounded by double amputees, paraplegics, but also the walking wounded. And Westy was shrewd enough to be the only VIP in the lead, surrounded by wheelchairs. No chance to shout, "You stupid murdering motherfucker." No choice but to applaud.

Found my unit. Viet Vets Against the War. Maybe fifty people at the beginning of the parade—a hundred by the end of the four-mile march. Counting cadence, "Dress right, dress," "give me ten"—all jokes now, of course. We actually felt defiant as we smoked cigarettes, the parade moving so very slowly.

Half proud, half defiant. No one asked me where I was stationed or when, and I did not ask either. We were a new unit.

Evan from CISPES was there. Strange little scholarly guy. We joked when we marched past the Federal Building that the crowd was so friendly, we should turn there for a Contra aid protest. We were arrested together there, exactly a year ago.

Good chants from Viet Vets Against the War:

> Ronald Reagan, he's no good.
> Send him back to Hollywood.
> Sound off, One-Two-Three-Four!

> If the generals want a war,
> Send them to El Salvador.
> Drop them on the jungle floor
> They won't bother us no more.
> Sound off, One-Two-Three-Four!

You get the general idea. Wasn't certain what to expect as we left Navy Pier staging area. Don't think anybody knew.

A half mile up the parade route a Black Veterans group preceded us. Beating a huge double-ended tribal drum—carried on four shoulders. Preceded by a sign: "No More Vietnams." "No More South Africas."

But the crowd loved us. Some because they were stupid with hysteria and would have screamed, "Welcome home, we love you!" to a passing garbage truck.

Others seemed to know who and what we were. They could read the VVAW banner with a symbol of a bayoneted rifle turned upside down. And the smaller Vets for Peace banner. People flashed peace signs. Even construction workers. And a lot of Black women seemed to know. A lot of the Black women did know.

And one of the marchers would go to the seven and eight-year-olds who waved flags and solemnly tried to shake our hands and told them, "No more Rambo, kids, no more Rambo, kids." One fatherly, graying VVAW person did that. I don't think the kids comprehended it in the middle of the bands, the ticker tape (actually computer paper). Maybe they noticed the wheelchairs.

There is no need to tell you at which points I cried. The stupidest time was hearing the bagpipes—but they always do that to me. Maybe some primordial Pavlovian reaction from childhood.

It was a perfect, crisp, sixty-nine-degree day. Almost an autumn-like quality. At LaSalle Street, the crowds were huge—maybe because we went through at noon hour. But the sun was finally warm and we were moving steadily. No need to call chants—the screaming would have drowned them out. Nothing to do but remember—the same warm sunny fall days in basic training twenty years ago at Fort Leonard Wood. There was a cute, gawky kid in our basic unit—almost painful to watch his sincere innocence, or was it vice versa? Saw him later in Nam—old from driving a gas tank truck. Later horribly burned in an explosion. Or did I just dream that last sentence?

As we crossed into Grant Park, a plane flew over the lake towing an advertising banner. "Welcome Home, Viet Vets—Hairline Creations." We are, I guess, a target market for toupees now.

Actually, I thought we were younger and more fat-looking than I expected. Some pretty grotesque beer bellies—a lot of gray, but hardly geriatric. An amazing number of the old fatigues and camouflage uniforms still fit. An inordinate number of longhairs, ponytails, etc. All those years of bitching about the long-haired protestors and now it's mostly vets wearing the long hair.

The group behind us was a disgusting bunch of bikers and their rifle-toting, flag-waving women. Awfully noisy machines, and they were throwing firecrackers. The biggest, loudest bike got jammed in ticker tape. Saw the guy pushing it at the end.

"Honor the warrior, not the war" was the VVAW motto. They invited the Pledge of Resistance [a group dedicated to preventing all-out U.S. involvement in the Central American conflict] to march with them. The Pledge couldn't decide and so didn't. Many were unsure of the motto's implications. Also, VVAW requested no additional or outside issues—or banners at least.

One group had a cloth "antiwar memorial" banner at Grant Park near the half-size Vietnam War Memorial set up there. I was told it was torn down by the crowd. The hardcore Pledge people were standing around with no signs or even buttons. I said hello but didn't want to talk to them. Not today.

After we finished the march, I went back to watch the parade following behind. Men seemed dazed. Many from New York and out of state were saying, "Thank you, Chicago. Thank you."

Some toy company must have given out the cute teddy bears with arms that hug. At least a lot the Marine units had teddy bears on their arms and on wheelchairs and poles holding flags.

Some of the men were marching arm in arm, a sort of drunken devotion or blurry, fatigued comradeship.

It could really have been the final healing. What a fantasy. If General Westmoreland and Jane Fonda had marched hand in hand. (Westmoreland refused to look at us from the reviewing stand. We stopped to chant, "Harold, Harold, he's our man! Turned Chicago on its can." [Mayor] Washington caught on and gave that big grin while Westmoreland inspected the motorcycle gang behind us.)

But a lot of men couldn't make it. Over fifty thousand dead Americans in the war, another fifty-four thousand suicides after the war, more than both figures combined in state, federal, and local prisons.

Would have been nice to have some whores there, and some Amerasian kids to meet their stepbrothers and sisters. So many things were only half remembered by us all.

I was startled at how much I remembered. The cheering of the crowds was intoxicating—if one drank it. But over 90 percent were too young to know what they were cheering. And what did the Continental Bank and Board of Trade people cheer? The good old days that maybe will come around again?

All these people who drove over eight hundred miles for this parade. Why did they come? Was it because this terrible horrible war was the last thing they did of consequence?

Why would one choose to wait twenty years for a thank you?

For one suicidal instant I wanted to scream out, "Baby killers!" and have a place in history as the last American casualty of the war. It was that kind of mock-heroic day.

GINSBERG (1926-1997)

(April 7, 1997, unpublished journal entry)

I am driving across central Indiana when the all-news radio station does a teaser, "The voice of the Beat generation is dead, details after these announcements." Since only two voices of the Beat generation remain and William Burroughs and his cats will continue to live forever in Lawrence, Kansas, I know who it is. "Allen Ginsberg is dead at age seventy." I cross myself.

In 1966 I was sitting in the student lounge at Wichita State University when an entourage of strangely dressed, long-haired men entered. We all stared—this was after the period of the button-down collars on pastel shirts in Kansas. The center of the attraction was Allen Ginsberg, in town for a poetry reading. The radical right (remember, Wichita was a major center for the John Birch Society) was outraged that he was there. After on-campus debate, the association of graduate students in philosophy dared to sponsor his reading on campus. There was a large crowd that night, including the vice squad conspicuously present with a huge reel-to-reel tape recorder awaiting even a hint of obscenity.

The performance was vintage Ginsberg, beginning with thirty minutes of chanting and gong playing. Then he read a new, long poem, *Wichita Vortex Sutra*. In essence, this was a stream-of-consciousness narrative of his recent drive from Wichita to Omaha, Nebraska and back. I was stunned as he described the same gas stations, oil refineries, and darkened farm houses which I had seen my whole life, but never through the eyes of a poet. He compared them to his visions of the villages of Vietnam—which he had seen, and I had not yet seen. He went on to say that young men in the farm houses in both villages bore each other no real malice and both lusted for life, for sex, something I could not dare say.

Somehow later in the week, I crashed a birthday party of someone I knew through contacts at Canterbury House and sat on the floor and chatted with Ginsberg, his partner Peter Orlovsky, and their "pet person," a mute childlike waif of a man whom they treated as "their baby." Ginsberg admitted he was also crashing the party. Somehow, I expected him to continue in his mad poet mode, but instead he rambled about rents in New York City and the difficulty of finding parking spaces.

There is a later, more hazy memory of talking with Ginsberg and Orlovsky on a sidewalk in New York City at some unknown date. He recalled his trip to Wichita, saying "lots of good poets come from Kansas but they all move away first." Aside from a brief visit to City Lights Bookstore in the Bay area at some other hazy dream time, this is the extent of my physical encounters with Ginsberg and his milieu.

Over the years, from snippets of scanning media, I picked up that Ginsberg had struggled with his homosexuality, had taken a white-collar job, and started psychoanalysis. His analyst told him, "Your only real problem is that you are gay, otherwise you are fine. Stop pretending and use your natural gifts and you will do well in life." This story, based on my reading a later autobiography, is only a very rough approximation of what really happened.

Someplace I read *Howl*: "I saw the best minds of my generation destroyed by / madness, starving hysterical naked . . ." It was a screaming critique of Fifties conformity. Bits of information about Ginsberg kept reaching me: he was "the Gay poet" and the "anti-war poet who wishes to levitate the Pentagon." And there was literary gossip: "but did he really have sex with the heterosexual Kerouac?" and strange stories of skullduggery at the Nairopa Institute and obscure Buddhist cults.

I pick up again on the Ginsberg story when my bookstore in Chicago goes bankrupt and I am unemployed, exhausted but with free time, enough time to read a new biography of him. Here is a man who does not fit. He challenges the literary avant-garde at Columbia University for being too readable, too explicit, too passionate. He reads *Howl* to a rich, hip audience in Southern California and, when heckled, strips off his clothing while screaming at the heckler, "my poetry is being naked and I challenge you to do the same."

He is passionately involved in the anti-war movement of the Vietnam era but also expelled from Czechoslovakia (where radical students had made him King of the May ritual), and he has joyous sex with student activists from Cuba and France. He is not really a gay icon, not really a left icon, perhaps not really a great poet.

I suspect him to be, or subjectively assign him, more to the school of Walt Whitman. Both loved males, Whitman hiding this love in his general love of land and nation, Ginsberg more explicitly stating his love of the soft down on a young man's stomach. Neither limited their love to "being" a homosexual or loving homosexuals, but to loving all men. This is why neither Whitman nor Ginsberg are true, in-house heroes to the modern gay community, but they retain their discomfiture for heterosexuals.

Certainly Ginsberg does not fit as an icon of the Left. He wanders off too much into spirituality, he is too much equally concerned with freedom in Prague and Havana as well as Paris and New York.

If Whitman wept for Father Abraham and loved the land and industry of America, so Ginsberg loved America as his uneasy home. "America I'm putting my queer shoulder to the wheel" is how he concluded one of his greatest poems, *America*, in which he described his anti-war stance as both a raging critic and yet true son of the Republic.

Although HarperCollins has reprinted huge editions of his collected poetry, I have no idea whether he is a great or even good poet. Sometimes I suspect he scribbled, used a tape recorder, chanted because he had no choice but to contain the inner and outer voices which flooded him and threatened to drown him as they had his schizophrenic mother.

The *New York Times* will do an extensive obituary, *The New Yorker* will give him space in "The Talk of the Town," and the remaining left press will note his passing, but with a certain incomprehension. I suspect that Ginsberg will be better remembered and understood in the Cathedral of Saint John the Divine in Manhattan. If his doorways of perception were often chemically entered, he seemed always able to remain focused on the vision, rather than the entrance. He remained focused on the spiritual journey.

Obviously this is a most subjective reminiscence. Of whom am I writing, the knowing will ask. But is this not a fair tribute, that one man's journey causes us to see our own?

Sweet Home Chicago to the World
Selected Essays, 1996–2008

ON THIS WINTER SOLSTICE

2001, *Hillsboro Free Press*

On this Winter Solstice, I will take United Flight number 551 from Chicago's O'Hare airport to Wichita, pick up an Avis rental car, wind through the unfamiliar bypass, and eventually find the familiar Thirteen Mile Road. I will check to see which farm implement Orval and Dean Suderman have lighted for the season. I hope my sister will have made the peppernuts and has the coffee ready when I arrive. As the shopping mall crooner sings, "I'll be home for Christmas."

On Christmas Eve we will go to Ebenfeld—the country church where my parents, grandparents, and great grandparents are silent participants in the service from the wind-barren graveyard.

Years ago, just before the sacks of candy were given out to children, the congregation would sing an old German hymn, "Nun ist sie erschienen." Once it was sung only in German and us young folks would fake the words, then there were a few decades of singing it in both German and English—and now it probably will not be sung at all. Maybe some Bill Gaither Christmas ballad will conclude the program.

Nostalgia is an uncertain guide for remembering the details of a childhood Christmas. The Welsh poet Dylan Thomas wrote in *A Child's Christmas in Wales*, "I can never remember whether it snowed for six days and six nights when I was twelve, or whether it snowed for twelve days and twelve nights when I was six." I do not recall the details of the year I got a bicycle. When I look at Christmas Eve family pictures, I squint and try to recall which year I wore that silly suit and tie.

Christmas away from home is more memorable. When I managed a bookstore in Chicago, we closed as late as eleven p.m. on Christmas Eve. Other merchants on the street would come in after closing their shops and begin shopping for their families at ten, at which point we just laid out the wrapping paper and in our mutual exhaustion let them serve themselves.

After I locked up the store, my next task was finding a restaurant still open. I often ended up eating Chinese food. Then, to Saint Clement's for Midnight Mass. Sister Caroline would hug me at the door. I am not Catholic but the people of Saint Clement Church were my seasonal family in Chicago.

I've worked more than one Christmas in locked psychiatric wards. I expected patients would be depressed from the holidays. Actually, they were rather cheerful—most of the patients were so sick that being locked up made them feel safe. Christmas blues are more serious for the worried well at home.

Now I work at the Harbor Light—a residential facility for men recovering from addictions, and men en route from federal prisons to their homes. Going through the lobby, I notice a plastic Christmas tree with a plastic Jesus, Joseph, and Mary thrown under its branches. I mention this while eating in the cafeteria to Chaplain Harris and my friend Rich. We agree it is wrong for the baby Jesus to be lying on the floor.

I go back to my office and describe this to some of my coworkers. Mr. Katiyar, my boss, suggests we make a crib from the cardboard boxes in which we get reams of copier paper. The office manager Milton suggests we can use paper from the document shredder for straw.

We assemble this and march solemnly to the lobby and make a social service crèche. In social services, this is the best we can do.

Decades past, at the old Partly Dave Coffee house in Elkhart, Indiana, we decided to have a Christmas dinner for the folks with no place else to go. Shirley provided turkeys. (Later I found they were rustled from a local turkey farm—but that is a different part of the story.)

There were maybe fifty people. The wife of a fireman and her kids. A couple of guys from the Rescue Mission. Kids who were having a tough time spending an entire day with their parents. A few hitchhikers passing through town. Some single men and women who just didn't happen to have a family.

Since I had baked the turkey, I was asked to say grace by this motley crew. Thinking and praying out loud simultaneously and spontaneously, I said, "Well, the first Christmas was two kids away from home—probably for their first time. They were not married. They had a baby. Thus began a family, which continues on to this very table. We are thankful for that. Let's eat."

9/11

2001, Hillsboro Free Press

On September 11, 2001 I turned on my computer in the morning and checked the news on AOL. There was a picture of a plane heading into the World Trade Center. I was irritated. Was AOL promoting a bad Jean-Claude Van Damme action movie? A few more clicks to news bulletins written in red and I realized this was real and shifted to TV coverage.

I went to work late. As I walked to the car, I realized every Mexican and Polish and English household on Huron Street had the same news blaring.

We were united that Tuesday in grief for a death in our common American family.

The Mexican family up the street put a sign up in their window. "We came to America late but we are Americans."

I first cried when I heard Prime Minister Tony Blair of Great Britain say, "This is an attack on all democracies—not just one nation."

And wondered if he muttered under his breath, "Welcome to the club. Some of us have put up with terrorism for forty years."

Grief and death unite families in a common emotion for a few minutes. Shocked, powerless, and awed, our old boundaries are transcended.

I recall being at Wichita State University when JFK was assassinated. An older woman spoke to college students and said, "You will remember this day well. The only similar day was Pearl Harbor." Now a third day has been added.

Grief and shock unite us. But this is not sustainable. We feel the need to do something, be it to fill up the car with gas before prices increase, or put up a flag.

Chanting "USA!" can make us feel good—kind of like when an opposing team makes a first down. But ultimately this will not do.

Then we start talking and trying to make sense of the event. President Bush showed all the eloquence and insight of a Texas teenager whose side window on his pickup truck was smashed on a Saturday night.

"This is a Crusade," he says—and manages in one breath to offend Jews, Christians, and Muslims in the Middle East who associate the crusades with a brutal European invasion of their region.

"This is war," he says. Well, yes, it will be a war—but more like the War on Drugs or the War on Poverty. Ask any high school sophomore about the results of war on drugs; ask any kid on the West Side of Chicago about the War on Poverty.

"This is a battle between good and evil." No, it is clearly a struggle with evil—and it remains to be seen if we are good.

"Victory is certain." No, the only certain thing is that battles will happen.

The judgmental moralists always show up at funerals. Our homegrown Taliban, Falwell, Robertson, and Dobson, chime in that New York City had it coming for being too liberal and tolerant. I don't know why they don't invite Bin Laden to join their Religious Round Table—they share a common view of society.

The Left recalls that America has done unwise and bad things in the world. As an imperialist power we had it coming—and what about the Palestinians, Hiroshima, slavery, and our treatment of Native Americans as past sins? We need to understand that this makes the terrorists very, very upset. (Odd, the Holocaust is never on their list of global sins against humanity.)

None of these folks can tell me how many more American firemen they want killed to finally satisfy their homegrown cosmic scales of justice. I think I will not return in my lifetime to the freedom and innocence we knew and took for granted a month ago. But after grief a family just keeps on going. My heroes continue to be the tough, tearful guys of New York City carrying off the ruins of the World Trade Center in plastic buckets, desperately seeking their fallen comrades.

Terrorists are like pirates. They once raided ocean travel and found harbor in North Africa. Pirates were from every country and yet part of no country. It's not as simple as a country. The second line of the *Marines' Hymn*, "To the shores of Tripoli," alludes to our fighting them as early as 1805.

These pirates seem to be a sect of Muslim fundamentalists. They hate rock and roll, women, and Jews. Their perfect world exists only in the eleventh century, and only a return to that will satisfy them.

To show our opposition to them, maybe we need to start by electing a Jewish woman as President who loves the Beatles.

NEW AND COSMIC BILLBOARDS

2001, Hillsboro Free Press

The first time I saw the billboard on Highway 56 reading, "Welcome to Hillsboro AND Marion," I almost drove into the ditch. Rerouting the highway was not the only change in Marion County.

I went to high school in the 1950s, during the intense rivalry between the two towns. If I were certain that the statute of limitations for criminal mischief to property had expired in the past forty years, I would admit that a friend and I changed the rocks on the Diamond X Ranch on old Highway 56 to read "Beat Mud" before the annual football game.

What seemed brave and funny then seems a little stupid some decades later.

Sports have been at the heart of small-town rivalries for centuries. As far back as a thousand years in England, there was a tradition of moving a ball between villages with each town's square being the "goal."

From fifty to five hundred men from each village moved the ball on a playing field that was from one to three miles long, depending on distance between the rival villages. The game could go on for days. (Stout clubs and the occasional dagger or sword were assets for each team.) Sports injuries meant the wounded and dead.

Cooler heads eventually prevailed and the playing field was shortened and defined as were the number of players per team and length of the game.

Spectators—with the exception of parents of Little League players—were forever forbidden to stay on the sidelines.

But the principle of sports being symbolic of serious rivalries between villages and cities continues to the present. Thus Chicago versus Green Bay, Marion versus Hillsboro.

Newspapers are judged and read by the quantity and quality of their sports coverage and not their coverage of local or international events.

Athletics were the result of local rivalries and not the cause. In the "olden days," we didn't get out much. Our worlds weren't much bigger than a one-room school, one local church, and a town which provided identity and Saturday shopping.

Beyond these safe and familiar places lay the unknown and the alien. And rather than risk knowing them and finding our commonality, it was easier to belittle, scoff, and pummel them.

I saw Kansas in a new way, through the eyes of the Beatnik poet Allen Ginsberg, when he read his poem *Wichita Vortex Sutra* to an audience at Wichita State in 1966.

In his poem, Ginsberg describes a nighttime round trip between Lincoln, Nebraska and Wichita. He mentions the Florence all-night truck stop and the lights of the McPherson refinery.

I was stunned to hear a New York poet appreciate the beauty and the drama of the prairie.

Ginsberg draws a radical conclusion in his poem. The small towns and farmhouses of the Plains states are, for him, similar to the farmhouses and villages of Vietnam. His ribald 1960s planetary consciousness of the unity of humanity is newly relevant as we move to war again.

But there is hope. The billboard welcomes travelers to both Hillsboro and Marion. Perhaps someday, new and cosmic billboards will be erected, welcoming us to New York and Kabul.

NICE

2002, *Hillsboro Free Press*

My coworker Fred caught me looking up a word in the dictionary. "Try looking up 'nice,' he said. "You will be surprised."

Fred learned English when he was fourteen by using a dictionary. He was a displaced person (or DP—nowadays called a refugee) from Lithuania, who came to Chicago via Germany.

I was certain I knew what "nice" meant. "Nice" is the ultimate Midwestern compliment. "Nice" is a beige-colored word—above average but not leading any victory parades or winning first-place trophies. I was raised to "be nice." I still use it as an easy compliment, such as "You have a nice home," and "Oh, what a nice drawing—now let's find a magnet and put it up on the refrigerator."

Midwesterners spend a lifetime looking for "nice"—the midsize Chevy, the suit or dress a step above mediocre but below spectacular or attention grabbing, the pleasant melody—not too sad, but not quite a "gloria" either.

But "nice" can also have a wicked, sarcastic underbite. "Nice move, Sherlock," friends yell when I drop an easy pop-up fly ball or hit my finger with a hammer.

(I won't get into the level of innuendo when "nice" is used in reference to certain aspects of the human anatomy.)

I looked up "nice" in the dictionary just to please Fred. Surprise! "Nice" originally meant "stupid, ignorant, slatternly" and other definitions best not explored in a family newspaper.

Now when I hear, "Oh, very nice," I ask myself: Did they look "nice" up in the dictionary, too? Which meaning are they using?

Learning about words is addictive. Browsing through the dictionary I found out the ladybug is an insect with a religious root to its name—it was thought to have the colors of the Virgin Mary, "Our Lady." The ladybug and the praying mantis are both insects with religious overtones. But the lady praying mantis bites off the head of the male while they make babies. The praying mantis is not nice; the ladybug is nice.

We are always adding new words to the English language—even though it takes a few years for them to make it into the dictionary. I learned a new phrase this summer at a backyard barbeque.

"So does your church do throw-up songs?" Adam asked Dan.

"No, we still use the hymnbook," Dan responds.

I was totally baffled by the phrase "throw-up songs." The mental image of some new horrific cultic practice corrupting the church with congregational vomiting alarmed me.

Apparently "throw-up songs" are the current rage to turn some congregations into bad subvariants of karaoke bars for those too geriatric or too young to get into the real bars, by projecting sing-along tunes onto overhead screens.

How nice.

"Beige" is a relatively new word first used in 1858—according to Mr. Webster—coming from the natural color of undyed wool. When people take a class in home decorating, or read two or more magazine articles on home design, or just watch more than three hours of HGTV, they may find beige cleverly disguised under trendy pseudonames such as "limestone," "desert rose," and "Arabian sands"—hiding its humble roots.

The popularity of beige in Midwestern design was explained to me by Milton, a Minnesotan. The Hubble telescope recently discerned that the overall color of the universe is beige—not blue, Milton said.

(Milton knows nice facts.)

"If you have a beige house," he argues, "with beige curtains and a beige couch, you blend into the universe—you are camouflaged, thus substantially decreasing your chances of being abducted by aliens. They can't find you." He claims this is true. Seems to work. The Midwest is safe.

How very, very nice.

THE WORLD IS ALREADY ALL AROUND US

2008, Hillsboro Free Press

Americans are increasingly singing, "Make the world go away." Folks are tired of competing with foreign companies, tired of dealing with immigrants, and tired of foreign involvements. These sentiments are fanned by hot election year rhetoric from politicians in both political parties who promise to keep America strong, its borders secure, and to protect Americans from foreign competition.

But the dream of building a border to keep the rest of the world at bay is a pipe dream that only makes sense if you are smoking Mexican giggle weed. Nativist, protectionist, and isolationist sentiments have strong roots in midwestern states. Certainly, Kansas is no exception.

The irony is that the only thing native about Kansas is its name—recalling a minor Great Plains Indian tribe. Contemporary Kansas is entirely the result of globalization.

Not many folks are supporting the wife and kids this winter by bowhunting buffalo, with corn and pumpkins as side dishes flavored with honey.

Farmers in modern Kansas raise wheat, milo, and soybeans with cows, horses, chickens, pigs, sheep, and a few goats as domestic animals. All of these are alien species and the result of past globalization. They are not native products. Even the odd llama is a South American import.

One could debate this while pheasant hunting—the annual local attempts to kill a few Chinese birds.

Or one could discuss globalization in church. Most Kansans will attend services at Methodist, Catholic, Baptist, Mennonite, or Orthodox services on Sunday and make at least passing reference to a Jew who lived in the Middle East. There are few native-born religions in Kansas. Denominations are European imports and not American.

Granted a few folks will attend American churches, but while the Jehovah's Witnesses, Mormons, Christian Scientists, and Scientologists can claim American roots, they are not popular in the Midwest. Even fewer folks will attend local services at a peyote meeting or go to a Sun Dance ritual that can claim to be a native religion. Most Kansans prefer European churches.

Prayers are said in churches for local prosperity, the blessings of good weather, and good commodity prices. But even these prayers have a global connection. I remember the late missionary anthropologist, Dr. J. A. Loewen, saying at the Ebenfeld Mennonite Brethren Church many decades ago, "Mennonite citrus growers in California hope for a good price for their oranges, then they can support missions and the denomination. But their prayers are really answered when crop failures happen in Florida." Today, I suspect he would use a more international image to make the same point.

Or, we can sit down alone and ponder globalism at the breakfast table. We drink a cup of coffee, most likely from South America, or tea from India or China. We eat a banana from Costa Rica or a few grapes, a winter product of Chile. We contemplate a shopping expedition to

Wal-Mart—the Chinese import store—and lament the cost of gas, a product of Saudi Arabia, for our drive.

Farmers are perhaps the most sophisticated globalists in Kansas. They can triage the nuances of Brazilian soybean production, Australian droughts, European farm subsidies, and increased demand for beef in China along with trade disputes with Japan. Their livelihoods depend upon predicting the futures. And the futures are global and not local.

Intuitively they understand the global markets are shifting to three spheres of influence: Europe, Asia, and America. The potential for growth is greater in Europe and Asia than in America. America knows how to export weapons and military forces. But increasingly we are selling what the rest of the world isn't buying.

Today, America, the breadbasket of the world, imports about as much food as it exports.

We may grow tired of the debate about globalism. Some politicians will promise to make the world go away. But we have always been an international and global society. We cannot be like the ostrich, an African bird, and hide our heads in the sand.

WANT MORE PEOPLE? BE "INTERESTING"

2007, Hillsboro Free Press

The population of Marion County hovers around 12,000 souls. What would it take to double this in the next decades? Or is slow population decline inevitable in this region?

The second question is, does the county want growth that matches the demographics of America? Meaning solid numbers of young persons in addition to retired persons?

Baby boomers are inevitably a growing segment of Marion County. The mild climate, good recreation facilities, wonderful senior programs and retirement centers, plus a low cost of living, all serve to make the area attractive. For some urbanites, low housing costs are the area's biggest magnet.

There are, unbelievably, inhabitable homes for sale in the county costing less than a remodeling job for a kitchen in Chicago.

I know this to be a fact. It is a major reason for my planning to move to Hillsboro once my Social Security checks start showing up in the mail.

Retired folks are wonderful new citizens for Marion County. (I will, doubtless, be the exception.) They do volunteer work, often attend church faithfully, pay their bills on time, stay out of jail, and don't make a lot of noise late at night. They pollute less than the average resident since they walk, ride bicycles, and don't throw away a lot of stuff in the garbage.

There is a downside to population growth based on aging. First, they don't spend as much money in the local economy as does a family with four kids.

Second, their frugality and thrift can make them opposed to change and a voting block for lower taxes.

Third, we don't stay around forever.

Vibrant growth is dependent upon retaining and attracting younger people to the county. The traditional way to attract them is to promise jobs and decent school systems.

Often overlooked is their subtle requirement that any place to which they relocate or stay must be "interesting." Younger folks demand both bread and circuses.

Urban planners are paying attention to this phenomenon and rural folks had best start paying attention.

"Why do college graduates consider Austin, Texas a great place for a new job while Kalamazoo, Michigan is considered a deathtrap?" asks the hotshot urban growth consultant, Richard Florida, in his book, *The Rise of the Creative Class*. After all, both are cities of about the same size with parallel pay scales. He goes on to ask why some urban neighborhoods are "hot spots" attracting new residents while other areas continue to decline.

His answer is simple. Austin is a funky and messy city with space for artists, musicians, computer geeks, and bohemians. Even the most respectable Baptists can find something interesting in Austin. Kalamazoo is boring.

Hot neighborhoods such as mine in Chicago are a crazy quilt of Hispanic and East European restaurants and churches with space for lofts, art galleries, and interesting shops. Rich folks love building million-dollar homes here.

If Richard Florida is right, then the secret for Marion County growth might be hidden in the annual arts and crafts fairs.

Add to the annual events and throw in more antique stores, pottery shops, and quilt stores, add a few more funky restaurants and bars along with some houses and shops skirting the edge of building code violations.

The county has too few eccentrics and cranks, too few Democrats, too few bohemians, and too few computer geeks to be attractive to most newcomers. (If they cannot be attracted, perhaps they could be hired to play these roles much like a duck decoy.)

The challenge for Marion County is not how to promote the area as a "nice" place to live but rather to identify how it could become an interesting place for new residents.

PUSHING FOR A TAX ON THE POOR AND STUPID MAY HAVE MERIT

2005, Hillsboro Free Press

Bob Knight, the "Music Man" from Wichita, did his song and dance routine brilliantly for the Marion County Commissioners.

He painted them a picture of a casino with 2,500 jobs and a twelve-story hotel generating tax revenue beyond their wildest dreams.

And all they had to do was allow a few tiny slot machines, roulette wheels, and poker games to come into the county.

Bedazzled by the promise of such riches, the commissioners said, "Shucks, let's ask the voters if they approve. Doesn't cost much to send them all a postcard."

This casino plans seems reasonable. After all, the middle class and rich folks have been taxed to the hilt with income and property taxes. Even "sin" is now taxed to the breaking point with booze, cigarettes, and gasoline costing extra to pay for the damage they create. Legalized gambling is the perfect solution. Instead of taxing "sin," sell it directly.

Gambling is a tax on the poor and the stupid. These folks just haven't been paying their fair share.

Thinking positively, imagine that the referendum passes and a casino is approved for Marion County. All that remains then is to find the best location for the new cash cow.

Converting a local grain elevator to a twelve-story hotel is feasible and the results would be dramatic. Plus, "The Co-op Casino" has a nice ring to it. But I am told the elevators are being used year-round and none are available.

Marion Reservoir has potential for development. One could plop a giant riverboat in the middle and run gangplanks to all four shores for easy access. (But I think parking would be a problem.)

Any of the county's retirement centers would be an excellent choice. Lots of older folks get up at night and have nothing to do. They could amble over to the gaming room and play slots at three in the morning and spend their kids' inheritance while waiting for their breakfast to be prepared.

Pilsen is an option for a casino with a polka band and bingo theme.

Another option is to push ahead with a landfill in Marion County and put the casino on top of it. That way everything that stinks would be in one place.

Or let the Arts and Crafts Fair people take over the entire operation. These ladies are geniuses at finding a place for four thousand cars to park once a year in Hillsboro and they understand hospitality and crowd control. But they only work on this one day a year. Let them use their expertise for the other 364 days.

Some of the local churches are building in the suburbs and putting in huge parking lots. But these are used primarily on Sunday morning. Perhaps the casino could share its parking lot and be called the Saints and Sinners Casino. Everybody would win. The casino gets cheaper parking. The church has more money for missions.

(Plus, the bad lounge acts that do contemporary worship music could find extra employment on the casino entertainment stage on Saturday night.)

Tabor College should take note and consider inviting the casino to campus. This would provide employment for students, plus internships. It would offer a chance to expand the business program to include a master's degree in gaming. (The cafeteria and snack bar could stay open all night.)

I suspect the final location of a casino in Marion County will provoke hate and discontent. Every landowner dreams of selling off sixty acres of his junk land for a fantastic price and retiring early. Every city council dreams of free money. Every gas station owner dreams of thousands of cars driving past his pumps.

Let me offer a gentle solution for the fight over the casino location. The county commissioners are considering building a new county jail. Why not build a multiplex and use the courthouse as a dramatic entrance for the casino and build the jail at the opposite end?

That way, if any of the millions of visitors to Marion County decided to act the fool when losing at the craps table, they could just be escorted down the hall.

FIGURING OUT THE MALE CONDITION AT THE O'HARE RAMADA INN

1996

There are about five hundred men age eighteen to seventy-plus. Maybe one percent of them are African American. I see one Asian and one American Indian in attendance. My impression is that a significant number have come to previous conferences in Chicago. A surprising number of women are here, all of them rather pretty and perky, usually accompanying a male partner. The women smile attentively but they're mostly silent. I am not explicitly aware of other gay men in attendance. I see men who might be gay (rather regrettable representatives), and men I wish were gay but unfortunately do not appear to be, and a huge percentage of men toward whom I feel a great deal of sexual indifference.

Earlier, as I drove to the conference with a former Voluntary Service administrator and ex-pastor, I mused that I already felt shy, lonely, and scared about this crowd—very much like an interloper and not a member at all. But then I feel that in most new situations.

The first plenary session opens with Dr. Robert L. Moore, a seminary professor in Hyde Park. He has short cropped hair and wears a black leather vest. He introduces John Lee, head of the Austin, Texas Men's Center. Lee is well-known on the circuit, featured at many other weekend gatherings, and author of nine books in eleven years—each book shorter and lighter than the first one, which was titled *Flying Boy*. Dr. Lee has a magnificent Alabama accent, a wonderful boyish gray beard, and an aw-shucks attitude. He says "fuck" a lot, and he deploys his bag of verbal tricks and mannerisms plus stream-of-consciousness patter to cover the lack of any discernible train of thought—let alone even a track. His father was a drunk and his mother was a wimp. They are still living. Recently on the phone they asked him what he spoke about at these conferences. "Mostly about you, Mom and Dad," Dr. Lee says. The essence of the forty-five-minute exercise in country humor, with appropriate poetry, is that one should know how close one wants to be to others and how long to stay with them. Dr. Lee has learned this from his twelve-year-old stepdaughter. As with Saul Bellow, each marital and partnership breakup seems to prompt Dr. Lee to write a new book with appropriate insights.

I go to a group session, "A Community of Two," about male friendship. As per usual there aren't enough seats so I sit on the floor. A North Shore psychiatrist and a younger North Shore psychologist, perhaps ages forty and fifty-five, respectively, give their fifth annual report on the status of their friendship. From the few crumbs of factual information given, it appears each is married and has children. They love and respect each other. The younger is taking flying lessons and shows clips from a movie about aviators to explain his situation. There is reference to his wife not liking him to take chances. The older man says he misses the decrease in contact with his friend but has come to realize he has been rather dependent and selfish. They read from assorted journal entries, Eastern poetry, show more video clips, and then, well after the allotted time, the session ends.

***

The ethos of the conference seems to be that one presents oneself as a "man with many feelings" rather than as a rich psychiatrist from Wilmette. Incidental details of class and vocation are the marks of a man with a false sense of himself—and the marks of a newcomer.

I head off for a session called the sacred community but have difficulty finding the press room in the basement where, according to the program, it is supposed to be happening. By the time I get there, everybody is shuffling slowly in a circle to the sound of a drum. I leave for a cigarette.

I run into an old friend who left Chicago some time ago. It is obvious he is in great pain as we sit together for lunch—trying to make appropriate small talk with the other men who have joined us for charred chicken breast and salad. The man on my right is a carpentry instructor for trade unions. Now approaching retirement, he is a veteran of these conferences. It feels good to talk with a craftsman for a moment. He talks about details of his furniture-building projects for assorted grandchildren.

My old friend and I take a walk. There's the usual stuff, marital problems, sexual issues, unresolved business from his family of origin. Now in a crisis state, he says his therapist sent him to the conference. I feel caught between wanting to renew the friendship and playing therapist or at least fairly decent listener to him. When we look at our watches, we see that we have missed an entire session.

I go to a workshop on male aggression. Once again Dr. John Lee and Dr. Robert Moore are presenting. Moore makes an interesting point about men and women—which I think I journaled about in the early 1980s. By roughly age forty, men are done being warriors and want to be lovers. I wrote about this phase as men fighting for vocational identity and social and economic power. Anyway, by around forty men want to play—often with their wife and kids. But women are lovers until forty and then become warriors. (Which often translates into her finishing a graduate degree, at the most harmless. My car companion is finalizing his divorce this month, on this model. After fifteen years as a hard-driving pastor and church executive, he recently came home to a simpler congregational assignment and his wife, a registered nurse, told him she wanted out.)

The workshop on anger is useful and even practical. Both Lee and Moore agree anger is a real emotion, like sadness and love, and it should not be dishonored. They suggest that immediate anger can be contained: "I need to talk to you because you missed a lunch meeting with me." When the expression of anger cannot be contained—such as talking about it forever, or with no boundaries—it is generally anger brought forward from the past. "You stood me up and my father was an asshole." There is another axiom: Rage is not a feeling but a state of being. Thus, men who abuse or kill, when asked, "What did you feel?" correctly answer: "I felt nothing at all."

We do some simple group exercises of squeezing a partner's fingers to express anger or else twisting a towel into knots. Don't laugh, this seemed useful to me. But I sense that my anger was not so deep or so buried as that of the men who packed the room. The paradox by appearance was that the most mild-mannered men were on the edge of uttering animal sounds and screaming "fuck" when the leader gave them the slightest opportunity.

***

On the drive home we have a long talk—mostly because I miss the Dan Ryan exit. As we bounce through Forest Park and other suburbs, the ex-pastor shares more of his life narrative. We get to my house and a young man from the Voluntary Service unit brings over some wine, and he and the ex-pastor exchange stories. Both are very bright; both have been pushed toward academic excellence by their families. I listen for a while and then make a fool of myself—talking about seminary, and the coffeehouse, and my army exploits, in a manic episode which I haven't had in a long time. As my monologue unspools, I gradually realize they're embarrassed by it, and so am I.

Much later that evening I figure out how exhausted and angry I was. The previous night I had listened to another friend talk about his needs for four hours. I had spent this day absorbing the ex-pastor's breakup crisis with his wife. For much of the conference in the past twelve hours I had been sitting on the floor in the back of the room like some errant schoolboy who had just been conned out of $180 to listen to men say what I felt I could say as well or better. So I was left bottled up, without a story, just the detached critical and affirming ear. My unsolicited and inappropriate monologue was anger, a demand to these two men in my house to acknowledge that I existed.

***

In the morning, I miss the brunch by a minute. (Note to self: cheap way to run a conference, offer brunch at 9:30 and run the conference until 4:00 without a lunch break). I attend two sessions. The first is by a leader in the men's movement who recounts the numerous spiritual retreats he has attended around the world. He now leads the New Monk movement, which is part of the New Warrior movement. Through staring at objects and a man in the room and saying "I am" to a partner, we are able to work alchemy or magic, which sounds suspiciously like cognitive reframing to me. Nevertheless, I find the opportunity to stare at a Wisconsin body builder in blue jeans and a flannel shirt is a welcome break.

The final group session is led by the international leader of the New Warrior movement. He is a North Shore lawyer, about forty years old. Frankly, he turns out to be the sharpest presenter and group leader at the conference. Simple tactic: we sit in a circle and as men come in, he insists we put out more chairs and include them in the circle. "We are a circle of men and we *will* find space for every man who enters the room."

He starts off with the question, "What does it mean to be a man? Okay, we all have a cock and balls, what else?" He gives an anthropological interpretation of initiation for young men, and says the best parallel was military service until the 1960s. Initiation is being ripped away from the mother, teaching and bonding with other men and discovering a spiritual dimension. He goes on to say that men are not initiated as a general rule anymore, and the New Warriors can in three days provide initiation for men from age seventeen to eighty-one, no matter what their stage of life or status in life.

Apparently seven thousand men in North America have undergone the ritual. I ask about the price of $580 for a weekend and say, "Doesn't that preclude men of a certain class?"

He fights back: "What price would you pay to be a man?"

I am tempted to bid about $28 but decide to hold that thought. He then talks in a rush about the nonprofit status, the extensive staff at each weekend event, and the option of monthly payments. He says he makes a real sacrifice since he is paid only a thousand dollars for each weekend he leads, far below what he could bill as a lawyer.

A serious point: The initiation weekend is followed up by small group work (for another $100), which can last for another twelve weeks. Otherwise, the initiation is solitary. "National Socialism initiated men also," the leader tells us, "but into a tribal identity. Since we have no collective identity but initiation into any religion, class, vocation, and sexual identity, there is no tribalism and no danger of tribalism." I find myself wondering about the potential harms which can be inflicted by both lone, non-tribal psychopaths and totalitarian tribalists.

At the break I sit and talk with an Oneida Indian from Oshkosh, Wisconsin. He is stunningly handsome, has been in recovery for ten years, and is now studying for addictions counseling and to be a tribal healer for addictions. A newcomer to the conference, he finds the pipes and drums for sale and the pseudo-Indian lore he has heard bandied about deeply offensive. We share our stories briefly. We decide next year we should sell consecrated communion wafers and wine on neck chains at a table right next to the drum shop.

Earlier in the day I had listened to Dr. Robert Moore tell of his trip around the world with wife number whatever. He had discovered both poverty and suffering in Asia but also seen the Temple of Shiva in Bombay. The god had a gigantic phallus, which allegedly went so deep into the earth that one could not go under it, and so high into the sky that one could not go over it. He was deeply moved by both the phallus and the poverty, although the connection was not entirely clear to me. He had said, "Men's community is no longer economic, it is now spiritual. Men's community is no longer culturally based, but spiritually based."

My foundational disagreement with the mythopoetic men's movement is its resistance to tribal, cultural, and economic analysis. It is also resistant to community building beyond the therapeutic weekend or seminar. We can debate if any spirituality can exist for long when it is independent of a cultural or economic foundation. At my most wicked, I suspect some part of the spiritual base is the rather high prices charged by the movement for admission to itself and its spirituality, and the ability of the participants to pay.

At the wrap-up session we form concentric circles. We sing nonsense words and dance in a circle holding hands. At the end we learn a fairly elaborate dance to Shiva—the creator and destroyer with the Big, Big Dick. It is all sort of charming in a New Age way.

Later in the evening I ponder if I am very repressed or very well. Most of the speakers had joked that they had spent over $100,000 for therapy so far in their lifetime. My bill is lower. My guess is that as a country boy I learned something about being a man from my father and my brothers. As a gay man I learned something about myself to survive and even love. As a recovering alcoholic, I have found some spiritual nature. None of this has been done in a self-conscious effort to be a man, but rather in an effort to stay alive.

I have always been insanely jealous of good straight men, able to move freely in vocation and love and family. Their road seems so much easier—and I still think it is. But apparently a PhD and a wife and kids doesn't give one as much comfort in being a man as I had presumed. Oh, well, one more thing I hadn't thought of.

I talk with my dad by telephone before turning in. He'll be eighty-nine this summer. He and Vi are concerned about raking leaves and getting the garden out in a month or so. He says there were quite a few people in church this morning and asks me twice how I am doing and then thanks me for my call. He has very little interest in long conversations. God, I do love that old man.

THINKING ABOUT THE MEN'S MOVEMENT

1996

I begin by calling your attention to three major movements in which males in America have self-consciously come together. Now I realize that larger groups of men assemble almost any weekend for sports rituals such as, for example, Super Bowl Sunday—the high holy days of masculinity in contemporary America—but they do not self-consciously assemble as they do at men's movement events.

Already almost fading from our memory is the 1980s men's movement with poet and teacher Robert Bly, guru of middle-aged, middle-class white males who gathered at seminars and retreats to beat on drums and lament the loss of their manhood.

Bly was very explicit that a grief process was needed in middle age to mark the loss of strong father figures, meaningful physical work, male intimacy, and men's weakness in the face of attacks from both primary women such as wives and lovers, mothers and sisters, but also attacks from the larger women's movement. Men, Bly said, needed to band together to collectively mourn, grieve, express anger, and ultimately find the "wild man" within themselves.

There were other articulate voices besides Bly, but the consistent approach was that men were in some form of negative space, collectively and individually, and that repentance and apology were necessary before men could move forward as healed—or at least more healthy—individuals.

The next self-conscious men's movement is even more controversial: the Promise Keepers. Founded by former University of Colorado football coach Bill McCartney, the organization has seen about a million evangelical Christian men gather in football stadiums to reclaim their roles as fathers, husbands, and heads of households. In their view, the aim is to become more faithful Christians. This movement, perhaps the largest of the three I describe here today, is the most controversial—due to its claim that men's authority is divinely ordained. But the movement also insists that men have collectively and individually failed to keep their promises and commitments.

The third movement is the Million Man March. In August 1995 a huge assembly of African-American men assembled peacefully in Washington, D.C., due principally to the charismatic leadership of Muslim leader and minister Louis Farrakhan. They gathered not to petition the government or the nation but to assemble for repentance and to reclaim their proper roles in the African-American community and in the nation.

So here are three unique and separate collective gatherings of men. At first glance they could not be more different: evangelical Christians, African Americans, and quasi-liberal if not New Age middle-aged white men. Yet some of the statements of apology and repentance, of collective and individual failure, are almost interchangeable. I would like to address two questions. First, why the apology? And second, to whom is the apology addressed? I hope my remarks will shed some light on the state of gender relationships in America today.

But before I can go further, I need to share a concept of gender community which is the foundation of my thinking and writing about gender. Briefly stated, every culture contains within it two communities: the men's community and the women's community. I generally draw this on a blackboard as two equally sized circles which are inside a larger circle. The larger circle is the cultural system—be it a tribe, an ethnic or racial group, or a stable regional community. The two circles inside the larger circle represent the men's and women's communities.

The two communities are at the most elemental level symbiotic—neither can survive biologically without the other. To an overwhelming extent there is a division of labor between the two. As a rule of thumb, in most historical and cultural situations the male community is more visible, takes on the task of defending the perimeter of the community through warfare and large game hunting, but also in public roles including trade and government. Traditionally the women's community has had a more primary focus on infants and children, the maintenance of the camp and home, and the so called "domestic life." If we had more time, we could explore the constant renegotiation which takes place in this division of labor—renegotiations resulting from economic and technological shifts, migration, warfare, and demographic disparity between genders.

Turning our attention to the men's community (and much of what I say here applies also to the women's community circle as well), an individual male has a multiplicity of tasks. First, there is the matter of membership through formal or informal initiation into the gender community. Second, one must maintain membership. Third, for men, one seeks increasing status in the men's community. Fourth, one must enhance or value the status of the men's community.

But as if this were not enough, the man must also relate to the women's community, both as an individual to women blood relatives, to secure a female partner if so inclined, but also to protect and provide for his children—who are presumably either male or female.

A man does have some options other than maintaining and enhancing his membership in the men's community. Most of these are seen as negative and are still vividly reflected in our slang and slander language. "Don't act like a child" means don't remain in a pre-gender state. "Don't be an ass" exhorts us not to descend to subhuman, animal status. "Don't be a sissy" or "Don't be a girl" emphatically prohibit defecting to or mimicking the behaviors of the women's community. "Don't be henpecked"—and you and I know there are much stronger terms for this—says in no uncertain terms, don't be dominated by the woman's community.

In most of human history, to be exiled from the men's community is to be an outcast, an alien, a stranger. A solitary man was the extreme sanction—often akin to the death penalty.

Uniquely in parts of Europe and America this solitary male is now seen as heroic.

To recap this part of my talk, let me share an anecdote. This past Christmas Eve I was at my brother's farm in Kansas—the same farm our family has had for well over a century. At the house, making his debut to assorted gathered relatives, was my brother's two-day-old first grandson.

The dogs started barking around 11:30 and my brother said, "There's a good chance the mountain lion is back at the cattle pens. Let's go."

So he, his son-in-law, and I got dressed. They loaded their 30-30s and we drove slowly around the pens and fields—to protect the perimeter. The women remained behind to offer ever more advice to the young mother. As we cruised in my brother's four-wheel drive, I had a sense that I was participating in a rite and division of labor which probably goes back to ancient prehistory.

With this highly oversimplified model in mind, let us see if it casts some light on the apology of these three different men's movements.

Economic Change

In general, the men's community has traditionally acted as the more public community operating to protect the perimeter of the larger cultural community. In recent American experience that meant the world of work was the men's community. Obviously, this has changed for virtually everybody today. Work is now the domain of both men and women. And while that is true, most men are experiencing what I call a two-dimensional loss in income status.

First, incomes are not progressing upward in the same fairly orderly way that they did for their fathers. Truthfully, men who are today in their seventies may tell you how they advanced toward home ownership and financial security through thrift, cleverness, and hard work. Larger economic data suggests that men with an IQ higher than their body temperature and ten fingers and ten toes rode an economic escalator up, almost unrelated to their skills and abilities. By contrast, men in today's work force are not progressing as well as their fathers did economically. I would note that if women use their mothers as a reference point, most women are economically more self-sufficient than their mothers.

Second, men are no longer the dominant economic force within the two-parent household. Only about 7 percent of American two-adult households can sustain their economic status on the male's income alone—and most of these are families approaching age sixty-five in upper-income brackets. Men are a less significant part of the economic pie. The economic situation of men, virtually across the entire spectrum of American culture, has slowly eroded. And I suspect that due to his individualism and lack of a self-conscious collective identity, each man has seen his decline as uniquely his own doing, his own fault.

In my work as a therapist, I often encourage clients to distinguish between their feelings of shame and guilt. Shame is what is imposed on us as individuals or communities, guilt is more the result of our own doing. The shame that American men feel economically is based on a radical change in economic situation, not of their own doing. Their guilt, on the other hand, may be their lashing out and seeking villains or scapegoats—be these women, minorities, or immigrants—to account for their shame. One does not need to apologize for shame—but I fear that the men's movements, due to a lack of economic self-analysis, might be doing exactly this.

On Homosexuality and the Men's Movements

Traditionally, homosexual and homosocial men were men who remained within the men's community. While many societies set strict limits on acts of sodomy, they also gave status to certain men who spent the majority of their lives within the men's community as religious leaders, warriors, teachers, healers, and shamans. Such men might be "different," but they were generally a part of the men's community.

Each of the three men's movements has taken a different stance toward male homosexuality. The Robert Bly mythopoetic movement claims to be pro-gay, but also states that the experience of gay men is so unlike their own, that gay men are precluded from membership due to being a third gender. There is some fragmentary evidence that the Bly men's movement owes much more to the earlier gay men's retreats than it cares to remember. Early seventies gay men's consciousness-raising gatherings, often rural, sometimes incorporating the sweat lodge, predate and anticipate much of the Bly movement, and suggest there has been more borrowing than is commonly acknowledged. The Bly men's movement with its emotional catharsis and physical and emotional intimacy feels free of homoeroticism since "that" is something done by the men in the other tribe.

For the Promise Keepers, homosexuality is an evil act. But taking seriously the "love the sinner, hate the sin" maxim, the Promise Keepers are probably no more distancing from homosexuality than the Bly movement. In fact, they are perhaps less distanced from homosexuality than the New Age otherness perspective of Mr. Bly.

The position of Minister Farrakhan on homosexuality is most interesting.

Homosexuals are denounced as a bad part of our men's community. Homosexual acts are bad things which many of us have done. But homosexuals are a part of the African-American community. The anecdotes suggest gay men participated openly in Farrakhan's Million Man March and were not harassed (though I need to go to the archive for more evidence of this).

The Million Man March and Malcolm and Martin

The American situation of the African-American gender communities is radically different from that of European, Asian, and Hispanic cultural communities.

First, there is the matter of matriarchal culture. I am not certain if I am willing to push this point. Is it the result of African origins or economics from the slave days on?

Second, the men's community in African American culture is in chaos—to the point of cultural implosion. Forty per cent of African American men are either on probation, parole, or incarcerated. Fatherhood seems to be a vanishing art.

American racism has a powerful gender component. Lynching was for "uppity" Black men. The insane double standard made Black women objects of white male sexual desire, while Black men were objects of fear and hatred. African American culture faces a unique—and that is much too weak a word—challenge. The men's community is feared, reviled, lynched, and rejected by the larger society. The women's community has had greater access, and continues to enjoy greater access, to the larger society. The result is a unique disparity between the men's and women's communities within African American culture—a disparity which appears to be growing rather than diminishing.

A huge percentage of African American women were in the public work force by 1900. They were motivated by poverty certainly, but they were also acceptable, non-threatening persons who could be allowed into a white-dominated cash economy. Today the wage gap between Black and white men with comparable education and experience is gigantic while the wage gap between Black and white women with similar status is small. In some cases, Black women earn more than their white female counterparts.

Our racism today as whites is divided by a clear gender perspective on the African American community. Don't believe me? Have two Black women approach you on a dark street on the South Side at night, then two Black men in the same setting, and tell me, you experience no visceral difference in your responses?

As I understand Martin Luther King, his push was for a less violent society in which all persons would be judged by the "content of their character" and not by the "color of their skin." It is less clear if he meant the same thing about the inward or outward nature of their genitalia. Malcolm X, perhaps because his perspective was shaped by the streets and not the church and the university, saw the gender problems of the African American community. The Black Muslim experience was to rigidly separate and rediscipline both the men's and women's communities. What appears regressive and repressive to white liberals is an attempt to rebuild a racial community through reshaping and healing the gender communities. The strict discipline and bowties for men, the white head coverings for women, are symbolic of powerful gender work being done, even if we might disagree with it. No wonder that Ossie Davis in his funeral eulogy for Malcolm X centered his oration on the notion that "Malcolm taught us how to be men."

The separatism of the Black Muslim movement is generally framed in terms of separating from a hostile white society. I suspect that another element is that only separation can provide the space for healing of the gender rift and conflict between Black men and Black women.

The oratory of the Million Man March contained an explicit theme that Black men have not maintained their own gender community and that repentance is required for this failure.

Despite eloquent and extreme attacks on the external enemies—mainly whites but with a subtext of anti-Semitism—the Million Man March deserves credit for being the most explicit and conscious attempt of a gender community to regroup in a self-conscious way.

The Spiritual Apology

The Million Man March had its soul in the Black Muslim movement with more pragmatic endorsements and support from mainstream black churches and civic groups. We do not normally think of Evangelical Protestantism as a woman-driven religion. The official lines about the non-ordination of women might lead us to believe it is the heartland of male dominance.

Similarly, we might believe, due to the high visibility of Black clergymen such as Jesse Jackson and Martin Luther King, that the Black church is a male-driven institution. Not true, buffalo brains. For more than a century, the Christian churches in America of all types have been an alliance of a minority of men in collusion with a majority of women.

Or so men have seen it. Your mother is spiritual, your father is pragmatic and strong and smart. (Hey, why do I have an image of Jewish faith as the last remaining bastion of male spirituality?)

Is there an attempt in all three movements to find a uniquely male spiritual expression?

Odd, but the media and perhaps we here today find such expressions as drumming, giving "three cheers for Jesus," and so on, as fascinating, hilarious, repulsive, and bizarre. But I suspect that we have no alternative to offer. The attempts of the men's movements to find a unique men's spirituality, and perhaps more profound, the recognition of the spiritual vacuum which individualism and stoicism have produced among men, may be a significant contribution of these movements.

Comments on Feminism and Men's Movements

I propose several key observations:

1. The women's movement generally serves to restore, strengthen, and renegotiate the women's community vis-à-vis the men's community.

2. Women's community has a stronger sense of collective identity than men's community. Paradoxically, the women's community stresses the collective nature of womanhood, while containing in the movement a wider range of individualism. The men's community stresses individualism and a sense that "I am not bound by men's collective standards," while containing less overt manifestations of individual style or expression of individualism.

3. I accept that inevitably any community retains cohesiveness by some degree of stressing an outward enemy. Additionally, any community acts in its own self-interest: get the best deal you can. For that reason, I have very little problem with women's critique of men's community or the so-called "old boys' network." Most men have reacted defensively: "I individually am not guilty of these things although my less enlightened male colleges are." Or it is claimed "the charges are overstated" or "wrong." Another response is ridicule.

I was deeply touched by a feminist academic writer who stated, "Women's studies are an urgent part of our responsibility to our sisters, daughters, and mothers." I am hard pressed to find an equivalent statement from a straight white male writer. I am no more impressed by the instances of feminist paranoia and ridicule of the men's movements than I am by men who ridicule and fear women. When a gender community comes together to rebuild, heal, and renegotiate its place in the larger culture, it is time for the opposite gender community to shut up and tend to its own business.

The Apology

I don't think the men's movements are clear about the nature of their repentance and apology. I think an apology to the women's community is insufficient, too late, and a poor move. What men may need to do is to apologize to their brothers, sons, and fathers—both genetic and social family. We have not tended to each other. This will take longer than a weekend retreat, a weekend march, or a weekend revival meeting.

The workplace is no longer the men's community. In America by the year 2000, only 20 percent of the entry level work force will be heterosexual white males. What for generations seemed the inviolate men's club is gone forever. As many men have experienced decreasing economic status and, for many, increased time with family responsibilities, they have sacrificed deliberate time with other men.

Because males took their own gender community for granted, they often failed to consciously identify its value for them. The rise of the visible gay men's community has driven the rising perception that men who nurture, display affection, and consciously enjoy the company of other men belong to another community altogether. This has further diminished the men's community. (I contrast this with the women's community in which lesbian women have served not only as role models but as strong leaders for women for more than a century. At present it is almost unthinkable that gay men could serve a similar role in the men's community.)

If the public arena and workplace are no longer the exclusive domain of men, how and where shall they now assemble? Since we as American men have hopelessly confused public policy with our gender agenda, we have almost forgotten how to speak about ourselves. I note that a woman advocating for women's issues is called a feminist, but there is no equivalent term for men doing the same thing for their own gender community. One sign of progress is the development of gender studies programs—particularly when they are authentically involved in gender studies. The fragmentation and objectification involved in women's studies, minority studies, and gay and lesbian studies too easily implies that there is a "normal world" understood by heterosexual, white male administrators, and pockets of deviance which can be objectively analyzed.

The apology of the three men's movements is ambiguous. One part seems to be unwarranted shame resultant from most men's downward economic status in the larger society and within the family. Another is an apology to the women's community. The third is vague awareness that men may have forgotten how to relate to each other—as friends, lovers, fathers, comrades.

I would hope that each of these men's movements will move from apology to doing solid gender work and celebration, for their own health and well-being as men's communities, for the well-being of the counterpart women's communities, and for the good of the larger society as a whole.

EUPHORIA AND BANALITY: THE QUEST FOR GETTING HIGH

2001

It is good to be here—even if this is a suicidal mission. I am from Chicago—and our first suburb is Evanston—the home of the Woman's Christian Temperance Union. I work at the Salvation Army. You may presume that I represent them. A few of you will recall me as a child of the 1970s, who now lives in Chicago, a work-hard and play-hard sort of town, the city of Al Capone and presently crack cocaine—and you're wondering what I am doing here.

I presume that I am speaking to an audience with diverse interests and perspectives about addictions. Some of you are comfortable—even smug—about your abstinence from drugs and alcohol. Perhaps you are like the persons Jesus referred to as "once born" who have no need for a physician. Hold on, I'll get to you later. Staff and faculty know that any reduction in drug alcohol use among students translates into an automatic increase in student retention—hence balanced budgets—and are praying I will have some modest success. I fear you may be disappointed. You need to know that drug and alcohol education has a very limited impact and can easily be counterproductive. Thus:

"This is my brain—this is my brain on drugs."

"Well, shoot, scrambled eggs are better than boiled eggs anyway."

"Alcohol is a dangerous adult activity and you should wait until you are much more mature and only use it after you are twenty-one."

"Great—two good things. First, a cheap and easy way to flirt with danger and death, and I can appear to be a sophisticated adult at the same time."

"In the euphoria of binge drinking you ascend first to heaven, then to the nonbeing of a blackout, followed by a morning after of projectile vomiting straight from hell."

"Most excellent! I can achieve cosmic travel for twenty dollars' worth of booze and a welcome escape from a boring life in a boring prairie town."

Others of you will say:

"If the odds are only one in ten that I will become alcoholic or drug-addicted, and considering that I am smarter and more clever than most of my classmates—let alone the general population—then the odds are excellent that I can successfully control any form of drug and alcohol use."

Others of you have this inner argument:

"I was raised in a dry town—in a dry church by dry parents. But I also notice the similarity between dry and dead. I want to be wet and alive."

All of these perspectives have enough legitimacy to deserve consideration. My own perspective comes from three sets of experiences. For twelve years I have worked as a counselor with men who have reached the end of the road from addictions—many of them the same people who make you afraid to visit Chicago. For six years I've worked part time in federal corrections doing drug alcohol education with residents— ranging from political and corporate leaders doing time for white-collar crime to mid and low-level drug dealers. Finally, there has been an endless dialogue with friends—ranging from those just out of college to others nearly illiterate—who have shared with me their reflections and experiences about their own drug and alcohol use.

I believe that drugs and alcohol must be considered not just from individual experience but also in terms of larger meta-analysis. Drugs and alcohol are a major intellectual issue as well as an individual problem. In other words, we need to see the big picture.

Most cultures, societies, and communities throughout human history have operated on two levels. First, there is daily life—the ordinary, the routine, the commonplace. The humdrum tasks of daily life—ranging from simple survival (food, shelter and clothing), to earning a living or finishing college are in the long term prosaic and banal. The daily routines in these cultures were periodically interrupted by a transcendent, out-of-the-ordinary state. Described sometimes as carnival, at other times as the Dionysian gods, this condition was achieved through ritual and celebration, often involving role reversals and even the violation of established taboos. Thus, spectacles, carnival, Feast Days, and theater stood in sharp contrast to the ordinary. Euphoria and a sort of "high" interrupted the banality and prosaic nature of daily life. Only grudgingly did the Christian tradition incorporate the joyous pagan traditions into the watered-down rituals of Halloween, Thanksgiving, Christmas, and New Year's Eve.

With the Enlightenment, the scientific revolution, the Protestant Reformation, and perhaps merely our experience of living on flat prairie land, we have elevated the banal and prosaic aspects of daily life into something we call the "good life." This consists of rationality and meaningful work and "correct relationships." Our individual quests for a "high"—to find a way, even for a moment, to "slip the surly bonds of earth and touch the face of God," as aviator John Gillespie Magee Jr. once put it, have not fared well. Religion is not much more than *New York Times* op-ed pieces mixed with Oprah Winfrey self-help platitudes with wall projector praise hymns which are neither sacred nor profane. Or religion is relegated to the cul-de-sacs of postmodernist anxiety. The near-sexual excesses of religious ecstasy are for most students merely cults to be observed. Sex is still passion. But now it is encumbered with technique, political correctness, and ideology.

We envy the genius of William Blake, Mozart and Van Gogh—but wonder if they might not have lived more serene lives with the benefits of modern psychotropic medications. Certain individuals achieve the transcendent—particularly in the world of aesthetics—the artist, writer, composer, rock star who is wild and crazy or cutting edge and represents us as celebrity or intellectual hero. But we are not them.

Still, all is not lost. Fear not. Today we can use chemicals to achieve euphoria and escape the banal and prosaic dimensions of our lives. The Weekend! We Party! (Never mind that we have turned a noun into a verb.) Today we are using chemicals to achieve euphoria. The more difficult routes are disdained and neglected.

At this point, please allow me to shift into my addictions-counselor mode and present the modern, grand unified field theory of using chemicals to achieve euphoria. First, there is more commonality linking heroin, alcohol, cocaine, crystal meth, Ecstasy, LSD, and marijuana than is commonly believed. They all produce immediate and fairly predictable "highs"—a sense of euphoria and a feeling of transcendence—followed by a crash or a low. For this reason, I am today excluding nicotine, caffeine, chocolate, and food-binging, since these things simply don't produce the same level of high and altered reality. Nor am I including Prozac and other antidepressants—which produce a long-term feeling of well-being but not a "high" or a "rush." Other so-called addictive behaviors actually fit more nearly into obsessive-compulsive disorders and are a separate topic.

Our distinctions between alcohol and addictive drugs are more culturally, regionally, and class based then they are reality. Thus, the tidy heroin addicts always look down on the sloppy drunks; the wine and beer drinkers feel smug and mainstream about their name-brand products used in fern bars versus the junkies shuffling around in alleys. Crystal meth is hillbilly cocaine. Alcohol is part of White House receptions and dinners, drugs are a Class X felony. But in addictions theory, these products are more similar than different. I repeat, they all produce a rapid high or euphoria, followed inevitably by a crash or down. This down is best alleviated by using the mood-altering substance again—in a few hours or days. In this way, a merry-go-round effect is produced.

All these products are widely used. In their lifetime, most persons will have used alcohol and or drugs at some point. Thus, my church serves wine every Sunday. More of your great grandmothers used morphine and cocaine—in the form of patent medicine—than you will.

Most people suffer few or no negative consequences from their use of either drugs or alcohol. But drug alcohol "use" can easily become "abuse." Abuse is defined in the dry language of the *Diagnostic and Statistical Manual of Mental Disorders IV*—the Bible of psychiatry, as "an unintended decline in functioning as the result of ingestion of drugs and alcohol." The most obvious example is a DUI. Unless your purpose in drinking was to drink enough to get up the courage to weave across the centerline of a highway and attract the attention of a Kansas Highway Patrol officer, a DUI is an unintended negative consequence.

By the way, a hangover is technically "alcohol withdrawal"—which is why more alcohol is the best cure for a hangover—but I am getting ahead of myself. Drug alcohol abuse is obviously most common in young adults—and secondarily in senior citizens—in the latter group for interesting and different reasons than in young adults. Perhaps a third or more of college students will not flunk out of college—rather they will drink and drug themselves out. Drug and alcohol abuse accounts for an estimated 75 percent of campus sexual assaults and 80 percent of campus violence. New research is underway which also indicates that drug alcohol use also radically increases your chances of being the victim of sexual assaults and violence as well as the perpetuator.

More overlooked are the longer-term effects of drinking and drugging. The weekend warriors are sober and often technically drug and alcohol free in a physiological sense by Monday morning. But their cognitive impairment, often in conjunction with mild to severe depression, probably lasts three to four days. Thus the frantic term-paper writing and cramming for tests on Wednesday and Thursday nights—when the brain fog has finally lifted. As an aside, I would add that modern psychiatry has made serious progress at alleviating clinical depression in the past decades. But the methodology for *producing* depression has been well known for millennia. Enough booze and enough drugs will induce and will produce depression.

Substance abuse is often self-limiting. The most common cure is called "growing up." Those of us over forty can probably list a dozen "party animals" from college days who are now temperate or abstaining—and seemed to make this transition with a minimum of fuss. In some cases, these often are also the friends who never quite got around to finishing their bachelor's, or master's, or doctoral program, or who in some way are functioning below their potential.

If there is drug alcohol use, and drug alcohol abuse, there is a third stage known as substance dependency. In popular terms this is "alcoholism" or "drug addiction." The best shorthand definition of substance dependency involves three factors: first, a loss of control over when to start the using cycle; second, a loss of control over how much to use; and third, a loss of control over when to end the using cycle. This is common to both alcoholism and drug addiction. The "using cycle" is a fancy way of saying, "Nobody uses 24/7." Periods of use may be separated by a few hours or a few months for substance-dependent persons. In my group work with recovering men, this "loss of control" model resonates with their experience. When I ask, "How many of you told yourselves you wouldn't drink or drug until Friday night, but found yourselves using on Wednesdays?" there is unanimous agreement that this happened. "Well then, how many of you said, 'Tonight I will only use a little bit and then call it quits for the evening'—but found yourselves crossing your own limits?" Again, there is unanimous agreement. "Well, then, how many of you said, 'Okay, I'll only use until the bars close, or Sunday evening or some other cut off time,' but crossed that line also?" Again, there is unanimous agreement this happened.

Now I don't know if this happens to college students—crossing your own intended line over when to start, how much to use, or when to quit. That is a question, however, that might be worth asking yourself. The disease model in addictions defines as addiction first as primary; second, chronic; third, progressive; and fourth, generally a fatal disease. The data is approximately consistent that about 10 percent of a population suffers from some stage of addiction. Of this population, perhaps 10–20 percent will achieve five to ten years of abstinence after the onset. None—or virtually none—will ever return to controlled use of mood-altering substances.

The disease model is one reason why addictions counselors like myself are so irritating to other disciplines—particularly the social sciences. If the claim that the disease of addiction is primary and not secondary—then it exists in and of itself. This has implications for social theory. First, poverty doesn't cause addiction—but we stubbornly refuse to see how addiction causes poverty. Both domestic violence and homelessness are essentially subcategories of addictions in North America and Europe. In terms of scholastic achievement, a huge number of students are not stupid; they are simply drunk and stoned. Crime is not alienation; it is the inner logic of addictions—accounting for more than half of all arrests and more than 60 percent of all parole and probation violations. Our friends the psychodynamic therapists often make a good living insisting you recline on their couch and talk about your bad mommy and presume that when you have resolved that trauma you will drink and drug less. While addictions may be concurrent with both neurotic and psychotic behaviors, these cannot be addressed within active addiction.

Anthropologists and apologists for Third World exotics often say, "These poor tribes people lost their homeland and therefore they drink and became poor." The disease model points to a genetic factor in which there is a four to six times higher level of alcoholism and drug addiction in certain families and genetic populations. Biographers and historians continue to irk me with their logic: "His last two novels failed and his third wife left him—therefore he drank more." (And they continue to suspect that his earlier genius was found in the amount of drinking and drugging he did.) The addictions people have a more dirt farmer explanation for the failed artist—the disease is progressive. It gets worse. Talent and addiction often coexist in one person, but in the end the progressive nature of addiction dominates.

I listen to addicts and alcoholics tell me what they consider the dramatic story of how they shifted from alcohol to heroin, then to crack cocaine, then back to alcohol and only marijuana as they sought a drug of choice they thought they could live with. The disease model dismisses this as people simply shifting seats on the same merry-go-round. When my clients tell me they can't stop using because of peer pressure—meaning they live in a dorm or the ghetto—I know I am no longer listening to the saga of a tortured soul seeking transcendent individualism but the banal and ho-hum progression of a disease called addiction.

I often hear the phrase: "I party a lot." When the noun becomes a verb, we have a problem. A forty-seven-year-old client now sober for seven months sits in my office. He has an insight not uncommon among recovering persons: "Hey, that wasn't a party. I screwed up the last twenty years of my life. I was just a drunk, wasn't I?" He speaks as one emerging from a long sleep or living in a cave—bewildered by daylight. All I can do is share in his grief during his awakening. At the end of his active addiction this client faces gigantic tasks. The first is dealing with the ordinary, banal, and prosaic tasks of everyday life. He must find food, shelter, and income. Second, he must find ways to achieve euphoria—but this time without mood-altering substances. But now a third task is required. Somehow, on a daily basis, he must remember his long sleep and not return to its tempting confines.

My own position has shifted. Alcohol and drug use seem increasingly part of the banal and the everyday. I am increasingly bored with college yarns of drunken sex, intimacy, and fights, the barely remembered theological and philosophical insights. I am suspicious that when drinking and drugging are reported as resulting from "peer pressure," this represents conformity, not radical individualism or authentic self-expression. I suspect that liquid courage is nothing more than a mask for numbing, unspoken fear.

For me, increasingly, the Chicago urban ghettos are places of numbing conformity and endless repetitive behaviors. There is no romance, let alone political ferment left in them—unless you are the wide-eyed innocent at the Urban Life Center or some other college field trip to see "the city." I see the endless cycle of Cook County Jail, disconnected utilities, children raised by grandmothers, shopping for shelters while homeless, being at the mercy of social service agencies, shuffling from treatment center to detox centers to psychiatric hospitals, while meanwhile your teeth are falling out. This is not the Chicago blues; it is a numbing silent shuffle. A friend of mine, now sober for two years, told me one night that his recovery from alcoholism was based on a simple premise. "I realized the gates of hell were locked from the inside." His simple declaration is the best summary I know of the personal and political implications of active addiction.

Heaven is not easily stormed. Religious and sexual ecstasy, intellectual dissent, violence, nakedness, confronting the principalities and powers, are all wonderful and legitimate forms of achieving euphoria—when done sober. Our common task as human beings is to find the courage to confront the banal and prosaic nature of our daily lives—both to write term papers and to grade them. Second, we must take the risks to achieve the extraordinary—the ecstatic, euphoric condition. Too often, we lack the courage to do this—so we seek it in chemicals. We must find the courage to drop out of college rather than to drink our way out, to come out rather than blame our behavior on "I was drunk last night—so what I said or did doesn't count." We must learn to confess, confront, amaze, astonish and horrify our peers and our elders—not because we were drunk or stoned but because we have found some inner strength to achieve radical actions.

The chemical quest for euphoria is the ultimate banality. Ten percent of the population is struggling with drug alcohol dependency. Of this population, perhaps 20 percent will achieve five years of continuous clean time. This 2 percent population—often found in Alcoholics Anonymous or other recovering populations—has something to say to all of us, both abstainers and users. For the most part, they are grateful for the prosaic. They are surprised by joy.

FIRST AMENDMENT IS A BROAD FREEDOM

2007, Hillsboro Free Press

Years ago, my old friend Jack was asked to appear as an expert witness in an obscenity trial in Cincinnati. Jack was a local radio personality and a stand-up comic genius.

When the defense lawyers grilled him before the trial they asked him, "Now, will you testify that this comedian was being artistic and not obscene?"

"Absolutely not," Jack replied. "He is totally obscene and lacks any redeeming artistic merit. That is precisely why I believe he should have the freedom to speak."

Needless to say, Jack was not called as an expert witness by either side.

I agree with Jack's absolute commitment to freedom of speech and freedom of the press. An open society does not censor words and images. An open society does not stomp on nor ban words, ideas, and images—even when they are offensive.

Today I worry liberals and conservatives are both equally willing to compromise freedom of expression for their perceived notion of what they perceive as a higher value.

Unthinkingly they grasp the blade of the sword, which is two-sided, and do not realize their own long-term risks for self-injury.

The American Library Association once again recently celebrated Banned Books Week. Most of their battles are about kids' books deemed too racy for younger readers.

But the battle over *Huck Finn* and Mark Twain's use of the N-word also continues. Do we allow a classic in American literature to fade out because the characters speak as people really spoke then—and unfortunately still speak today?

Does it make a difference if the-N word is used by an award-winning Black novelist such as Toni Morrison in *Beloved* or by a crusty old white guy (equally award-winning writer) William Faulkner in his short story portraying Southern degradation, "A Rose for Emily"?

Is the word different when used by a rap artist or a poorly informed college freshman in a classroom discussion?

These are the actual questions that my friends who are editors, teachers, and parents face on a regular basis.

Recently the Bureau of Prisons, fearing that prisons could become recruiting centers for Muslim extremists, decided to remove all potentially offensive religious books from their chaplain's libraries.

With all the brilliance of government bureaucrats they also removed the writings of the Christian apologist C. S. Lewis and many other standard Christian writers.

Only the unified howls of protest from Christian, Jewish, and Muslim chaplains and religious leaders reversed this dangerous precedent.

Hate crime legislation on a federal, state, and municipal level is now the vogue. If you paint a swastika on a synagogue you are charged with both criminal damage to property and a second charge of committing a hate crime.

On the surface, hate crime legislation seems like a good idea. Folks who use insult and threaten racial, ethnic, and sexual groups should be punished.

But wait a minute. If I decide to spray-paint my feelings about the war in Iraq on an Army recruiting center, am I also at risk of being charged with a "hate crime"?

For a decade I managed a community bookstore in Chicago. My primary role was as the book buyer who selected new titles for all departments.

As a rule of thumb, I rejected romance novels, because they were bad literature; blatant pornography, because we were a family bookstore; and titles like *The Anarchist Cookbook* that offered a practical guide to making homemade explosives, just because I didn't like the customers who were shopping for it.

About once a week I dealt with some customer who was irate because of books we carried or did not carry.

Was I banning books or violating community standards by my decisions? To this day, I don't know. But the experience has given me greater sympathy for librarians and teachers.

I remain certain that the First Amendment allowing freedom of expression is the best part of the American Constitution.

It is the solid foundation for an open society. But the practical ways in which we apply this to our libraries, bookstores, classrooms, and mass media will be an ongoing battle.

"DUMB BOMB" FALLOUT STILL EVIDENT

2007

Maybe there was a secret, second terrorist attack six years ago on 9/11. The entire United States was hit by a Dumb Bomb causing us to take leave of our senses. This Bomb produced irrationality, amnesia, moral blindness, and a sheep-like acceptance of political absurdity.

Conspiracy theories about the Al Qaeda attack on the World Trade Center were inevitable. All tragedies, from Pearl Harbor to the assassination of JFK, have produced nonsensical explanations. But even nonsense may contain an element of truth.

The consequences of a Dumb Bomb hitting the United States help to explain events of the past six years. The Dumb Bomb is completely different than the computer guided Smart Bombs that strike with pinpoint accuracy.

Therefore, when citizens of Saudi Arabia trained in Afghanistan and Pakistan attack the United States, the government gears up for a takeover of Iraq. This makes as much sense as invading Argentina after Pearl Harbor.

Saddam Hussein was a devilish dictator, but he was a secular dictator with as much to fear from the religious zealots of Al Qaeda as any secular state.

Now as Iraq disintegrates into an aimless collection of warring religious, tribal, and political factions, our president appeals to the collective amnesia of Americans by waving the bloody shirt of Vietnam as a rationale for another decade of military sacrifice.

(I do not hold President Bush at fault for his error in "misremembering" Vietnam. He was in a chemical fog during much of that war and reading history books was never his strong suit.)

The Dumb Bomb has made us feel that we have been inducted into a War on Terror. As recruits we have alternately been told to buy duct tape, go to Disneyland, keep on shopping, keep on the lookout for odd packages and powders, and not to worry about our civil liberties.

A trip to any airport is now an Orwellian experience. Anonymous loudspeakers blast terror alert levels. Like sheep we stand in lines, take off our shoes, abandon our shampoos and nail clippers, and try not to think about the fact that our most advanced airport security technology still cannot distinguish between a Wisconsin cheese and a plastique explosive.

If, at some future date, we are told to strip naked and hold our hands over our heads and march single file through the metal detectors, we will grimace a bit and accept this as part of the price of being recruits in the war on terror.

The Dumb Bomb made decent Americans accept the erosion of their civil liberties and moral decency. Maybe a little bit of torture isn't so bad. Maybe prisoners can be held indefinitely without recourse to trial. Maybe the government does have the right to eavesdrop and threaten you with prison if you tell anybody you are under investigation.

When we express doubts about the War on Terror, the government turns up the fear level like the faucet on a sprinkler system.

When a decent guy like Pat Tillman abandons a football career and enlists in the Army in a moment of patriotic fervor and ends up taking three bullets to the head at close range from his fellow soldiers in Afghanistan, we can just wrap his body in a flag, give him a medal, and collectively forget the gruesome details.

Nobody knows how long a Dumb Bomb affects thinking. There are indications its effects are wearing off. If you catch yourself smelling a whiff of absurdity, feeling some fatigue from the political rhetoric and the shouting heads on Fox News, and have a growing suspicion that Comedy Central is giving you more accurate information than the president, maybe you are awakening from a collective national nightmare rather than abandoning the War on Terror.

If the Dumb Bomb is wearing off, maybe we can tell every presidential candidate—in both political parties—and every hotshot general and elected official, "Enough with the rhetoric and blowing smoke. We are waking up."

RAKING LEAVES WAS HARD WORK TO AVOID

2007, Hillsboro Free Press

My sister asked me to rake the leaves in her yard when I was her guest at Thanksgiving. I schemed to find a way to continue to eat her good cooking while doing no work.

For two days I was able to persuade her that raking leaves put me at risk of heat stroke due to the nearly eighty-degree temperatures.

Then I pointed out the impending cold front would produce sixty-mile-per-hour winds, making leaf raking an exercise in futility.

My final gambit was to suggest than a pending snowfall would cover the leaves on her lawn and make removing them irrelevant.

"Could you just go rake the leaves today?" she said in the tone of voice an older sister uses. Dialogue ended and I put on my gloves and found a rake and some trash bags. Her corner lot is a huge expanse of leaves covering well-tended grass. Mostly these were alien leaves, illegal immigrants from trees blocks away. Some were so odd I suspected they blew in from Oklahoma or Nebraska. I started to sort them by species with the intent to bag and return them to their original owners.

For a moment I became a Republican: folks should take responsibility for their own leaves and all aliens should be expelled.

Modernists believe nature must be rearranged into perfect lawns, controlled bushes, and trimmed trees. Hauling leaves to a compost site, where in solitude, away from the prying eyes of the community, they can return to mulch and not spoil the faux landscape, is a critical part of the modern landscape. The leaf blower is the high-tech status symbol of modern leaf control.

I considered going over to good neighbor Oliver Mohn and borrowing his leaf blower. Then I remembered that when I borrowed his electric hedge clipper a few years ago, I cut his extension cord in half within ten minutes. I continued to bag the leaves, feeling increasingly a victim of modernity.

My sister has a lovely arrangement of dried leaves in a decorative pot near her front door. "How can these leaves on your porch be an art form, while you force me to do slave labor removing unfettered leaves from your lawn?" I asked during my second coffee break.

"Maybe the leaves on your front yard should be thought of as a postmodern art exhibit's metaphor for the beauty of brown carpeting on a forest floor. Consider this: Henry David Thoreau did not rake leaves when he lived at Walden Pond. He learned to live in harmony with nature."

She would have none of my philosophy.

"If you would talk and think a little less you would be done by now," she said. "This is not a high-tech job. Even small children know how to bag leaves," she added, as she pointed to the door.

Several junior high students walked by and did not offer to help rake.

I considered burning the leaves but remembered that both the city and county now forbid leaf pyres. (Years ago, Hillsboro forbade burning trash and leaves only on Mondays since that was the day that women hung laundry out to dry. But now most laundry is dried indoors and an anti-burning ordinance is no longer really necessary.)

If it is carbon emissions we are concerned about, the total emissions from hauling leaves in a pickup truck, plus the use of heavy equipment to maintain the city compost heap, might almost equal the pollutants of raking them to the curb and setting them ablaze.

Eventually I gave up the idea of such civil disobedience and continued to rake leaves and put them in plastic bags. Mr. Kreutziger, another good neighbor, came by and chuckled, "It is a lot of work to bag leaves. You could have just raked them and put them in the back of my pickup."

I thanked him for his generous offer but I was nearly finished with my arduous task.

The next day it snowed, concealing my labor. The black bags of leaves formed a wonderfully abstract sculpture on my sister's front lawn.

Sadly, I was persuaded to dismantle this and haul it to the composting center.

GOAT GLAND BRINKLEY

2001, *Hillsboro Free Press*

Does anyone remember the story of Dr. John R. Brinkley, better known as "Goat Gland Brinkley"? He was a noteworthy Kansan and his legacy lives on—in unexpected ways. As Paul Harvey would say, "Stay tuned and I will tell you the rest of the story."

Brinkley was born in 1885. He was orphaned and made a living as a telegraph operator and snake oil salesman of patent medicines. He spent less than a year in Chicago and was run out of town for fraud. He picked up a medical degree from a diploma mill in Kansas City for $500. (No unpaid student loans for this fellow.)

He set up practice in Milford, Kansas, near Topeka. Either in Arkansas or during his brief period as a company doctor for Swift and Company meatpacking plant he observed billy goats doing what billy goats do with zest and vigor. He also noted in 1917 that many middle-aged men did not have this same zest and vigor.

His idea was brilliant: transplant the glands, which give billy goats so much joy, from the goats to men. Result—Happy Men, Sad Billy Goats.

Soon Milford was the Fountain of Youth for men from Kansas and Oklahoma. Never satisfied, Doc Brinkley looked for ways to let more people know about his operation. Radio was untested and new. Brinkley started one of the first radio stations in Kansas, KFKB (Kansas First, Kansas Best) and played hillbilly music. He and his wife talked to farmers about feeling a little peaked. Soon the Brinkley Clinic was the biggest business in Milford.

There were few regulations on either radio or medicine at the time. Brinkley would turn the wattage up on his station and knock down whooping cranes in Nebraska and sparrows in Oklahoma.

He decided he could treat any sort of illness by radio. Just mail in your symptoms on a postcard and he would read them on the air and tell you to go to your local pharmacist and pick up Brinkley patent medicines #7 and #18 and #19. Small town pharmacies in Kansas flourished from his patent medicines. (He was sort of an early HMO provider.)

His enemies were the Kansas Medical Board and the American Medical Association. Brinkley went to trial for fraud but the jury was persuaded by the testimony of satisfied customers. Brinkley figured, why not control the Kansas Medical Board? He ran for governor in 1930. Too late to file, he ran a write-in campaign. Hour after hour he spelled his name out for listeners tuned in to his radio station and instructed them on the proper procedure for a write-in ballot.

He did well. He carried Kansas and won five counties in Oklahoma for good measure.

Local Democrats and Republicans were not happy and enough Brinkley ballots were discarded to allow his Democratic opponent to win—the lesser of two evils. Brinkley realized his welcome was wearing out in the Sunflower State. Resourcefully, he moved his transmitter across the Rio Grande River and started radio station XERA while living in Del Rio, Texas.

Now at night he could knock down pigeons in New Jersey and eagles in Idaho. He sold time to every other faith healer, including those selling autographed pictures of Jesus. He played hillbilly music—upgraded to country and western music—a phrase first coined by his station. Brinkley died in 1941.

But station XERA lived on. I remember listening to it as a little kid. Strange sounds of whooping and hollering. I didn't stay up late enough to hear the really good stuff. Since the station would sell time to anyone, an itinerant disc jockey known as Wolfman ("Howlin' on the Air") Jack started playing music late at night. This was music banned by mainstream radio stations. This was wild music. Rock and roll. More than one rock musician tells the story of listening to a Mexican radio station as a teenager late at night and realizing his dream was to play music like this.

The license of KFKB wandered around a little. Eventually it landed in Wichita and became KFDI.

So old Bob Dole is not the first Kansas politician to pimp virility in commercials.

And now you know the rest of the story.

THE GROENINGS, THE SIMPSONS, AND THE MENNONITES

2007

The Simpsons is the best satire of contemporary American culture. For those interested in Mennonites involved in mass culture, it is also a case study of a family—that of *Simpsons* creator Matt Groening—morphing from the Mennonite immigrant experience to pop culture celebrity in four generations.

For two decades *The Simpsons* has made people laugh and groan at the antics of this dysfunctional—but ultimately loving—family. Homer and Marge Simpson and their three children, Bart the brat, Lisa the child genius, and Maggie the pacifier-sucking infant, along with Grandpa Abraham, live in the mythical city of Springfield. Groening has been coy about Springfield's location, even suggesting it might be Winnipeg, Manitoba, because his father was born Canadian. He has alluded to the Mennonite and German language origins of his family. Groening also has recreated his own family tree in the names of his cartoon characters. Most obviously, his real-life parents are Homer and Margaret Groening, and he does have a sister named Lisa.

The show is preoccupied with religious, and some might say sacrilegious, themes. From Reverend Lovejoy to born-again neighbor Ned Flanders, Groening wrestles with issues of faith and meaning in all his characters. When Bart's tree house burns down, the Amish show up for a barn raising. Marge says, "Oh, those Amish are so industrious, unlike those shiftless Mennonites," and the scene shifts to "Mennonites" shooting dice and smoking cigarettes. In-jokes like this go over the heads of most viewers.

Reconstructing the genealogy of Matt Groening, one finds a fascinating saga. The story begins in the 1870s, when Abraham Groening immigrated from the Ukraine and became a leading member of the Gnadenau Krimmer Mennonite Brethren church southwest of Hillsboro, Kansas. He was a board member for a one-room school district and hired his sixteen-year-old son, Abram Abraham Groening—soon known as A. A. Groening—to teach a room full of youngsters, most of them his siblings.

In 1908, A. A. Groening was among the first thirty-nine students at Tabor College in Hillsboro. Seven years later, he graduated and began graduate work at the University of Kansas and taught part-time at his alma mater. He was a promising young lad.

But there was a shadow on the horizon. War fever was breaking out because of looming conflict with Germany. The Groenings spoke both High German and the Plautdeutsch dialect. They were pacifists by religious conviction. A. A. Groening got a draft notice. Vigilante groups were out to prove their patriotism to their German neighbors. One night, they picked Abraham Groening as a target. He got wind of this and drove his family to his brother-in-law John Siebert's house.

The vigilantes came on horseback with torches and guns, circling the house but not entering. Shortly thereafter, on September 18, 1918, Abraham Groening had a quick farm sale and moved his family to Hepburn, Saskatchewan. Apparently, they later relocated to Main Centre, in the same Canadian province.

According to government records, an agent from the Bureau of Investigation, the predecessor of the FBI, came to Hillsboro looking for A. A. Groening. He interrogated John Siebert rather firmly. Siebert claimed he did not speak English well and did not recall ever discussing religion or politics with Groening. He said Groening went to Canada because he thought farming would be easier near the Arctic Circle.

The draft-dodging A. A. Groening married in Canada, began a family, and had a son named Homer. When the war was over, he did more graduate work at the University of California and returned to Tabor as a professor in 1920. By 1930, he was dean at Tabor and instrumental in starting the athletic department. His parents also returned to Hillsboro and retired there.

In 1930, A. A. Groening and family, including ten-year-old Homer, moved to Oregon where A. A. taught at Albany College. Homer married Margaret Wiggam. He had strong aesthetic interests and worked in advertising but also made films and wrote poetry and cartoons, thus bridging the worlds of advertising, media, and illustration. He fought in World War II as a pilot, which probably produced some interesting conversations with his father.

Homer and Margaret had a son, Matthew Abram Groening, born in 1954. Matt remembers his father's encouragement for sketching and cartooning. Matt graduated from Evergreen College, got a job in a record store, and began selling his cartoons from the front counter.

He got an offer to do a cartoon series, and *The Simpsons* began. He named his son Matthew Abram Groening, the fourth generation to use this biblical name.

In 1972, A. A. Groening returned to Tabor to receive a distinguished alumni award. He and his wife walked through the old church building where he first took college classes. In the 1980s, Homer Groening returned to Hillsboro and took assorted cousins and relatives to lunch at the Iron Kettle Restaurant, the hangout of townspeople and farmers. He thanked them for their kindness to his family.

This is an intergenerational saga. Abraham Groening was an immigrant from the Ukraine to central Kansas and he was part of the larger Mennonite migration. He was a leader in the Krimmer Mennonite Brethren Church—a group somewhat more conservative than even the pietist Mennonite Brethren. The faith that prompted him to relocate his family a second time to Canada to avoid the drafting of his sons into the military is complex and unknown. His son Abram Abraham Groening was equally complex and is worthy of more research. He went from teaching in a one-room school at age sixteen to a doctorate in science with time spent at the University of Kansas, the University of California—probably Berkeley, and the University of Chicago. Somehow, he was able to return to his Mennonite Brethren alma mater as faculty, even briefly as dean, without controversy. He moved on to Oregon and continued a distinguished career. His religious affiliation later in life is unknown.

Matt Groening certainly knew the story of his family. While it is said that "Grandpa Abraham" was a mere coincidence presented by his scriptwriters, certainly Groening has retained control of names used in the show.

How much of this is coincidence and merely the whimsy of a creative genius remains open to discussion. One suspects that a more careful examination of the life of A. A. Groening as the bridge figure would solve part of this puzzle.

YOU KNOW YOU ARE A CRIMINAL IF:

2006

On job applications you write in your BOP inmate number rather than your Social Security number.

You stand flat against the wall when somebody in a suit or uniform comes down the hall.

When you enter an office, you request permission to sit down.

You have a driver's license in six states—but not for the state in which you currently reside.

You plan to use your PSI (Pre-Sentence Investigation) as the framework for writing your memoirs.

You cannot pass the math section of the GED but you know the metric system of weights.

When you call to inquire about renting an apartment, you always ask if it is more than five hundred feet from a school or playground.

When a cop turns on his lights, you automatically get out and put your hands on the trunk of your car.

You know the maintenance steps for storing a Cadillac for six years—and the maintenance steps for starting the same car after six years.

Your resume lists twenty jobs—each lasting exactly six months doing things like, laundry orderly, kitchen aide, grounds keeper and library assistant. You insist this is career development by noting, "Working in a variety of jobs for the federal government has broadened my skills base."

You have a cellphone, and a woman—mother, girlfriend, wife or daughter—owns the cellphone.

You have five children aged seven and none of them are twins.

You know the precise boundaries of the North Illinois Judicial District.

You can correctly identify and rank for severity the spectrum of colors in the USPO drug screen system. (You know your own color and the color of 80 percent of your closest associates.)

You have more than three arrests for driving on a suspended license with no insurance.

You think doing telemarketing is an office job offering a chance of advancement.

You understand the Federal Guidelines for Sentencing point system—but have never heard of Google.

Your cell phone directory lists the numbers of your mother, wife, three girlfriends, lawyer, probation officer, bondsman but no business numbers and no numbers for friends.

You know the Greyhound Bus rest areas between Yankton, South Dakota and Chicago.

You think doing data entry and working in a steel mill are still career options in Chicago.

You have heard you can find dirty pictures on something called the Internet.

You have done enough job readiness programs that you feel you could teach them yourself.

You think drinking two six-packs a day is social drinking.

You know how long cocaine, marijuana, and heroin are detectable in a drug screen.

Every time you urinate, you wonder if you should be filling a sanitary plastic cup.

GALILEO'S HERESY PREDATES DARWIN'S

2007, Hillsboro Free Press

Evolution has been in the news lately. During a presidential debate last month, three Republican presidential candidates shyly raised their hands to say they did not believe in evolution. This past week, Senator Brownback wrote a vigorous op-ed diatribe denouncing evolution in the august pages of the *New York Times*.

In the past few days, the Creation Museum costing $27 million opened its doors to the public in Kentucky. For $19.95 (less for children and tour groups) one can see displays of children cavorting with dinosaurs and the friendly vegetarian dinosaurs boarding Noah's Ark. (I am unclear as to whether the most famous dinosaur of all, Barney with his purple pajamas, is included in the exhibit.)

The creationists insist the world was created a little over six thousand years ago, the Grand Canyon is the result of a week's worth of erosion after the great flood, and most things are pretty much the way they were originally created in six days.

The creationists may be right. I was very young when the world was created and therefore forget most of the details. Today, at my age, I forget even where I left the remote control for my TV.

But increasingly I suspect our modern-day creationists are mistaken when they blame Darwin for foisting evolution on unsuspecting scientists in the 1800s.

The world fell into error much sooner than Darwin. Remember some crazy Italian named Galileo in the 1500s spread the newfangled notion that the earth revolved around the sun? (Granted, Galileo did recant when the Pope threatened to have him burned at the stake.)

But ever since childhood I have held to the perspective of a stationary earth that is flat with the sun revolving around it. I remember a vigorous argument when I was about five with my older sister. She tried to convince me the earth was round and that it revolved around the sun.

She had the advantage of age and being able to read. But I trumped these by using the Laws of Observed Evidence. "Look outside! Clearly the land is flat and goes on forever. And the sun shines into the bedroom in the morning when it rises and into the living room in the evening when it sets. And if the earth were spinning, we would feel the wind and get dizzy and fall down." I was brilliant.

But she was stubborn in her book-learned nonsense. I think I eventually won the argument by crying and telling Mom she was picking on me.

But this is serious stuff. Both Martin Luther and the good old Popes believed in a geocentric worldview—that the sun revolves around a stationary earth. They had the story of Joshua making the sun stand still, references to the foundations of the earth, and other scriptures on their side.

But today only a few beleaguered scholars and very few scientists remain who have not fallen for the heliocentric claptrap.

They need your help. Should Senator Brownback ever return to Kansas (I read he is mostly living in Iowa these days), constituents can demand that he amend his anti-evolution position to include a stationary and flat earth with the sun circling it every twenty-four hours.

Folks could write the Kansas Board of Education and insist that prior to stopping the teaching of Intelligent Design they should first insist schools inform children the earth does not move. Perhaps even local schools could be investigated for evidence of teaching this heresy.

Once the concept of our stationary orb is firmly established for every citizen, I suspect the trivial discussions of Darwin will fall by the wayside—maybe even roll off the edge of the earth.

OSAGE ORANGE TREES DESERVE RESPECT

2007, *Hillsboro Free Press*

When I was a kid, Saturdays revolved around hedge trees—more properly called "Osage orange trees." There was trimming hedge, burning piles of bulldozed hedge trees, cutting out hedge posts, and later nailing barbed wire to them for fences.

I even have a few memories of bringing in hedge wood when we had a wood-burning stove. In those days, Kansas had 96,000 miles of hedgerows.

Long after my father had retired, he would often head out to the farm to "trim hedge" out of force of habit.

My grandfather Suderman once told me about his memories of planting hedgerows and how the saplings were woven together to form an impenetrable barrier. In Texas such hedgerows were defined as "horse high, bull strong, and pig tight."

Increasingly, the Osage orange tree fascinates me. I have a carved Osage orange vase in my office in Chicago that I bought at the Arts and Crafts Fair in Hillsboro some years ago.

And this year, I gave Marion County hedge apples as Christmas gifts to my friends. (They complained that hedge apples rotted rather quickly. I told them they were given a "seasonal" gift, not a permanent gift like a fruitcake.)

While in London some years back, I went to the Kew Gardens—an astonishing collection of plants from around the world. There I saw a hedge tree—a sickly looking specimen one could cut down with a Weedwacker.

A few weeks ago, I was in Philadelphia and went to St. Peter's Episcopal Church. In the cemetery behind the church are five of the tallest hedge trees I have ever seen—with trunks that would take two adults to embrace. Apparently, these trees are from cuttings sent back from the Lewis and Clark expedition in 1804.

But the history is not entirely clear. There is a reasonable chance the hedge tree in London is also from the specimens brought back from Lewis and Clark.

To confound the problem, at the home of Patrick Henry in Virginia, there is a giant hedge tree believed to be three hundred years old—which would predate the Lewis and Clark expedition by a century.

"We put up signs every year warning people about the dangers of falling hedge apples," said a nice lady who was in church waiting for her daughter to finish choir practice.

The hedge tree has a remarkable part in American history. The Osage Indians and other Plains tribes used its wood for making bows. Thus the early French explorers called it "bois d'arc"—the bow of the arch. (This term is still used in eastern Kansas and Texas.)

Before barbed wire became common, hedge trees were part of settling the frontier. Around 1850, Texans were exporting hedge seeds to Ohio for a peak price of fifty dollars a bushel. Since the Osage orange is first cousin to the mulberry tree, when attempts were made to do silk production in America, it was discovered that silkworms thrived on hedge trees. Alas, the entire silk industry never became profitable.

The hedge tree today ranks somewhere between a nuisance and an oddity. Bow hunting, fences and silk all depend on other materials. Fireplaces are decorative elements in homes and rarely part of central heating. Hedge trees are an invasive species in pastures and fields and take valuable space and moisture.

In 2004 the United States congress declared the oak tree the national American tree. The oak tree is a decent enough candidate—good for furniture, flooring, and paneling. It grows slowly and produces acorns that are hardly more useful than hedge apples.

Today even the most ardent tree huggers rarely hug a hedge tree. But the hedge tree is a part of American history. It is tough, persistent, and almost useful. It also deserves some respect.

A MEDITATION ON CARL JUNG

1998

Discussed in this essay: Richard Noll, *The Aryan Christ: The Secret Life of Carl Jung*, Random House, 1997.

1.

One suspects the author, a clinical psychologist, now a lecturer in the history of science at Harvard University, is a disillusioned Jungian. Certainly he writes with all the passion of an abandoned lover. Nevertheless, this is an important but critical look at what the author calls the Jung Cult, the title of an earlier work by Noll published in 1994. I shall quote at length from Noll in the interest of summarizing with fairness. I'll conclude with my own memories, dreams, and reflections.

This is how Noll outlines the current state of Jungian historical work:

> The Jung portrayed in *MDR* is a clairvoyant sage, a miracle worker, a god-man who earns his apotheosis through his encounter with the Dead and with God. His is a morality tale of mystical evolution, as his life becomes the exemplum of his theories, the heroic saga of an "individuated" man who survived a terrifying encounter with extramundane beings (the archetypes) from a transcendent reality (the collective unconscious). Unfortunately, *MDR* has served as the basis for all subsequent "biographies" of Jung since its first publication in 1962. Until recently, the truthfulness of this preferred version of Jung's myth has gone unquestioned. There is great resistance to altering the myth, which would mean tangling Jung in time and space and restoring him to his German cultural milieu, a humiliating descent from mythopoesis into history. (xiii)

Noll is convinced that Jung regarded himself as a "religious prophet with extraordinary powers," and "that despite his multiple professional personas of physician, psychotherapist, and social critic, he consciously devoted his life to promoting the growth of a religious community centered on his personality and his teachings" (xiv). Even more radically, Noll asserts that, "In later life, after studying the ancient mystery cults and alchemy, Jung openly told more than one person that he—and those who follow his methods—were chosen to be the redeemers of God" (xiv).

Jung was a pagan who saw the Judeo-Christian tradition as his enemy, and who saw myth as more important than fact-based history. For Noll, the problem is that Jung is an Aryan Christ who promises redemption—but in a world deracinated of troubling historical facts. Noll protests:

> the most troublesome part of this story comes from asking you, the reader, to do the morally impossible: to imagine a world—fin-de-siècle German *Kultur*—in which the words "Hitler" and "Nazi" and "Holocaust" do not exist, a world in which spirituality is fused with blood and soil and the sun, a world in which an Aryan Christ could find apostles—and sincerely promise redemption to his redeemers. (xvi)

By way of background, Noll examines the lives of Carl Jung's ancestors. His great-grandmother was rumored to have had an affair with Goethe—resulting in Karl Gustav Jung, a German nationalist, pietist, Rosicrucian, and physician born in 1794. In the absence of serious documentation, even Carl Jung did not know how seriously to take this story about his grandfather—but his belief in reincarnation did include a belief that he was, perhaps, the spirit of Goethe (18).

In 1817, at the age of twenty-three, Jung's grandfather Karl took part in a traditional ceremony at the Wartburg castle, sometimes known to its celebrants as a "*Thing*—what the ancient Germans called their annual tribal gatherings" (5). It began with a torchlit procession up to the fortifications, the participants decked out in the traditional garb "of their native regions" (5). Then, Noll goes on to describe:

> At the foot of the Wartburg, the men built a huge, blazing bonfire and other pillars of fire that could be seen by the people of Eisenach. Encircling the central fire, with an excitement driven by a sense of the sacred and the dangerous, the men sang the traditional hymn "*Eine Feste Burg*" ("A Mighty Fortress is Our God"). One of the leaders then offered a few inspirational remarks about justice and invoked the important symbol of the German forest of oaks. The mighty oak was sacred to the ancient Teutons and indeed was the "cross" upon which Wotan (Odin) underwent his revelatory self-sacrifice....

> More hymns were sung and a patriotic sermon was delivered. Then . . . the young men joined hands around the fire and took a collective oath of allegiance to one another and to their group (*Bund*). They also pledged to preserve the purity of the *Volk*. Before the Wartburgfest concluded, for the first time in recorded German history "un-German books" were denounced and burned in the great central fire. (6)

Grandfather Karl considered this event a peak experience of his life and preserved the black, red and gold wrap from this event—the colors of the modern German flag. The wrap would become one of his grandson's prized possessions (7). Karl renounced the Catholicism of his birth and became an Evangelical Protestant, and significantly, the baptismal certificate was signed by Friedrich Schleiermacher, one of the formative thinkers in the history of Pietism, the so-called "religion of the heart" (8, 9).

This is not Pietism as I had imagined it. But Noll delivers his verdict with devastating simplicity: "Religion mated with German nationalism in the eighteenth century and produced a fever in the people called Pietism" (8). He elaborates that

> Pietism was born of disgust with orthodoxies, dogmas, and church hierarchies in the traditional Protestant denominations. . . . Pietists dared to question authority and to be suspicious of foreign interpreters of Christianity. They called it a *Herzensreligion*, a "religion of the heart," a spiritual movement that emphasized feeling, intuition, inwardness, and a personal experience of God. The function of thinking, indeed reason itself, was disparaged and could not be trusted. . . .
>
> . . . It was the fire of the Holy Spirit that must burn within: indeed, it was often said that "the heart must burn." They emphasized the burning experience of "Christ within us" instead of the inanimate, automatic belief in the dogma of a "Christ for us." Such subtle distinctions had profound distinctions for German nationalism, for the belief arose in the feeling of group identity bound by common inner experience, a mystical blood-union of necessity, rather than as something external existing for an individual. Hence the Pietist emphasis on service to others as a method of serving God. (9–10)

"By the middle of the eighteenth century," Noll argues, "German nationalism had become so intertwined with Pietism that the literature of the time blurs distinctions between inner and outer

Fatherlands" (10). In this way Christian and German icons and symbolism intermingled and fused:

> The "internalized Kingdom of Heaven" became identical with the spiritual soil of the German ancestors, a Teutonic "Land of the Dead." In these patriotic religious tracts the sacrificial deaths of Teutonic heroes such as Arminius (Hermann the German, who defeated the Romans in the Teutoberg forest) and the mythic Siegfried are compared to the crucifixion of Christ, thus equating pagan and Christian saviors" (10).

Carl Jung was familiar with the format of the pietist diaries of spiritual struggle or *Wiedergeburt*, and his *MDR* is a parallel story of rebirth. But Noll contends that Jung's story is one of pagan regeneration (11).

2.

Grandfather Karl Jung was arrested for his nationalist sentiments and resettled in Basel to teach medicine. He became a wealthy man but always with a feeling of exile from the German homeland. He discovered Freemasonry in Paris and continued that practice in Basel. The first wing of Freemasonry was the Illuminati—more concerned with political nationalism—and hence banned in Bavaria. The second wing was Rosicrucian—with its unique mythology of the red cross entwined by red roses. Grandfather added the Masonic symbols of a gold star to the Jung family coat of arms. The grandson Carl would paint these symbols on the ceiling of his Tower in Bollingen and continue the use of Masonic, particularly Rosicrucian symbols, at the Tower (14–15).

Though the son of a Lutheran minister, Carl Jung felt stronger affinities for his grandfather Karl, and Noll tells us that "it was the legend of his grandfather, not the living example of his father, against which Jung constantly measured himself as a young man" (19). By age twenty, Jung and several female relatives were conducting séances to contact the dead. Several months earlier Carl's Uncle Rudolph, his mother's older brother, had died, and as the séances got underway, his father Paul, the Lutheran minister, lay mortally ill. Jung's maternal grandfather, the Reverend Samuel Preiswerk, also seems to have exercised an effect on young Carl during this time. Noll explains that Preiswerk

> was a man of many talents. He was chief of the Protestant clergy of Basel, a professor of Old Testament exegesis and oriental languages at the Evangelical Institution in Geneva, an acclaimed Hebrew scholar, a poet, a composer of religious hymns, and a man who regularly spoke to spirits. The Spirits of the Dead were everywhere among the living and could be addressed, but only if one knew their language. He believed that Hebrew was the language of heaven (he was not alone in this regard!), and he fully expected to speak to the Old Testament prophets and his savior in their divine tongue. (24–25)

According to the Jung family legends, Preiswerk "would talk to the spirit of his deceased first wife in weekly séances while locked in his study, much to the dismay of his second wife and the fascination of his children" (25). Preiswerk taught his favorite daughter Emilie and her siblings "to stand behind him and chase away the spirits when he gave his sermons, for he and the family earnestly believed that the air around them was crowded with the chattering masses of the Dead" (25).

Given this background, it's not surprising that Jung and his cousins began their séances in June 1895. Two of the cousins were Uncle Rudolph's daughters, twenty-one-year-old Louise ("Luggy"), and a thirteen-year-old, Hélène ("Helly"). During the first session, Helly went into a trance and channeled the voice of Grandfather Samuel. A glass of water shook violently on the table (26).

These sessions were stopped for two years during the confirmation period of Helly into the church but resumed in 1897. By this time Jung was well read in spiritualist literature while at medical school. To his dismay, his cousin-medium was recreating images and characters from books he had sent her on spiritualism. In particular, she recited stories from a book written by Justinius Kerner that detailed the "extensive case history of a young clairvoyant woman in the German town of Prevors" (34)—the Seeress of Prevorst—a peasant woman who around 1829 was consulted by theologians such as David Friedrich Strauss and Schleiermacher for her ecstatic wisdom and healing powers.

Jung realized that by giving his cousin the book he had created the material for her séances.

> He learned a valuable lesson about the power of "hidden memories" and textual material to reemerge in an entirely novel form in consciousness. In fact, material that one has "forgotten" can reappear in thoughts, fantasies, or dreams and have all of the emotional force and visual clarity of actual memories. At the turn of the century, this quite normal phenomenon was called "cryptomnesia," literally "hidden memories." (39)

Yet, Noll says, "Despite his awareness of the influence of cryptomnesia on Helly's performances while he observed them . . . he did not use such psychological terminology to characterize them until he finished his medical training" (39). Even more damning, in Noll's view, Jung "was later to deny seemingly clear cases of cryptomnesia that if acknowledged would threaten his most central theories" (39).

Apparently Helly had fallen in love with Jung and was faking psychic experiences to keep him involved. Jung would later use materials from these séances for his doctoral thesis, reformulating the experiences as a study in "hysteria." Since his thesis subject was widely known to be his cousin, her chances of marriage were destroyed because of the implied mental illness, at the time "thought to be the result of 'bad blood' in a degenerate family" (50). Helly died unmarried, a dressmaker in Paris, at the age of thirty.

By 1900, Jung was a medical doctor at the Burghölzli—the mental hospital in Zurich where he would work for the next nine years. The term "schizophrenia" was coined here by its noted chief, Eugen Bleuler, in 1908. Many of the long-term patients suffered from some variation of schizophrenia. The institution was world-famous and many psychiatrists from Europe and America rotated through it (45). Noll describes the general atmosphere:

> Since many, if not most, mental disorders were considered at that time to be diseases caused in part by hereditary degeneration, Jung and his colleagues were cloistered in a veritable hothouse of human degeneracy twenty-four hours a day. New physicians at such asylums saw things few outsiders could even imagine. Constant exposure to the bizarre delusions and hallucinations of psychotic individuals . . . to the sight of raw sexual acts and overt seductions, and to irrational responses

to reasonable questions could only have a subtle but seductive destabilizing effect on the rigid, intellectualizing, bourgeois young men who were the standard-bearers in Western European civilization's war against degeneracy. (45)

By 1906 Jung was a promising young research doctor known in Europe and America. Using what today would be called a word-association test, Jung examined patients to see if their word associations reflected experience in life or some other form of memory.

3.

In March 1907, Carl Jung met Sigmund Freud in his Vienna flat. In January 1913, they agreed to have no further contact (53). According to Noll,

> The mythic tale of Freud and Jung is one of the best known of the twentieth century. Most people know the skeleton, if not the flesh, of the truth ... that Freud, the father of psychoanalysis, anointed Jung as his heir apparent, and Jung, perhaps like an ungrateful son, rejected his mentor and went his own way after a terrible clash. Jungians reframe the story by claiming that Jung could not accept Freud's exclusively sexual theory of life and broke with him to fashion a theory that took into account the essential religious or spiritual nature of people. For ... Freud's disciples, Jung's defection was an apostasy, a rejection of the science of psychoanalysis marked by Jung's lapse into narcissism, psychosis, mysticism, and anti-Semitism. There are elements of truth in all these versions. (53–54)

Noll proposes a truce in the Freud/Jung conflicts—and the overanalysis of their relationship. He suggests that Jung sought out Freud for the "clinical utility" (54) of psychoanalysis, but he "could not abide by its secular claims: in the psychoanalytic movement he envisioned, for a brief time, a scientific religion of the future" (55). Freud needed non-Jewish and non-Viennese followers, and Noll observes, "Previously seen as only a Jewish affair, that psychoanalysis aroused the interest of Bleuler and his largely Swiss, Christian staff was a major coup for Freud and broadened its appeal" (57). Jung's role, then, as the first president of the International Psychoanalytic Association founded in 1910, was strategic.

For a time, Jung and Freud agreed on the psychodynamic approach as a refreshing alternative to the theory of "degeneracy," which implied that implacable, hereditary factors lay at the root of mental illness. "This made psychoanalysis especially attractive to those considered 'tainted' by their ethnicity, such as Jews" (55). Second, psychiatrists at the time were increasingly able to diagnose mental problems but had precious few treatments at their disposal that actually seemed to work. Psychoanalysis seemed to be a promising tool.

But there was an intense personal dynamic between the two men that complicated matters. In a letter to Freud in 1907, Jung told him that "my veneration for you has something of the character of a 'religious crush.'" He went on to speak of an "undeniable erotic undertone," and told Freud, "This abominable feeling comes from the fact that as a boy I was the victim of a sexual assault of a man I once worshipped" (62).

Indirect evidence suggests that Jung had sexual advances made on him by a friend of his father's when he was eighteen and he was never able to process the experience. Freud spoke critically about Jung with fellow psychoanalyst Sandor Ferenczi, recalling how he confronted Jung about his problem with male friendship: "I spared him nothing at all, told him calmly that a friendship with him couldn't be maintained, that he himself gave rise to the intimacy that he so cruelly broke off; that things were not at all in order in his relations with men, not just with me but with others as well" (63). Even followers of Jung acknowledge that. His friend and pupil Jolande Jacobi noted in 1927, "I discovered why Jung was at the same time afraid of men; to accept men as best friends or as his best pupils" (62).

This must have been a fascinating time. The founders of psychoanalysis did therapy on each other, knew each other's sexual histories and peccadillos intimately, yet were also forming what Jung and Freud saw as a movement with world-changing implications. Little wonder that those who left the "church" of either Freud or Jung were seen as apostates and that suicide was common among those who departed or were ejected (59–60). Noll contends that both Jung and Freud were founders of cultlike movements, but each took a very different direction. Jung was committed to a "charismatic religious cult centered on his own personality and teachings, offering modern individuals the promise of redeeming themselves 'spiritually'—a process he called 'individuation'—and offering them the opportunity to become part of a select spiritual elite" (64). In a telling summary, Jung wrote to Freud after both received an invitation to join the International Order for Ethics and Culture group:

> I imagine a far finer and more comprehensive task for [psychoanalysis] than alliance with an ethical fraternity. I think we must give it time to infiltrate into people from many centers, to revivify among intellectuals a feeling for symbol and myth, ever so gently to transform Christ back into the soothsaying god of the vine, which he was, and in this way absorb those ecstatic instinctual forces of Christianity for the *one* purpose of making the cult and the sacred myth what they once were—a drunken feast of joy where man regained the ethos and holiness of an animal. That was the beauty and purpose of classical religion. (65)

Freud's response was to shut down Jung's enthusiasm. "But you mustn't regard me as the founder of a religion. My intentions are not so far-reaching. . . . I am not thinking of a substitute for religion. This need must be sublimated" (66).

4.

By age thirty-two, Jung was an outwardly successful man, married with two children, a third on the way, promoted to associate director at the institute, the heir apparent to Freud, and on the cutting edge of psychiatric innovation. Then Dr. Otto Gross, a mere footnote to history, but a colorful and influential character, entered the picture. Gross was the wayward son of Hans Gross—the father of modern scientific criminology. Otto started out as a traditional physician but by 1898 he was addicted to morphine and cocaine. He wrote a book expressing a positive opinion of Freudian thought and Freud returned the favor, cultivating his friendship. From 1906 to 1913, Gross practiced a wild form of psychoanalysis in all-night Bohemian coffee shops, holding audiences of writers and artists "spellbound" and developing a reputation. He told his clients to "Repress nothing!" and according to Noll, "They obeyed" (74). Years later, his cures among the Dadaists and avant-garde were regarded as miraculous by other psychiatrists.

Gross's flamboyance knew no bounds. He openly practiced polygamy and impregnated two sisters—friends of the sociologist Max Weber—while married to a long-suffering wife. In 1908 his father pleaded with Freud to treat his son for addiction and it was arranged for Jung to conduct the preliminary treatment at the Burghölzli, after which Freud would do the final sessions of analysis.

Jung oversaw the traditional treatment of the patient's gradual withdrawal from opium and cocaine while Gross ranted and raved—appearing to mimic what today would be called manic-depressive symptoms. What is striking is that in the intensive sessions the "analysis" was mutual between Gross and Jung for two full months. Jung wrote Freud on June 19, "in Gross I discovered many aspects of my true nature, so that he often seemed like my twin brother—except for the dementia praecox" (84).

Noll speculates that Gross taught Jung about the counterculture Bohemian world of sun worshippers, of sexual escapades, neo-pagans, and Theosophists who had formed colonies in Switzerland and Germany. He probably introduced Jung to the writings of Johann Jakob Bachofen—who believed that society had a matriarchal origin, but had moved to the patriarchal style which now dominates. To live and love freely, instinctively, and polygamously was the way to unleash the ancient creative energies of man, according to Bachofen, "who claimed to have archaeological evidence for his theories" (85). This would prove a lasting influence on Jung.

Gross certainly gave Jung the concepts of introversion and extroversion—which Jung attributed to him in his book *Psychological Types*, published in 1921 (88). It was the last time Jung would mention Gross, who was never able to shake his addictions. Gross's father consigned his son to an asylum from which he escaped in 1913, ending up in Prague where he met Max Brod and Franz Kafka. His last known whereabouts were a Berlin warehouse where he was discovered alone and ill. He died shortly after in March 1920, most likely from pneumonia (89).

Jung had his first affair with a female patient, Sabina Spielrein, in 1908. Gross had prepared the way. She had completed treatment, was now a medical student, and she recorded in her journals how Jung felt permission from Gross to begin the affair with her (89). From 1909 onward, Jung not only practiced polygamy in his own life, but he also recommended it to his male patients. Among the first to receive and document such advice was Medill McCormick, part owner of the *Chicago Tribune*. "McCormick suffered from severe bouts of alcoholism and depression," Noll writes, "for which Jung prescribed polygamy as a way of overcoming his despair and saving his soul" (91). Jung himself had a forty-year relationship with Toni Wolff, a former patient, research assistant, and lifelong confidante, who, according to Noll, "was deeply involved in the development of his personality typology and in the writing of *Psychological Types*, which appeared in 1921" (95).

In a theoretical sense, Jung disagreed with Freud about the most powerful life force. "By September 1912, he made it clear to Freud and to his own circle in Zurich that this powerful energy of life was not only the sex drive... but should be viewed as a more generalized force of nature whose currents carried ancestral spiritual longings through biological channels" (99). Jung formulated a model, says Noll, positing that

> since the most potent ideas of human concern are religious ones, we should discover the spiritual symbols of our ancestors deep within the unconscious mind of each individual. That is, looking at the evolutionary development of the human species, the most recent therefore most powerful, influences on present human experience would be racial or tribal ones. In Jung's new view, religious needs were biologically based. The peoples of pagan antiquity, closer to our prehistoric ancestors, celebrated their sexuality in their spirituality and were therefore less plagued by neuroses and psychoses than modern Europeans. Jung forged these insights into the theory that a life could only be meaningful if one's religious beliefs and sexual practices resonated with those of one's racial ancestors. (99)

Noll contends that Jung merged elements of Pietist thought—principally the "light within"—with the ancient practice of sun worship (107). And by 1912, Jung was no longer a Freudian, nor was he "a Christian or a monotheist" (109). Noll observes that, "By this time Jung had converted most of his Swiss-German and Christian colleagues to the notion that organic memories of ancestral impulses were more important than individual memories." In short, "This was the beginning of an Aryan science of psychoanalysis in Zurich. It was the beginning of Jung's return to his *Volk*, and to the inner fatherland" (109).

Freud was displeased. Writing about the Jungians, he trenchantly observed:

> They are now doubting the influence of infantile complexes and are at the point of already appealing to racial differences in order to explain the theoretical disparity. Jung must now be in a florid neurosis. However this turns out, my intention of amalgamating Jews and goyim in the service of [psychoanalysis] seems now to have gone awry. They are now separating like oil and water. (109)

Jung was not out of step with his time. He was borrowing from the philologists of his day such as Friedrich Max Müller and Ernst Renan, who saw in all languages living relics of ancestral thought. Muller referred to a "mythopoetic age" which predated civilization and Christianity (111). Noll describes the milieu:

> From the racialist right to the anarchist left a culture of "progressive reaction against industrial capitalism was on the rise. All of the values that formed the foundation of the industrial order—repressive Judeo-Christian antihedonism, utilitarianism, and rational thought—were confronted with new philosophies of life or of pure experience that exalted myth over history, impulsive action or deed over conscious reflection, and feeling or intuition over rational thought. (115)

The picture gets progressively darker as Noll paints it:

> The multifaceted Volkish movement (*Volkstumbewegung*) had a broad plan for Germanic society: at the individual level, the taking of cures, abstinence from alcohol, nudism, vegetarianism, the eating of health foods, contact with the ancestors through spiritualist practices, and hiking through Nature were all remedies to erase the sense of profound loss that so many suffered. At the level of culture, a cleansing of the Aryan race through eugenics and deportations was proposed. (115)

The publication of Jung's *Psychology of the Unconscious* (1912, English translation 1916) made Jung a folk hero in Bohemian circles (117). In December 1913 Jung began inducing trance states within himself which he called "active imagination" (121). During these experiences, he saw himself becoming a lion-headed God in the cult of Mithras. Noll contends this was Jung's initiation to a personal experience of the god within and a sense of his own deification which he only revealed in a 1925 lecture to followers (121–123). And while Jung claimed to have had no independent awareness of Hellenistic and Mithraic initiation rites in 1913, Noll says that during that 1925 lecture he "inadvertently" admitted to the wide reading he had done prior (125). Noll goes on to document these sources rather exhaustively. It would seem that Jung once again ignored his own writings on cryptomnesia (143). In Noll's view, "the collective unconscious may still be said to exist, but only on the shelves of Jung's personal library" (133).

5.

Noll argues that German intellectuals such as Wagner, Nietzsche, and others saw a weak, Jewish Jesus imposed on a strong Aryan people. Thus in the Parsifal myth and other yarns, there was a quest to find the "real" Jesus—who certainly was not a weak, subordinate Jew. Houston Stewart Chamberlain, according to Noll, one "of the inner circle at Bayreuth after Richard Wagner's death" (144), helped to popularize such a perspective, writing in 1899: "The probability that Christ was no Jew, that He had not a drop of genuinely Jewish blood in his veins is so great that it is almost equivalent to a certainty. To what race did He belong? This is a question that cannot be answered at all" (144) Of particular interest to many Europeans at the time was an Old Saxon manuscript dating from 830 C.E. that had first been published in 1830 under the title *Heliand* (Savior), purportedly "the first rendering of the New Testament gospel into the language of the ancient Germans" (146). (An English translation from the original Saxon by Ronald Murphy, SJ, was published as *The Heliand: The Saxon Gospel*, by Oxford University Press in 1992.) The work combines elements of Wotan and Christianity. Noll says that "Jung cultivated a special relationship to Wotan, whom he believed to be the true god of the Germanic peoples of Europe," and that "Wotan came to him in a dream in the form of a wild huntsman" (146).

By 1916 Jung had about forty disciples who shared his views of renewing society. In lectures to this group Jung made reference to his Seven Sermons to the Dead and other material from his trance states. He was using techniques which would today be called automatic writing and channeling. I also see parallels to "journaling," in which a follower is to write a book of one's own, which functions as a spiritual journal and contains dreams and drawings. Jung was now operating at three levels:

> To make his spiritual movement a success, Jung had to adopt at least three false faces or masks. In his professional talks, his professional publications, and his books (at least until the 1930s), he equivocated. He could not talk about the living mysteries of the gods and of the ancestors in a public forum if he wanted to be taken seriously. To get around this problem, he constructed a confusing but somewhat poetic pseudoscientific vocabulary to cover up the true meaning of his experiences. Terms that he used in print and in lectures in 1916 such as "personal unconscious," "collective unconscious," and "persona" were in reality *Decknamen*, or cover names, that hid the true nature of the phenomena from outsiders. (159)

For the inner circle in the Psychology Club, he spoke in directly spiritual terms—but only fragments of these speeches and lectures exist. For a middle level he wrote elliptically and ambiguously, according to Noll. For the followers of Jung, "The world-redeeming process had now officially begun. Patients became apostles. Analysis became initiation. Cures became secondary to conversions. Their formerly mundane and spiritually bankrupt lives took on cosmic dimensions. They were on the path" (158).

In *Memories, Dreams, Reflections* there is a haunting story. In the summer of 1916 Jung's doorbell began ringing but no one in the house saw anyone at the door. Jung stated the house was full of spirits and he inquired what they wanted. They responded, "We have come back from Jerusalem where we found not what we sought" (161). The spirits were Christian crusaders come back from Jerusalem who had not found salvation. Jung wrote the Seven Sermons to the Dead to offer them an alternative pagan philosophy, featuring the god Abraxas, "a god both good and evil" (161). Noll explains, "Jung tells the howling Christians that after death the soul does not go to the Christian promised land but toward God as the sun or the star within" (162). The symbol for this vision, based on the fiery sun, is the mandala, which in Sanskrit means "circle" (162).

Jung's disciples were primarily women. Edith Rockefeller McCormick and her daughters and husband spent years in Zurich and funded the country club where Jung and his followers met. The

McCormick family also underwrote the publishing costs of many of Jung's publications. A few disciples defected to Ouspensky and the Theosophical Society, but Jung continued his practice. Then, "After almost twenty years of being relatively ignored by the German media," Noll writes that

> suddenly in 1933, 1934, and 1935 Jung enjoyed a popularity north of the Swiss border that was unprecedented. He was courted by German scholars as never before. He gave seminars in Berlin and lectured in other German cities. According to Jolande Jacobi, one of his closest disciples from the thirties on, "His idea [about the Nazi movement] was that chaos gives birth to good or to something valuable. So in the German movement he saw a chaotic (we could say) pre-condition for the birth of a new world." In response to a letter to him expressing her concerns about the dangers of Nazism, Jacobi said, "He answered me: 'Keep your eyes open. You can't reject the evil because the evil is the bringer of light.' Lucifer means light-bringer. He was convinced of this, you see. That shows that he didn't see and didn't understand the outer world. For him this [Nazi movement] was an inner happening which had to be accepted as a psychological pre-condition for rebirth." (274).

In 1936 Jung spoke at Harvard on the college's three hundredth anniversary. The following year he lectured at Yale. Noll describes the way Jung's reputation expanded and entered the mainstream:

> In Zurich, Jung's community of disciples began to swell with physicians and spiritual seekers from England and America. These disciples began, and in many cases continue today, the sanitizing of Jung's image from a Germanic mystic or charlatan with anti-Semitic leanings to that of a wise old man. The Second World War and the Holocaust forced Jung to downplay his Volkish utopianism and Aryan mysticism. (277)

When his long-time disciple Jolande Jacobi converted to Catholicism, Jung wrote a furious letter, telling her: "With me nobody has his place who is in the Church. There you have your confessor. I am for the people who are out of the Church" (278). Noll ends his book by allowing Jacobi to have the last word. She said: "He himself behaved as if his psychology was another religion" (278).

6.

A Personal Reflection on The Aryan Christ:

1. A lawyerly rebuttal could be written to Noll's book. The mysticism and spiritualism could be the excesses of a young genius. Who among us would want to be held responsible for our belief systems in our early twenties? The mature, and the post-war, Jung should be our focus, and an old man can certainly be forgiven some convenient rewriting of his own personal history. Jung was a product of the intellectual climate of his time and should not be judged apart from it. Noll's rage that the Jung family will not release more of the personal writings of Jung, particularly his "Red Book," is perhaps merely the petty peevishness of an academic who believes he is entitled to the contents of every attic. Jung does not advocate "polygamy" in the standard anthropological sense; more non-monogamy for males as a way of getting in touch with their primitive side does not meet the definition. Nor is there concrete evidence that he engaged in more than a psychological form of paganism—perhaps only a spirituality which was not traditionally Christian. Some of this argument is sustainable.

2. Just as we are all Keynesians now, so today we are all Jungians. The belief in drawing on inner resources, getting in touch with feelings, feeling "power," writing one's journal, and developing our own symbolism as a part of finding meaning in life—all this is dominant in both pop psychology and the social services—which are often indistinguishable. The sanitized and simplified Jung is presented without the arcane language. We all "know" whether we are introverts or extroverts. We all find ways to get in touch with our masculine or feminine side, and understand that our dreams are both a descent into a universal symbolic system and are also fraught with some sort of vague spiritual meaning. We worship the Sun and Nature and watch our diet. We feel some sense of contact with our ethnic and spiritual ancestors, be they the writers of the *Martyrs Mirror* or of Irish poetry. The gender movements are rife with the men from Mars, getting in touch with their primitive inner male and listening to the gods in every man, while our sisters do the same with more blood and more planets. We all read Joseph Campbell and find that with enough journeying work we can find the mythic meaning to our individual lives

and become, as Jung said, "individuated" and complete persons. We are every bit as ahistorical as Jung—forgetting or not caring about the origins of our ideas. Perhaps that is a fitting tribute to him.

Jung is the guru of the Christian psychologists and their pastoral imitators who have gotten in touch with their own myth in clinical pastoral education. After all, Jung is almost Christian, and he offers a convenient way to be daringly hip and scientific at the same time. And Bible study is much more fun when it is a mutual search for archetypes. The spirituality of the inner life offers a wonderful way to combine our Pietist and psychological yearnings—and offers a way for Evangelicals and Catholics and liberal Protestants to engage in a mutual but still highly individual quest with the oil of a common ahistorical, "spiritual" language.

3. Jung was a Nazi or part of that mindset. But how far can one go with this line of reasoning? Is every socialist responsible for Stalin's gulags? Every Christian a part of the Inquisition and historic anti-Semitism? We can draw careful lines of intellectual and religious ancestry and establish that we, or our heroes, had no real part of such horrors. Or, perhaps we can acknowledge a mature sense of collective historical recall and admit that very good things have horrible shadows.

4. The choices facing practitioners in psychology are limited. Freud offers spirituality only as illusion and neurosis, and a world seemingly limited to the individual's primitive reaction to his mother; behaviorism is essentially reductionist to the point of strict biochemistry; Jungian thought and its derivatives offer the most room for taking the search for meaning seriously.

Sam Keene at the Midwest Men's Conference in April threw down the gauntlet to the Jungians who dominate the men's movement. His argument was that archetypes conceptualized as "hardwired" are bullshit. If the archetypes are "metaphors"—such as king, warrior, magician, and so on—they are useful—but only as any metaphor might supply insight. But a similar question could be raised about "spirituality." If spirituality is merely metaphor, we are all free to write our own poetry. Then again, if "spirituality" is part of some larger historical or ahistorical existence—there are obvious implications.

From Christian to pagan: Jung came to adulthood in reaction to a rational, industrial, professional world constricted by three generations of middle-class Christianity. He clearly moved beyond that toward a mystical paganism which involved personally acting in non-traditional sexual ways. I simply do not know what he was like as an older man—and Noll provides no information.

My own psychological theorizing and personal story (both very much in process) includes a belief that one must get in touch with more primitive feelings, experiences and encounters with life—either in parallel with Christian faith or as a distinct stage of spiritual growth. For many men this is a part of life which is missing. There is a sense in which I am polytheistic—I take principalities and powers and the daemonic seriously. And I am increasingly aware of the dangerous shadows which exist in all of these—even in the seemingly benign, such as "liberal democracy."

I am grateful for the liturgical Christian tradition. On Sunday, we bring our collective mythologies and quests for meaning and subordinate them to a larger reality. Every knee bows. We recognize a larger spiritual drama than our own—and yet, somehow, we are part and not part of that drama.

Carl Jung wrote a letter to Bill Wilson, the founder of Alcoholics Anonymous, which Wilson cherished all his life. Jung pointed out that the alcoholic was on a spiritual quest—in spiritus—which could only be completed by sobriety.

I remain sober and Episcopalian. And still alcoholic and pagan.

—Dale Suderman, August 1998

THE AGE OF ABUNDANCE

2008

Discussed in this essay: Brink Lindsey, *The Age of Abundance: How Prosperity Transformed America's Politics and Culture*. HarperCollins, 2008.

Preface: I am not smart enough to write a feature article for The Common Review. *My mind, at best, runs in word squirts of six hundred to two thousand words and not in four to six-thousand-word ejaculations of any sort. Age, a spent youth, and being easily distracted are the root causes. Did I tell you I met Tammy Faye Baker once at a trade show? Anyway, this is a damn shame because I have learned some interesting stuff while not writing this article.*

***

In *The Age of Abundance*, Brink Lindsey sits on his libertarian economic perch and describes a fascinating economic map for analyzing contemporary American and, to a lesser extent, European society.

The forces of capitalism along with open markets have in the past half century produced a society of unprecedented widespread wealth that has moved beyond scarcity and even beyond affluence. The problem is that those who defend capitalism and free markets—generally known as conservatives—love the original system, while despising what they regard as the excesses it produces: diverse lifestyles, cultural relativity, and the "blooming of a thousand flowers" in the rich soil of material wealth. They fear that the Protestant work ethic of delayed gratification, accompanied by the absence of savings, will undermine the entire economic applecart. They plead for a return to what they regard as traditional cultural values which they see as the underpinnings of the free-market capitalist system.

At the same time, social progressives love the new cultural mix of the past decades while decrying the economic system that produced it. While feeding from the capitalist trough, liberals raise their heads long enough to squeal about domestic income disparity, the plight of the Third World, and rampant consumerism. They make their obligatory noises about porcine excess and then, without irony, continue their feeding.

Lindsey optimistically finds a bridge between the modern inhabitants of Red and Blue states. Both sides share a concern with lifestyle and the quest for personal meaning—be it spiritual health and fitness or psychological well-being. Lindsey references Maslow's hierarchy of needs—beginning with food, air and water—but as one ascends the pyramid, the "needs" become more ill-defined— whether one talks about the quest for meaning or spiritual purpose. Lindsey suggests this is our present condition: a quest for meaning that goes well beyond an individual's political or economic persuasion. He shares a wonderful yarn of the elderly Abraham Maslow and his wife accidentally ending up at the Esalen Institute in Big Sur one California night and being the horrified but honored guests of a sybaritic lifestyle that went well beyond the basics of food, water, and shelter.

Lindsey recounts two powerful stories from 1968. (I am not certain he fully comprehends their full significance.) In Haight-Ashbury, the summer of love was proclaimed with an invitation to tune in, drop out, and begin a new social order based on play and the Age of Aquarius. At the same time in Tulsa, Oklahoma, a crowd of 30,000 people gathered for the dedication of a new university called Oral Roberts University. The Reverend Billy Graham gave the address. Several symbolic events happened at this event. A new institution was launched, demonstrating a shift away from poor-folks Pentecostalism gathering in tents and by creeks. Second, American evangelicalism honored the older Pentecostal movement. But the conservatives did not rejuvenate existing institutions— rather they gathered the abundance from a conservative society to create new ones—just as they would pioneer new political tactics including direct mail, the Christian Coalition, and the adroit use of media to further their goals. They did not rejuvenate old denominations. Rather, they began megachurches and parachurches of every stripe. At the Haight-Ashbury declaration of Free Love an enthusiastic crowd was encouraged to sing the old worker hymn, "Solidarity Forever." But since most of the youth in the crowd didn't know the words, they instead chimed in with, "We all live in a Yellow Submarine."

The youthful counterculture declared capitalist and consumerist economy to be the enemy, but never created more than passing institutional alternatives. While they lamented corporate America borrowing their graphic design, music, and language for hip ad campaigns, this may be more of their legacy than they realize. (The light bulb in my refrigerator burned out and I found a replacement bulb at Jewel supermarket this afternoon and now it works again.)

The abundant society—as distinguished from the merely "affluent" society of Galbraith in the late 1950s—was the economic foundation for radical cultural change in America. That feminism, gay rights, and the Vietnam protests were based on a surplus of time and ideas— the key elements of an abundant society—is almost beyond debate.

Affluent women, articulate gays, and college students who could not be bothered by the draft were the foundation for these movements.

The Civil Rights movement is more complex. Certainly its impetus started in the rising expectations of African Americans in universities and northern urban areas. When it showed signs of becoming subordinated to the goals of white activists, Black separatists sent them packing. And it remains unclear to this day if the struggle for racial and ethnic justice is an idea based on abundance of multicultural inquiry in academic settings, or a street-level fight to move from survival to affluence.

The campus debates about political correctness are today at least as complex and subtle as the court etiquette of Louis the Fourteenth, a more narrowly based abundant society. The cultural and intellectual foundations of a nation with broad-based affluence need to be examined. First, is postmodernism perhaps nothing more than a surplus of ideas? In an age of scarcity, literacy and a modicum of religion were deemed necessary for economic and moral survival. In an age of affluence, the best civic and political ideals needed to be taught along with the vocational skills necessary to maintain the means of production. But in the age of affluence, all ideas are interesting but few are necessary for survival or production. Indeed, if one holds to any values of religious faith, or any grand unified theory of the universe, or passionate human value, one runs the risk of being déclassé. "We are all so past that," the postmodernists attest, and busily go about their task of flushing out the last residual elements of a true believer.

The postmodernists make an exception for Marxism, particularly of the vaguest and most banal type—a tool for critical analysis to be wielded not by an unemployed worker but by the clean and soft hands of an idealist, an intellectual, or an academic. The exception for religion is more narrowly focused. One can appreciate one's Catholic, Jewish, or Baptist heritage only as that which we have moved beyond. If any replacement is allowed, it must be of some form of spirituality—ideally with no roots in any historical epoch. Thus for postmodernists the present task of understanding the Islamic world exists as something of an intellectual quandary. If it does not fit into a Marxist model of class struggle it is almost unintelligible. One can be a little bit Marxist but not a little bit jihadist.

The postmodernist surplus of ideas is actually subordinate or aligned with the concept that lifestyle itself is a purchasable commodity in an abundant society. Lifestyle—the combination of dress, language, housing, the maintenance of health and place in the world—now has moved well beyond the callous climbing of the class ladder toward not just personal choice by picking from class-based lifestyle served family style but by an endless picking and choosing from the abundant buffet line set out in American society.

Social conservatives will contest the claim that they have purchased a lifestyle. Instead, they claim they have remained anchored in traditional family values, Americanism, and a respect for the Protestant work ethic. Meanwhile they blithely go to the same gymnasiums to work out, are only slightly more obese and divorced than their liberal counterparts, and are equally committed to cosmopolitan international travel. But theirs is cause-oriented. More than a million American evangelicals go on "short-term missions" every year. If they do not smoke and drink it is unclear if this is the old Puritanical streak or the new health consciousness. While claiming to preserve old institutions, they create new religious universities and megachurches and casually abandon old European religious creeds. They are about as equally concerned about health care as their liberal counterparts. Social conservatives have pioneered developing their own media with television and radio sources long before the Internet. Is learning child-rearing techniques from James Dobson rather than Dr. Spock any less of an abandonment of traditional techniques of childrearing learned from grandparents?

If one wants to preserve a folk festival or a local historic landmark, one might do better to look to liberals than conservatives for funding. The commodification of lifestyles stands in sharp contrast to older, more rigid analysis of class. Indeed, upon rereading Paul Fussell's pointed satirical book, *Class* (1983), I was struck by the almost quaint hierarchy in which one is locked into the class system and will almost inevitably be betrayed by a social faux pas if pretending to move beyond one's stratum. The only way out is through Class X. "X people are better conceived as belonging to a category than a class because you are not born an X person, as you are born or raised a prole or a middle. You become an X person, or, to put it more bluntly, you earn X-personhood by a strenuous effort of discovery in which curiosity and originality are indispensable. And in discovering that you can become an X person you find the only escape from class" (212–213).

Nearly a decade later, Douglas Coupland wrote his novel *Generation X* (1991). Borrowing from Fussell—but not acknowledging him—he tells the story of a "slacker" who dismissively works a "McJob." Almost too post-anything to frolic in youthful sex, drugs, or rock and roll, he and his two friends sit around talking dismissively of friends who have sold out to post-college corporate America—while taking advantage of parents who fly them back home for the holidays. The slacker senses he is doomed eventually to find a livelihood—most probably in some creative but well-paid role.

Indeed, the abundant society values inconspicuous consumption almost as much as the affluent society and its predecessors in the Gilded Age valued conspicuous consumption. The new urbanism with its passive regentrification of homes where it is chic to be in proximity to an ethnic or artist neighborhood increasingly replaces a vision of suburban McMansions. The simple country home or summer retreat trumps ostentatious travel in the abundant society.

David Brooks in *Bobos in Paradise* (2000) captures the gestalt of the mixed class and lifestyle choices of the bohemian bourgeoisie and how these are shared values of people on both the right and the left. But he whiffs when he insists that Bobos are an elite group. In fact, they constitute a widespread modern phenomenon. Richard Florida in *The Rise of the Creative Class* (2002) perhaps captures this better with the trendy mix of creative areas in urban America. Thus the phenomenon of the starving playwright who produces an original play but depends upon patrons and paid attendees for a subtle form of support. A friend of mine who is a sculptor and committed to a radically downward mobility says that he lives off commissions from the very persons he often holds in contempt.

The simple life is key to understanding this mindset. The option or at least the appearance of downward mobility and some sort of simple life or environmentally sound lifestyle is held in the highest esteem even while fraught with the perils of paradox and ambiguity. Perhaps it is important that 57 percent of persons who bought the hybrid Prius stated the fact that the name of the vehicle clearly announces they drive an environmentally sound car. But like most things which appear to be new, the value systems in the abundant society are not, really. David Shi, in *The Simple Life: Plain Living and High Thinking in American Culture* (1985), sketches a long intellectual tradition in America beginning with the Puritans and Quakers, who believed the deliberate simplification of life allowed more time for religious and moral activities. This was amended by the Transcendentalists toward a broader definition of the good life—but still based on simple living and high thinking.

The problem was that this turned out to be a largely intellectual and academic exercise. For when these well-intentioned souls attempted to align with those who lived the simple life out of necessity, they discovered their neighbors possessed precious few "high thoughts" and were more concerned with their own economic betterment. Jane Addams baked bread for two weeks in an attempt to identify with poor tenement women. She quit when she noted that her hands were tired and her correspondence was piling up.

Perhaps no case study illustrates the inherent tensions in the abundant society better than the issue of travel. The Grand Tour of the Gilded Age was made increasingly commonplace by Cooks Tours—cheap, fast travel done by common folk beginning around 1870. The aristocrats noted that the unique grandeur of their view of the Matterhorn from their resort balconies was starting to become diminished—by the sight of their maids marching below them, led by an umbrella-wielding tour guide. So, the aristocrats found a solution: travel to ever more exotic and unaffordable destinations. One could do a safari or amateur explorations of the Amazon. If not remote, at least travel could be difficult—beginning with mountain climbing and concluding in ever more exotic whitewater rafting. Indeed, the very discovery of nature and a sort of proto-environmentalism came from the first arrivals to the abundant society at the end of the nineteenth century. Their hardy, inaccessible wilderness areas stood in stark contrast to the immigrant vacations at places like the Catskills.

This has become commonplace. The children of the abundant society are in the Himalayas while insisting that snowmobiles and roads be kept out of pristine wilderness—since only they have the time and energy to feel they are the first visitors to these areas. In fact, one does not really "go on vacation" in the abundant society. This is too reminiscent of Disneyland and Branson, Missouri. (Las Vegas is a gray zone—one can go there for the sake of paradox and irony.)

And more than a million evangelicals go on short-term missions outside of the United States each year. A friend tells me about twelve retired couples from a local church who are planning to fly to Thailand with the task of landscaping a church and an orphanage there. The fact that there may be no shortage of Thai landscapers has escaped them, he says. But how different is this "mission tourism" from probably an equal number of Americans who go on eco-tours, educational tours, or as progressive members of affinity groups to sit and identify for a week or two with poor and oppressed peoples?

The fact that the children of both the right and the left bump into each other at the Louvre on their respective college tours is worth noting. Often the purpose of the trip is to find what is authentic and identify with it. Thus a conversation with a primitive medicine man, a simple tour among the Amish, a weekend retreat at the abbey of a religious order, or a longer stay in the Peace Corps all produce the common refrain. "I admired this culture so much and I was changed by my encounter with it." One's self is enhanced by encountering those living in scarcity or who have made lifelong commitments to a lifestyle—often based on religious ardor. But the postmodern encounter with the primitive and the committed primarily serves one's own highest good—personal growth.

The problem is that one cannot escape one's own postmodernism nor one's own purchase of a lifestyle. Indeed, they have become like assholes or gender—everybody has one. In this way the age of abundance shades into the age of invective—both bold as a scream or subtle as an innuendo, or the compulsive noting of the paradoxes and ironies of other people's lives. The hipster who stands in defiance of capitalist society is whispered to be a Trustafarian. The academic with his worn tweed coat has lived modestly on the detritus of capitalist society and had three months' paid vacation annually—often funded by foundations for the majority of his lifetime. Those who seek to be original and creative are whispered both in their own self-doubts and the muttered words of others to be derivative. We are Green as we fly around the world to see and perhaps help sea turtles or whales or polar bears.

The conservatives are at least as innovative as liberals and probably at least as exploratory in their lifestyles—both culturally and sexually. What may remain consistent and perhaps eternal in human existence is what René Girard calls mimetic envy. The language of inconsistency betrays this. The way out may be an acceptance that few lives are lived in an abundant society without irony and paradox—or even hypocrisy. This is best explored in the friendships of personal narrative rather than shopping for a new lifestyle or that elusive something called post-postmodernism.

MOODY, THE MEDIA, AND THE BIRTH OF MODERN EVANGELISM: A CAUTIONARY TALE

2004, Books & Culture

Discussed in this essay: Bruce J. Evensen, *God's Man for the Gilded Age: D. L. Moody and the Rise of Modern Mass Evangelism.* Cambridge University Press, 2003.

The death of D. L. Moody in 1899 was a headline story for the American press and the final installment in a thirty-year symbiotic relationship between the evangelist and daily newspapers both in America and Great Britain. Bruce J. Evensen, a communications professor at DePaul University, masterfully recounts both how the newspapers elevated Moody to celebrity status and how they came to occupy a central role in modern mass evangelism. Less satisfactory is the author's portrayal of the religious, economic, and social forces which swirled around the Moody revival campaigns. The author's adulation of both Moody and his twentieth-century spiritual heir, Billy Graham, makes this a bright shining portrait of urban revivalism unclouded by even a shadow of irony.

Evensen meticulously mines the minutiae of press coverage to portray six urban campaigns conducted by Moody: the ascent to fame in Britain in 1873, the faltering Brooklyn revival, and the success stories in Philadelphia, New York, Chicago, and Boston.

Moody and musician Ira Sankey arrived in Britain in 1873, unheralded by the press on either side of the Atlantic. Two years later Moody returned to New York as an international celebrity. With growing expertise in each successive city in Scotland, Ireland, and England, Moody had mastered a technique for drawing crowds by a rational process of uniting Protestants across denominational lines, using saturation publicity in both the secular and religious newspapers. The stir created by this skillful strategy attracted unbelievers who might otherwise never have attended a local church service.

Moody returned to a bidding war for his next American campaign. Unwisely perhaps, he accepted the option of church-dominated Brooklyn over Philadelphia. The Brooklyn revival drew newspaper coverage and crowds, but Moody was preaching to the choir of the converted and the event was almost overshadowed by the cause célèbre of Brooklyn preacher Henry Ward Beecher, who had been caught in a messy scandal of alleged adultery. Beecher—by this time a sad, anxious man—lurked around the edge of the crowds drawn to Moody.

The nine-week campaign in Philadelphia was a greater success. The city's powerful business establishment—led by John Wanamaker, George Stuart, Anthony Drexel, and Jay Cooke—was firmly behind Moody. Wanamaker had 300 of his department store employees "volunteer" as ushers. Indeed, Wanamaker secretly owned the Grand Depot where the revival was held, and two months after Moody left, converted the tabernacle into a new location for his department store. The campaign neatly coincided with the city's centennial, and President Grant and other national political figures attended while in town, further heightening the hype surrounding the revival.

In 1876 Moody went to New York City, transforming the newly bankrupt P. T. Barnum's Hippodrome into a tabernacle for revival. Again the barons of the Gilded Age, this time headed by J. Pierpont Morgan and Cornelius Vanderbilt, underwrote the campaign. Evenson admits their possibly mixed motives for such benefice. "Certainly they hoped for a spiritual revival in their city, and almost as decidedly did they pray that the excitement might overwhelm the public's growing disaffection with national scandal and depression."

Later that same year, Moody returned to Chicago, this time as a prophet with honor in his own land. The *Chicago Tribune* and rival papers boosted Moody's revival as a point of civic pride. The city, recently devastated by a horrendous fire—which destroyed Moody's first attempt at building a tabernacle—could not be outshone by East Coast cities. When the crowds faltered, Moody devised theme promotions to renew public interest. For instance, there was the special night for "fallen women," intended to attract prostitutes who worked less than a mile away. Evensen is coy about whether this was a crass publicity stunt to increase newspaper coverage, or a sincere outreach to suffering women. Even less clear is what welcome would later await the converts who went to the inquiry room in local churches.

Seventy-eight local churches organized the Boston campaign in the winter of 1877. The two competing local newspapers made Moody a headline event with daily transcripts of his sermons on their front pages. Unitarians kept their distance, but a wide range of Congregationalists, Episcopalians, Methodists, and Baptists united behind Moody. The Tremont Tabernacle, with seating for seven thousand souls, was built in the shadow of A. J. Gordon's Baptist Church. When attendance flagged, special trains offering free or half-price fares brought in small-town and rural folks to fill the seats. By the conclusion, a million people had attended the revival, and six thousand new converts were reported. (Evensen ignores the fact that Boston was no stranger to systematic citywide revival. The 1858 Boston revival had used techniques similar to Moody's.)

The raucous Gilded Age free press was underfinanced and desperate for copy to attract local readers. No longer house organs financed by political parties and factions, newspapers needed advertising and market share to sustain themselves. They combined crime stories, local scandals, and gossip with boosterism and competing visions of civic reform in attempts to claim reader loyalty. All this was happening in an urban market that was increasingly foreign-born and developing its own foreign-language press.

Moody used the press brilliantly. He placed reporters front and center at a reserved press table complete with inkwells, paper, candles, and press aides to whisper the names of pastors who led prayers. Reporters were even allowed to bring their girlfriends with them to sit in the choice seats. To accommodate the stenographers who struggled to keep up with his machine-gun delivery, Moody slowed his preaching to 220 words per minute. He held afternoon meetings with the press to share anecdotes for the evening press. (A daily schedule of events was an early form of the modern-day press release.) Moody said, "I don't know what will become of me if the newspapers continue to print all of my sermons"—while at the same time making every effort to continue to be front-page news.

The press reciprocated Moody's accommodations. Walt Whitman, drawn to Boston to see the celebrity preacher, noted "Moody's wonderful murder of syntax" and too frequent use of the word "I." For Whitman, Moody was a newspaper commodity in the style of police reports and patent medicines. But the press cleaned up Moody's syntax when they placed entire transcripts of his sermons on the front page; and when crowds thinned, reporters ignored the empty seats. Moody's civic spectacle was simply too good for circulation and local pride.

Preaching in American cities to immigrants, mostly Irish Catholics, who shared desperate poverty and a growing sense of their own political power, bringing with it new political machines, worker unrest, and attempts at urban reform, Moody largely ignored these issues. With no apparent sense of its emblematic implications, Evensen quotes from a press account of a young girl working in a factory, recently converted at a Moody revival, who stoically sang a revival hymn while her fingers were methodically cut off in an industrial accident. Moody's one notable contribution to social reform was preaching temperance. (Francis Willard—soon to expand her range of reforms to include an editorial position on a Christian socialist magazine—was working alongside Moody in Boston with afternoon temperance sermons but is ignored entirely by Evensen.)

Unfortunately, *God's Man for the Gilded Age* makes only passing mention of Moody's involvement with the 1894 Columbian Exposition in Chicago. Evensen does not tell us that the World's Fair board offered Moody a site for a revival campaign—and obtained for themselves the fringe benefit of keeping the Fair open on Sunday. After all, this was a religious event. Moody's preaching was now in proximity to the world's first Ferris wheel, the glitter of the Midway carnival, and the spectacle of electric lighting. Evensen makes brief mention of Moody's competing for attention with the World's Parliament of Religions. But perhaps a bigger story, another detail unremarked by Evensen, concerns Turlington W. Harvey, local lumberman and longtime Moody funder. Harvey used the gatherings to sell lots for his alternative suburb south of Chicago. This effort exists today as the impoverished city of Harvey, Illinois.

Evensen has done landmark research on Moody and the urban press. Missing is a sense of Moody's Gilded Age context and of what it might mean to be God's man in a time so named. The result is a book full of facts, but insufficiently grounded in the kind of critical theological or historical reflection that could tease out those facts' larger significance.

GRUMPY OLD MEN

2007, Hillsboro Free Press

The second oldest joke in America goes like this. A young boy is taken to the barn and shown an eight-foot-high stack of manure. He immediately takes a pitchfork and starts digging into it frantically.

When asked the cause for his energetic digging, he says, "Well, with this much manure, there must be a pony in there someplace."

This lad stands in sharp contrast to the grumpy old men who daily place their bets that there is no pony. "Yup, not only is there no pony, but tomorrow there will be another pile of manure, even if you clean that one up today," they lament.

And they sip their coffee and chortle on about the naïve idealism of the kid. Grumpy old men wager every day that each and every new idea, concept, and lifestyle will not work. And mostly they win their wagers. Indeed, for centuries they won their argument. They were right, heavier-than-air machines cannot fly—until the kids from Dayton, Ohio proved them wrong.

They are kin to the fellow who proposed closing the United States patent office at the turn of the nineteenth century because all the important things had already been invented. Grumpy old men are not true conservatives. Conservatives try to preserve and utilize traditions, pass on old values, and tell the story of old times. Grumpy old men do not contribute to historical preservation societies, they do not pass on memoirs, they do not participate in folk festivals. "Probably not much use in trying to talk about the past parts of the old days," they say. "These younger folks wouldn't appreciate it anyway."

Nor are they progressives looking to create change. They just make bets that no new idea, product, or concept might have value. For them the future is doomed to fail and the past wasn't much better.

Probably if they had their way, we would still be living in trees, afraid to come down and hunt game, plant crops, and build cities.

So eventually the kid leaves town to seek his pony elsewhere. He crosses the Rio Grande at night. He leaves Warsaw and Krakow on a visitor visa and sleeps on his cousin's couch until he finds a job in Chicago. He packs up his stuff in his car and leaves rural America—and heads to New York, San Francisco, and Chicago to seek his fortune or die trying. He skips out of the plantation system in Mississippi where there is no future in picking cotton.

With few skills, no street smarts, and sometimes not even basic English, admittedly many don't survive. Nevertheless, the immigrants who have fled the realms of grumpy old men have very often been the infusion of hope in their new worlds. This is not a new phenomenon. For example, my friend Ben Hartley did historical research and found that an amazing number of the new churches and religious institutions in Boston were started after the Civil War not by native born Bostonians—who were perhaps too prim and proper to risk new stuff. Rather naïve immigrant idealists from Iowa and rural Canada and Ireland began them.

This spring some grumpy old men will watch commencement ceremonies and slap their knees and laugh at the pony-seeking kids marching across the stage. "Well, they sure ain't gonna make it in the real world."

They may fail to note that fewer kids stay in rural America after they graduate. When grumpy old men are wrong, they are really wrong. And sometimes the kids looking for a pony where there should be no pony are onto something.

McDONALD'S GOES BUST

2007, Hillsboro Free Press

McDonald's was a landmark institution in Hillsboro. Its neon lit sign was the third-tallest structure in town—overshadowed only by the grain elevator and the water towers. The news of its demise spread like a prairie fire among the View-From-Afar gang. This motley crew of friends, some expatriates from small towns—including

Hillsboro—and other armchair pundits, was true to form and quick to opine and speculate on the crisis.

"I presume the McDonald's had already driven out the locally owned restaurant and is now getting its just desserts," wrote Brian from Paris.

I had to explain that when the hometown restaurant, the Iron Kettle, burned down, many of its patrons just walked across the highway to encamp at McDonald's for their morning coffee.

The most outrageous interpretation shocked me. "Clearly, the Nancy Pelosi-loving, Hillary Clinton-supporting, white wine-sipping, fern-bar devotees of Hillsboro have achieved what the citizens of Berkeley, Boston, and Taos were unable to achieve in their battles with McDonald's. Hillsboro has fought and won a cultural battle to prevent America from becoming a gigantic, boring strip mall. Could the city be emerging as a Blue pimple in a very Red state?"

This purple prose from a nameless alumnus of Tabor College demonstrates the very limited value of graduate degrees in English. He fails to understand that in Kansas strip malls are symbols of progress and nobody even knows what a fern bar is. Another Kansas friend wrote me, "These folks need to go for local products. Didn't they realize that McDonald's buys beef from Argentina and their milk shakes are made with seaweed?" he lamented.

Even if his facts are a bit skewed, I had to give him points for his provincial pride. My international friends from Iraq and Sudan asked about what restaurants remain in Hillsboro.

"There is a place serving pizza, a new place with Mexican food, and an established business with a German buffet," I said.

"Clearly you are becoming an international city serving Italian, Mexican, and German foods. Why not exploit this and get the city declared a UNESCO world heritage site, fly the United Nations flag over the high school, and attract tourists from all over the world?" they suggested helpfully.

Ideas like this leave me silently rolling my eyes.

"So now where do the farmers go for their morning coffee?" asked Tim, the caring, peace-loving person.

"I understand some of them go to Ampride—the gas station and mini-mart owned by the farmers' cooperative," I said.

He became very excited. "You mean the peasant farmers in the county gather at a worker-owned cooperative for their morning consciousness-raising sessions? Do they join in solidarity with the campesinos of El Salvador and Nicaragua as they drink their Fair Trade morning coffee and discuss the presidency of Daniel Ortega?"

His excitement about this option continued unabated until I explained that most of these farmers were landowners—not peasants—and that they drive pickup trucks worth more than the GDP of El Salvador and were probably mostly skeptical about raising the minimum wage.

Adam, the elitist, saw the situation from a unique perspective. "Clearly the farm economy is booming with higher grain prices and Marion County folks are ready for a bit more upscale coffee. Why don't they open a Starbucks coffee shop franchise? Once they have tasted a Grande Low-Fat Caramel Macchiato their lives will be forever changed," he said.

"And about how much will this cost?" I asked.

"Well, about $3.65 plus tax," he replied.

"Sorry, I suspect these folks would sooner drink recycled swill for under fifty cents a cup than pay that sort of price," I said.

The View-from-Afar gang has lots of opinions but very few solutions for life's persistent questions. I shudder to think what they will say about more troops going to Iraq.

ON READING PAUL FUSSELL

2003, Journal Entry

Journal, July 30, 2003—Wednesday morning before work and a few minutes remain for reflection. Remodeling for the third summer in a row disorients me. Once again, "things" are not in their place. Projects seem half-finished or barely begun. I catch myself delaying unrelated parts of my life, such as journaling, paying bills, keeping in contact with friends. Remodeling is the excuse. "When I get an office space I will take care of paperwork, and when the kitchen tile work is finished, I will start cleaning." The concept of multitasking has been a theme in recent months. This is best illustrated by looking at the bedroom floor one morning and finding a hammer, tape measure, and lecture notes for Northwestern among dirty clothes all jumbled together beneath my feet.

Remodeling this year is complex. It mostly feels like a juggling act on interior work—coordinating beam and wall stuff in the front rooms, installing bookcases, figuring out a curtain system and some system of getting plaster and painting done, all of this in the context of an unknown schedule for new windows and siding. Add to this the variable of a new front door system and possible deck installation. I've set an arbitrary date for interior work to be mostly finished by August 21 when, I hope, Adam comes to visit. This may not be realistic. September is Boston for a week with Ben and time in the archives. I've pushed back doing an in-service on Men and Recovery to October to leave the entire month open. Am headed to Bluffton to see John Kampen and Carol on August 9. Will then return with walls torn out and beam installed by Doug Bermudez and Steve—and maybe Michael.

Random Images of Past Days:

Did a walking tour of area around Harbor Light for six Northwestern students and their adjunct professor, Doug Hostetter. Not certain if they learned anything, but the exercise pulled a lot of stuff together for me. Cities are a place of endless recycling with vestiges of different historical, economic, and cultural layers overlapping each other. This is as true in Chicago as in ancient cities like London and Jerusalem. So we walk around Harbor Light and discuss the Laflin farm site, stockyards, Skid Row, robber barons, Romanesque architecture, Theodore Dreiser and *Sister Carrie*, the Bauhaus movement, African-American immigration patterns, crack, and mayors—with attention to the Carter Harrison (Chicago mayor 1879–1887) empire, land values, and postindustrial America. All of this within four blocks.

When Doug raises the question of affordable housing in Chicago, I realize that affordable housing is usually not much more than a niche or stage in land utilization—much the same as affluent housing is usually only a stage in land use. In the larger scheme of things, cities are more nearly like a forest with cycles of growth and decay and subtle ecosystems. The mighty redwood and the most fragile mushroom equally become compost for the next stage of growth. The hubris of developers, preservationists, and affordable housing advocates is their belief that cities are static, a naiveté akin to that of a junior botanist who attempts to fix a forest glen to keep it forever as he found it on a warm Saturday afternoon in late May.

This is part of my own justification for working with individuals rather than systems. Human beings are more adaptable than ecosystems. For me, the priority is not affordable housing but equipping persons to be able to afford to pay for their own decent housing and to better navigate and adapt to the urban forest.

Jesse was my last client on Tuesday. He just turned twenty and is of Hispanic and German heritage. He is a long-time gangbanger and drug dealer with multiple felonies for dealing and weapons possession. He was referred to me by Boot Camp because he used drugs while on probation after completing the Boot Camp program. In three months, he has moved out of his parents' home on the Southwest Side to live with more functional siblings in Rogers Park. A relative has given him a job on a construction crew that pays $13 an hour—although he has zero skills for this. He has a strategy for life: save money and get an associate's degree and ultimately a B.A. in psychology.

Last night he asked me, "So what is a 401(k)?" He dropped a new casual sexual partner because he found out her friends are "gangbangers." He continues, "I can't do that. She was pissed." Along with affirming him for his decisions, I also did some ethnic storytelling with him to establish a context for his story. "So, this is the upward move. Your siblings and larger family are helping you out—just like the new family in AA is doing. You fuck up, they will kick you to the curb rather than go down with you. But you also now have a larger obligation, to give a leg up for other folks—this may take decades to really happen—but you know you owe them." At his request we will continue sessions even after the mandated probationary treatment terms are completed. I agree to jiggle the paperwork to make this happen. Yes, a thing can both "be" and "not-be," and furthermore, one can both successfully complete addictions treatment and still remain in treatment.

The larger tragedy is, why do Hispanic clients ask about 401(k) plans when they enter mainstream systems and African-American clients rarely, if ever, ask the same question? Jesse will navigate the city forest quite well if he remembers the principle, "No guns, no drugs, no booze." Chicago does offer affordable housing for failures. "Jails, institutions, and death" is the Narcotics Anonymous chant at their meetings. I am constantly startled by the adaptability of relatively functional individuals in cities—ranging from Jesse on the young end to old guys in recovery who figure out how to use recovery programs as retirement systems. The endless nooks and crannies that immigrants find as a base in Chicago astonish me—from Korean drycleaning shops, to shared housing by Hispanics, to Polish guys who work in crews to install windows.

Paul Fussell

I will review a new book on World War II by Paul Fussell for *The Common Review* magazine. This is a slight book in which he reworks his older themes about men in the military. Fussell is a former Marine who saw combat in the Battle of the Bulge and expected to be shipped to the Pacific for the invasion of Japan. He used the GI Bill to get a doctorate, wrote solid academic books, and published papers on obscure (to me) English-professor-type stuff. He got tenure (at Rutgers and then the University of Pennsylvania), was married, and had kids and a nice house.

He broke out of the pack by writing *The Great War and Modern Memory* (1975). His revisionist perspective on World War I was that male bonding, homoeroticism, and the nonsexual and sexual admiration of younger men is a core theme in the poetry, literature, and memoirs by the combatants in that conflict. Thus, erotic poems about the beauty of younger men were reworked after the war as eulogies to fallen warriors. (It is always safe for men to love each other in the most intimate way, provided one of them is dead.)

Later, in his book *Class: A Guide Through the American Status System* (1983), he plays with class distinctions by categorizing Americans into nine groups ranging from the *Lumpenproletariat* to the most elite. He is hilarious and mocking and makes most readers uncomfortable as we see how we are prisoners of culturally defined "objects of desire." (I am moving my TV set to the living room so that guests do not see it immediately upon entering my apartment—and consequently I move up one class.) The only escape he offers from this status trap is the elusive goal of a tenth category—"category X"—persons who mix and match both furniture but also relationships in ways that upend predictable class markers. As Fussell says, "you are not born an X person, as you are born and reared a prole or a middle. You become an X person, or, to put it more bluntly, you earn X-personhood by a strenuous effort of discovery in which curiosity and originality are indispensable" (179). His example is a female anthropology professor with a mix of curios, kitsch, and functional objects in her home along with a range of sexual partners—diverse in gender and age.

Fussell's influential collection of essays titled *Thank God for the Atom Bomb* (1988) has a powerful lead essay. He describes how the alternative to the atomic bombing of Japan—a conventional land invasion of the Japanese islands—would have played out. He envisions what the human cost would have been for both Allied forces and the Japanese, and in his telling, the atomic bomb provided a quick, cruel, but ultimately less lethal ending to the war. For Fussell personally it offered a chance for a doctorate rather than a marker in a veteran's cemetery.

Written during a wave of anti-nuclear protests, the essay shows Fussell in his most iconoclastic mood. It is a reminder that Fussell does not identify as part of the pristine, moral purity of the academic left. He describes himself as a traditional middle-class kid, knocked out of his square by the horrors of combat in World War II, who now seeks to balance family life and academic life. In her memoir, *My Kitchen Wars* (1999), his first wife Betty recalls their life together differently. She writes about an open marriage, drunken group sex at faculty parties, and, for her, the final straw: finding her husband naked with an equally naked male graduate student—from the engineering department, no less. The experience led to her filing for divorce. Most recently appearing in Fussell's oeuvre is *Uniforms* (2002)—again not much more than an expanded essay in which he points out how men use clothing to define themselves for themselves and for each other.

The Boys' Crusade: The American Infantry in Northwestern Europe, 1944–1945 (2003) retells but also reshapes the familiar saga of the "the greatest war." As Fussell describes it, the infantry from D-Day on were boys, usually seventeen to twenty years of age. Most were poorly trained and away from home for the first time. They were virgins in every sense of the word—innocent of sex, violence, and death. Fussell turns them into living bodies—with violent diarrhea, intestines opened by gut shots, brains splattered. They are crying and confused but they somehow manage to continue on. They died from German weaponry but also from misplaced aerial bombing by their own Allied forces. They were sent on preposterous missions from which few survived. Fussell mocks the military historians who depict this as a giant endgame in chess with forces advancing on Berlin from the West and the East, or in terms of simple bravery—the Steven Spielberg approach. These were a bunch of kids lurching through hell.

Fussell has a sort of fondness for General Dwight D. Eisenhower. He is the ultimate boy, from Abilene, Kansas, with a boyish grin that did not leave him in old age. Eisenhower describes a "crusade"— oblivious to the political incorrectness of the term but also seemingly without much more depth for the term than a Pentagon marketing slogan. Ike's discovery of the death camps reframes the crusade. Only as the war neared completion did the boys and their boy-chief find an event which gave content to the term "crusade."

I have felt a kinship with Fussell for almost two decades—and never really understood why. He stubbornly refuses any act of self-revealing. Even his autobiography keeps the reader at arm's length. Yet he has always struck me as a fellow participant in an arena of men who have other men as both friends and as lovers. The complexity of this defies the simple categories of gay and straight. He knows men can be young and beautiful. But the same young male who resembles Michelangelo's David also shits in his pants from sickness and fear. Fussell understands that boys will be sent off to die—either in combat or by living to an age when they are too old to be desirable. Fussell could be described as a grizzled humanist—but this would not capture how he pays attention to other men. He both sees and values men—without resorting to the reductionism of gay and straight. He sees history and culture through a lens unencumbered by political correctness, the so-called grand sweep of history, or war as the illusion of a cosmic chess game.

The Boys' Crusade is a small book yet difficult to categorize. It is neither history, nor advocacy for or against the military. It is not memoir. It does not advance, at least for Fussell, a new thesis. Rather it is a still, small voice. It reminds us that boys killing boys is another word for war. See Iraq, see Liberia, see Bosnia for additional chapters.

A Straight-Shooting, Plain-Spoken Texan and Our Iraq Adventure:

Two column ideas for August. When the fuck did we start using the term "straight-shooting, plain-spoken Texan"? If anybody should know better it is my fellow Kansans. Texans are tall-tale tellers. They are profligate spenders who have no sense of the future and a wildly absurd recall of the past. They are practically an American synonym for variations on non-truth telling. Iraq is a bit of a mess. The set-up of weapons of mass destruction in Iraq was false. The middle chapter of the invasion and takeover went nicely. The third chapter being written now—occupation and exit—is a total fiasco. Since conservative Americans are anti-interventionist and actually isolationist they will soon be marching (or voting) to support our troops—to bring them home.

The NGO types can't admit it, but out of humanitarian concern, they are actually asking for *more* troops—under a United Nations flag to bring some sort of relief and order to a suffering people.

Footnote: Baghdad hasn't had 24/7 electrical service for decades.

EXPOSING THE DEMONS OF WAR

2004, *The Common Review*

Reviewed in this essay: Paul Fussell, *The Boys' Crusade: The American Infantry in Northwestern Europe, 1944–1945*. Modern Library, 2003.

Boys—often between seventeen and twenty years of age—fought the final ground battles of World War II. Many had been either recently drafted or shifted from desk jobs, and their commanding officers were often barely older than they. In this thin but by no means slight book, Paul Fussell cuts like a skilled butcher with a short knife through the fat of "military romanticism" to the hard bone beneath. There we find what Fussell calls "the history of real human action and emotion, especially as triggered by intimate horror, death, and sorrow."

The typical American infantryman was a small-town boy with, at most, a high school education. He had received less than seventeen weeks of training before he went into combat. He vomited from seasickness aboard the ship taking him to the United Kingdom. He was better paid and supplied than his British counterpart—for example, being issued 22.5 sheets of toilet paper per day while the Brits had to do with a mere three sheets. In many cases he had his first sexual experience with a London prostitute, armed with the safety of army-issued condoms, before crossing the English Channel to the Continent.

General Eisenhower told these youths that they were about to engage in a "Great Crusade" when they landed in Normandy. This is not to be understood through a veil of irony, as practiced readers of Fussell might expect, for the author does like Ike. The bellicose, prissy Patton and the narcissistic Montgomery are not his heroes. Eisenhower, with his Abilene simplicity and lifelong boyish grin, is both a popular and representative leader in a narrative about the "boys' crusade," although Fussell also illuminates how the war's endgame in the Nazi concentration camps bludgeoned Ike's moral disposition. Probably few young soldiers understood Ike's historical reference at all, and only a handful of sophisticates would have thought of the ill-fated Children's Crusade of 1213. For the most part, these boys were fighting in strange lands for their own survival rather than consciously partaking in any geopolitical strategy or acting in pursuit of an ideological goal.

More than 135,000 of them died in combat. Those who soldiered on endured pointless patrols and death from friendly fire—particularly misplaced aerial "support." Even "victory" was gruesome. Eisenhower, in his memoirs, describes the results of the battlefield at Falaise as a "killing field" and states, "It was literally possible to walk for hundreds of yards, stepping on nothing but dead and decaying flesh." According to novelist Kingsley Amis, even an aerial-spotter pilot vomited from the stench as he flew over the battlefield.

Fussell quotes an infantryman: "People didn't crumble and fall like they did in the Hollywood movies. They were tossed in the air and their blood spattered everywhere. And a lot of people found themselves covered in the blood and flesh of their friends, and that's a pretty tough thing for anybody to handle." One medical historian of the time says, "Veterans remembered—and sometimes dreamed of, years after the war—bodies literally torn to pieces, of intestines hung on trees like Christmas festoons."

To end such scenes, some American soldiers shot themselves in the hand or foot to be taken off the battlefield. Others deserted or feigned mental illness. Most fought on—often as much to avoid losing face among their peers as anything else. Because of green troops entering from Replacement Training Centers, Fussell contends, "the Allied ground army grew worse as the war proceeded."

Only as the war lurched to a close and the horrors of the death camps became known and visible to GIs was there some sense of idealism and cause among them. Fussell notes that by the time they entered and saw the death camps for themselves, they had begun to realize that "they had been engaged in something more than a mere negative destruction of German military power. They had been fighting and suffering for something positive, the sacredness of life itself."

The irony of a war in which some residual idealism is found near the end rather than the beginning of the campaign is more complex than most chroniclers of World War II have been able to comprehend. Now the Germans—including those who surrendered—were perceived as subhuman, much the same as they had regarded the Jews and Poles. In one liberated concentration camp, Fussell writes, U.S. troops machine-gunned to death 122 SS guards and then turned over the other guards to the surviving prisoners for appropriate treatment. In pondering these facts, Fussell tempers his affirmation of late-stage idealism in the war with a terse statement: "There is nothing in infantry warfare to raise the spirits at all, and anyone who imagines a military 'victory' gratifying is mistaken."

Paul Fussell as a person remains offstage in this narrative. Only in a brief biographical note do we learn that during "the Second World War he was severely wounded in France as a twenty-year-old second lieutenant leading a rifle platoon in the 103rd Infantry Division." Thus he invokes the authority of memoir while refusing to impose upon the narrative the first-person voice and ego. Yet in spite of this conscious choice for restraint, Fussell is, if anything, more focused, passionate, and intense in *The Boys' Crusade* than in any of his previous books about war. The near impossibility of using words in any meaningful or honest way to make sense of, let alone recall, the horrors of combat and the near homoerotic beauty of naïve, unscathed "soldier boys," is a theme Fussell has visited before, beginning with *The Great War and Modern Memory* (1975). That book described the trench warfare as recalled by writers and poets who fought in World War I, and it broke Fussell out of the academic pack, earning him a National Book Award.

Fussell returned to these themes in *Wartime: Understanding and Behavior in the Second World War*. Both civilians and many military personnel were often protected from the horrors of war by a sanitized media and the need to preserve morale. That book's final chapter, plaintively titled, "The Real War Will Never Get in the Books," presages his attempt to accomplish this nearly impossible task in *The Boys' Crusade*. *Thank God for the Atom Bomb and Other Essays* (1988), published near the peak of antinuclear sentiments in this country, revealed Fussell not as a hawk or a dove but more as a pox on all ideology. The net result of the bombing of Hiroshima and Nagasaki, Fussell argued, was to save the lives of infantrymen doomed to a land invasion of Japan—but it also probably saved the lives of Japanese civilians. Yet Fussell's book also offhandedly offended American Legion patriots by recalling the racism inherent in such GI atrocities against the Japanese as collecting gold teeth from still-living enemy soldiers and using their boiled skulls as souvenirs.

Fussell tells his own story of moving from a naïve, pampered, middle-class California life to combat and back to academe as a student under the GI Bill in *Doing Battle: The Making of a Skeptic*. His own combat experiences are horrific, but he studiously cuts himself off his opportunity to present himself as hero or villain. Elsewhere, the Fussell persona is best revealed as the detached, ironic—and wickedly funny—observer in two books, *Class: A Guide Through the American Status System* (1983) and *Uniforms: Why We Are What We Wear* (2002). *Class* mercilessly dissects the way Americans typically embrace class differences while denying that such differences exist. Fussell makes it impossible to avoid seeing ourselves and others as locked into endless mimetic desire and pretense. In *Uniforms*, Fussell exercises to fine effect his gift for aphorism, finding inspiration in Thomas Carlyle, who observed that "[s]ociety, which the more I think of it astonishes me the more, is founded upon cloth." Here Fussell holds forth on uniforms ranging from those of McDonald's service workers to academics and the clergy.

The Boys' Crusade crisply addresses three recurring and consistent themes that are dominant in Fussell and should be urgent for all thoughtful readers. First, what does it mean to be male? More particularly, what does it mean to be a young male? Michelangelo's David—the self-contained, serene warrior in thoughtful repose—is the western ideal from the Greco-Roman world via the Renaissance and into the popular modern imagination through Johann Winckelmann. Fussell dares to take this David apart, and to show us his anguish, horror, vomit, and excrement exposed by fear. He dares to leave his intestines and brains splattered on the ground. In *Doing Battle*, he approvingly quotes Phillip Caputo, who, when he trained as an officer in Vietnam, was told, "Sir, you're going to learn that one of the most brutal things in the world is your average 19-year-old American boy." Fussell loves his male comrades; *The Great War and Modern Memory* is dedicated to a technical sergeant "killed beside me in France, March 15, 1945." He is not afraid to describe the innocence and beauty of young men. But his male gaze is far more knowing and complex than simple admiration for other men. He leaves us with the inchoate mix of fear, brutality, idealism, and cynicism that war brings out in men— but leaves unanswered the question of whether this is a temporary condition or the core of masculinity once the veneers of civilization are peeled away.

Second, Fussell confronts us with the problem of memory—both personal and collective. He consigns popular films such as *Saving Private Ryan* to the "purgatory where boys' bad adventure films end up." After combat, Fussell suggests, the protective gauze of ideology tends to be applied. As far as he is concerned, both patriotism and pacifism conceal the particulars of combat experience. The armchair battlefield historians, like football coaches in the postgame review, with their arrows converging on Berlin from the West and the East, provide no pleasure for Fussell. And even though he is a distinguished and credentialed member of the "Greatest Generation," Fussell makes only fine and nuanced distinctions among the sacrifices and suffering of soldiers from 1914 to Vietnam.

Finally, and most important, before we read the great philosophical and religious treatises on human culture and human nature, we need to consider Fussell's insistent demand that we see the horrible primitive scenes of violence and death as an urtext of human experience. Paul Fussell is our greatest portrait painter of wartime. He exposes the demons but does no exorcisms. If he provides us with some glimpse of the truth, it does not bear translating, least of all into any kind of lesson.

SUPERMAN

2008, Hillsboro Free Press

"People of earth, this is Dale Suderman." The entire world watches the breaking television news story as a Michael Jordan type sports hero—also rumored to be an alien—announces he will leave the sports world to seek the planet of his birth.

Dale Suderman, a.k.a, Super "Man," was an orphan raised by Darrel and Edna Suderman in a farm community north of Wichita. His superpowers scared his mother to death and he was sent to an orphanage where his basketball skills emerged and he eventually starred on a team owned by a malevolent Lex Luthor. Dale Suderman disappeared from the basketball arena to once again find love and wisdom among the simple folks in his hometown in Kansas and announces he is leaving the world stage. As the story ends, he is enrolling under a new alias, "Clark Kent," in a journalism class taught by Lois Lane.

Well, at least this is how the comic book, *Superman, Inc.*, published in 1999, presented the yarn—in sixty-four pages of vividly colored cartoons. How do I know this? About 47 percent of computer-literate Americans "auto-Google"—they check out their own name on the Internet. (I suspect the habit is more widespread than reported, since many folks are not self-disclosing their own private vices.)

I admit to auto-Googling. Today I get 285 hits for "Dale Suderman." There is a marathon runner in Texas and a conservationist in British Columbia using my name. My own history of scribbling for magazines, the Free Press, and giving speeches results in more than a hundred "hits." But the majority of the references for "Dale Suderman" refer to this prequel story about the legend of Superman.

After discovering this coincidence a few years ago, I paid $6.95 at a comic book store for a copy of *Superman, Inc.*, had a cup of coffee at a sidewalk café, and read the book. It was a creepy experience. I really was raised in a small town in Kansas north of Wichita—although not an orphan—so far as I know. My parents really were Dan and Edna Suderman, not Darrel and Edna Suderman. As a child I did not scare my mother to death with my superhuman powers, in fact, my physical clumsiness and constant daydreaming were cause for concern by my real-life parents.

Nor did I move on to the world stage as a sports superstar. But like the comic book hero, I have, at times, returned to Kansas to find wisdom and a center for myself. And journalism has fascinated me for decades—even though there is no academic program to blame for my scribbling.

To paraphrase the rap song, "It's hard out there for a superhero." I showed the comic book to friends who accused me of having it printed as a vain tribute to myself. "Sorry, I will admit to being a narcissist, but I don't have the money to pay for a four-color graphic tribute to myself."

I contacted an authority on the Superman saga and pointed out the coincidences in the story. He wrote back laconically, "Yup, it is strange," and cut off contact. But sometimes in my Walter Mitty moments, I daydream that maybe I really am a superhero now so cleverly disguised as a pudgy old man that I have forgotten my true identity.

"It's a bird, it's a plane, it's Suderman." Well, maybe.

WHEN THE BIBLE DIVIDED THE LAND

2007, The Common Review

Discussed in this essay: Mark Noll, *The Civil War as a Theological Crisis*. The University of North Carolina Press, 2006.

Prior to the Civil War, the United States had evolved into a more or less monolithic Protestant nation. This had come about partly as a result of the rapid growth of Evangelical Protestant churches supplanting older Anglican and Establishment congregations. Of the fifty thousand places of worship in the land, roughly 95 percent were Protestant, dominated by Methodists, Baptists, and Presbyterians. More citizens attended weekly church services than voted in national elections. There were as many Methodist preachers as there were postal workers, and overall, twice as many clergy as members of the military. Only the railroads had a larger net worth than did the churches. Church receipts nearly equaled those of the federal government.

According to Mark Noll's latest book, *The Civil War as a Theological Crisis*, the denominations themselves were the earliest nerve centers of American national identity, long before national political parties framed debate around issues of national import. Noll contends that Evangelical Protestants in antebellum America shaped the national debate leading to the Civil War, but they failed to agree on how to use the Bible as a definitive text, and were unable to develop any kind of theology as an organizing principle for reading it. As a result, they could not provide lucid answers to the national debate that they had helped initiate. In Noll's account these shortcomings contributed after the war to the rise of secularism and the decline of Protestantism as a moral force in American society.

Indeed, actual church pulpits preceded the bully pulpit of the modern presidency as a primary source of values and information. Today's cable television talking heads had their antecedents in public discourse from the educated clergy. In 1845 the clergyman Jonathan Blanchard publicly debated an emancipationist opponent for four days in sessions that each lasted eight hours—outdoing even the longest modern-day presentations of C-Span. An American citizen in the nineteenth century was more likely to hear a sermon on Sunday than read a newspaper, and the vast majority of college students attended institutions administered by religious societies or denominations.

The Evangelical Protestant faith, Noll argues, provided the ideological dress for the new republic. The reverse also seemed to be true—Evangelicals believed the Republic proved the rightness of the Evangelical Protestant worldview. For them, America was in a covenant relationship to God, there was a relationship between private character and public well-being, and the Bible and (secondarily) the Constitution were both incontrovertible texts. Just as important, most Protestants thought the Bible's meaning to be clear and uncomplicated. The Bible, as the Methodist Holiness teacher Phoebe Palmer wrote in 1865, is a "wonderfully simple book." The Bible was best understood through common sense available to any ordinary person. Protestant believers generally discerned that it supported Republican government and the market economy, and also forecast the providential destiny of the United States. All this was done with the self-confidence of Enlightenment thinking, "a nearly infallible ability to perceive clear-cut connections between moral causes and public effects."

And yet ordinary readers of the Bible were hardly finding the meaning of the text to be so straightforward. Already by 1844, Methodists and Baptists each had split into northern and southern factions precisely because they could not agree on what the Bible said about the omnipresent problem of slavery. In 1863, President Lincoln proclaimed a "national day of humiliation, fasting, and prayer" for the healing of a fractured country. In Brooklyn, one of the country's most mesmerizing preachers, the Reverend Henry Ward Beecher, declared from his pulpit that the "most alarming and fertile cause of national sin" was slavery. According to Noll, Beecher believed that "the Bible could not speak [about slavery] with less ambiguity." But weeks earlier, just a few blocks away, the Presbyterian Reverend James Van Dyke denounced abolitionism as the national evil. So confident was he of the Biblical rightness of slavery that he could only conclude that men like Beecher were scoffing at Biblical authority. On the same day as Lincoln's appeal for national humility, the Rabbi Morris J. Raphall addressed the Jewish Synagogue of New York and conducted a thorough exegesis of Exodus, Leviticus, and Deuteronomy. His conclusion was that the Hebrew Bible irrefutably supported slavery.

Abolitionists such as William Lloyd Garrison claimed the truth of personal freedom trumped any single biblical text—and hence became a bogyman for Evangelical Protestants. Garrison took a different approach to reading the Bible than the Evangelicals were used to: not a system of supporting arguments with decontextualized scriptural quotations, but one of articulating theological first principles prior to reading the Bible.

The biblical case for the institution of slavery as reported by Noll may be surprising to the modern reader. As he so clearly points out, neither the Old nor the New Testament explicitly condemned slavery, and both accepted it as a cultural norm. More clever and nuanced antislavery arguments brought up the problem that Jewish and Roman slavery was not based on race, and asked provocatively why there were no Caucasian slaves. (Lincoln picked up on this theme while campaigning in Cincinnati in 1859.) Still, even though defenders of slavery conceded the attendant violations of biblical norms—the sexually predatory nature of slave owners, the breaking up of marriages through the slave trade, and the inability of slaves to practice religion with their masters—all violations of biblical norms—they nevertheless insisted the concept of slavery was biblical.

The arguments—replete with scriptural "evidence"—by the proslavery debaters were persuasive. Even when they conceded flaws in how slavery was practiced in the South, they "proved" to their listeners that the institution was biblical. This will not sound unfamiliar to anyone who has debated some evangelical Protestants today on issues such as abortion, gay marriage, or the practice of nonviolence, and who has run into the same buzzsaw as practiced by defenders of slavery—an onslaught of chapter-and-verse biblical quotation that appeals to the so-called plain meaning of the text. Such a strategy—commonly known as *prooftexting*—is generally conducted devoid of historical context, and its practitioners tend to view any appeal to larger biblical principles as a weakness or diversion from what they perceive as obvious and timeless truths.

Noll states, "The primary reason that the Biblical defense of slavery remained so strong was that many biblical attacks on slavery were so weak." He goes on to say that the "biblical antislavery argument seemed religiously dangerous, and the nuanced biblical argument against slavery in its American form did not comport well with democratic practice and Republican theory."

The African Methodist Episcopal Church, made up of freed slaves, used the same Bible and the same language as other Protestants but had no difficulty in proclaiming the evil of slavery—starting with the golden rule and common sense. And it went a step further by casting doubt on how republican ideals themselves could be perfect if they were also to support slavery.

Noll consistently raises two seemingly secondary questions in the theological debates about slavery. He demonstrates persuasively that the problems of race and economics—both foundational issues to the debate about slavery—were given minimal attention by all sides. The question, in Noll's analysis, was not merely the buying and selling of slaves, but the concept of "buying and selling in general." Freed slaves faced racial discrimination and economic marginalization no matter where they lived and worked. And even many abolitionists had problems seeing Blacks as beloved brothers and sisters.

Was anybody able to get beyond economic self-interest in the lofty theological discussion about slavery? Noll points out that Harriet Beecher Stowe's bestselling novel, *Uncle Tom's Cabin*, may have helped spur the debate over slavery, but in the end, ironically, it contributed to secular cynicism by showing so many characters using self-serving biblical quotations to prove their position. If the Bible could be used to prove anything, to the secular mind it wound up proving nothing.

One of the valuable contributions of this book is that Noll has combed the archives of Canada, Britain and the European continent to see how other Christians saw the American crisis at the time. Non-Americans who held the Bible in high esteem were far more likely to see how the problem of slavery was also a problem of race, economic practice, and American ideology. Thus when the Episcopal Bishop of Vermont defended slavery in a German Protestant newspaper, the editor retorted that he could use the same arguments to defend polygamy. This was not an uncommon European response; the Jesuit journal, *La Civilta Cattolica*, made a parallel claim, suggesting that private interpretation of the Bible and Republican Protestantism could lead to both Mormonism and slavery. The High Church Tory *Times of London* taunted Northern self-righteousness, asking if Yankees would be willing to give up slave-grown cotton, sugar, and tobacco as well as the profits of Yankee shipping. Furthermore, they inquired why the abolitionist Horace Greeley failed to employ a single freed Black person at his newspaper.

British Evangelicals under the leadership of William Wilberforce, with the same view of scripture and theology as their American abolitionist counterparts, had successfully fought to abolish the slave trade in 1807, and banned slavery in all British territories in 1833. Noll notes this only in passing and provides no explanation of how British evangelicals came to such a clear agreement of the Bible's opposition to slavery when their American cohorts remained so deeply divided. (If the authority of the British Parliament over the American colonies had not been severed by the American Revolution, slavery might have been abolished in North America in 1833 and the Civil War averted—a point seldom pondered.)

One intriguing aspect of Noll's book is that he reserves his highest praise for conservative ultramontane Catholics. If, at the time of the slavery debate, they questioned modernity, individual conscience, and freedom of speech, their special contribution was that they freed the Bible from the certainties of common sense, separated race from slavery, and questioned the liberal economic order. For Noll, this group represents a more pessimistic but also further-reaching theological perspective, in contrast to the shortsighted optimism and reductionism of American evangelicals on both sides of the slavery debate. One wonders where Noll's validation of Catholic higher-order thinking comes from, though it is worth noting here that the author recently left an evangelical bastion of higher education, Wheaton College, for a position at the University of Notre Dame.

Noll's conclusion is unsettling. He writes that a nation ostensibly sharing a common text and faith eventually had to turn to the generals to resolve their inability to achieve a common biblical understanding. If the Bible had contributed to the creation of the American national culture, then the Civil War marked the beginning of the book's decline as a common moral authority (p. 159). During the Gilded Age that immediately followed the bloody War between the States, the pietistic Salvation Army and those in the vanguard of the Social Gospel would attempt to challenge unfettered capitalism. But it would remain for Karl Marx, a little-known international correspondent of the Civil War, to write new texts exposing the relationship between religious self-interest and politics with a clarity and insight that most Christian theologians utterly lacked. A century later, Martin Luther King Jr. would invoke both Gandhi and the Bible as he led his moral crusade. But "deeply rooted religious conviction" would no longer be the foundation of American moral debate.

Both those who pray for an Evangelical majority in America and those who fear the rise of the religious right will find something of importance in this book. Both will benefit from learning how an era of biblical authority and Evangelical Protestant cohesion was tried—and culminated in civil war.

ALL STRAUSS'S CHILDREN

2005, The Common Review

Discussed in this essay:
James Mann, *Rise of the Vulcans: The History of Bush's War Cabinet*. Penguin Books, 2004.
Anne Norton, *Leo Strauss and the Politics of American Empire*. Yale University Press, 2004.

Leo Strauss taught political science at the University of Chicago. He was revered as a teacher by many of his students, engaged in the usual faculty politics, published difficult-to-read books appropriate to his discipline, and won academic laurels. He died in 1973. Traditionally such men leave a legacy: a small portrait hung in a department foyer and footnotes in doctoral dissertations that will eventually be available on microfilm.

But today Strauss's name is at the center of discussions about American foreign policy and the impact of neoconservatives in government. The spectrum of speculation about Leo Strauss and the Straussians is huge. In the most extreme version of the story, a global conspiracy extends from the post-Weimar Republic in Berlin, through the Quadrangles of the University of Chicago, onward to Washington, DC, and, finally, to the Green Zone in Baghdad. By this account (scripted it seems for a Hollywood film to be directed by Oliver Stone and starring Gene Hackman), Straussians hijack the ancient wisdom of Athens and Jerusalem, turning philosophy into secret teachings for the initiated. They now run amok in the sacred halls of the academy—leaving faculty hiding under their desks in terror. More important, in this scenario, the Straussian minions, not content with academic laurels, begin their campaign to take over the government. Led by Paul Wolfowitz, deputy secretary of defense, they comprise a secret neoconservative cabal in the White House, the Pentagon, and the State Department.

A less bug-eyed version of the story is that a mild-mannered Jewish scholar from Germany spends his life studying and teaching ancient philosophical texts and believes that both natural rights and natural law exist. He stands in opposition to historicism, the value-free scientific study of human behaviors, and American pragmatism. His students and disciples find that they have a natural affinity with American political and social conservatives and become preeminent voices in the neoconservative movement.

Finally, I would suggest that an anti-conspiracy perspective is possible for understanding Strauss if we use a wider historical lens. This would place both Strauss and the Straussians in a larger landscape of natural law and natural rights along with a unique role for America—ranging from Manifest Destiny to the jingoism of "Remember the Maine" to the muscular Americanism of Theodore

Roosevelt. Academics giving national events a mantle of intellectual respectability and the cachet of a moral high ground are not unique to modern times.

Unfortunately, the burden of proof for challenging any conspiracy theory is nearly insurmountable, which is one reason such theories flourish. All evidence that a conspiracy does not exist in the form presented can also be reframed to serve as evidence of how fiendishly clever the conspirators are at covering their tracks. Anne Norton's approach in recounting the Straussian tale relies on a carefully crafted story in which she, the youthful student, is sometimes taken advantage of: "I was made, somewhat against my will, the carrier of an oral history." This assertion creates an immediate cloud of ambiguity about her motives for writing the book. She was the student of Joseph Cropsey, a student of Leo Strauss, while she attended the University of Chicago. We learn assorted kinds of personal information: that other Straussian faculty members took her into their offices and whispered stories into her innocent ears about the old days, that she has received funding from the same foundations that fund the Straussians, and that she has drunk champagne and eaten strawberries at the luxury Lincoln Park, Chicago, apartment of Albert Wohlstetter—a believer in nuclear weapons during the Cold War. (As opposed to the luxury Hyde Park, Chicago apartments of the traditional Straussians.) Her secondhand description of the master is that he was "a timid man, wary of physical harm, and not good at managing the practical matters of daily life."

Leo Strauss was born near Marburg, Germany, in 1899 into a rural Jewish family. He came to America from France in 1932, first teaching at the New School for Social Research in New York. In 1948 he was appointed by Robert Hutchins as professor of political science at the University of Chicago. He courted Hannah Arendt—ex-lover of Heidegger—but she rejected him, Norton contends, speaking in the very best tradition of faculty lounge conversations.

As a scholar and teacher, Strauss advocated the close reading of texts—in the style of the shul. For Strauss the classical texts spoke for themselves, and secondary sources were entirely dispensable. His thinking and scholarship covered a prodigious span of intellectual history—the classical writings of Plato and Aristotle; the medieval Jewish philosopher Moses Maimonides and his more obscure ninth-century

Muslim counterpart, al-Farabi; the dawn of modern political thought as found in Machiavelli, Hobbes, and Spinoza. Strauss worked to address the philosophical issue that so preoccupied him: the persistent tension between reason and revelation.

Strauss identified a tradition, running from Socrates to Thomas Aquinas, that affirmed what he called the "classical natural right." This tradition assumed a sharp distinction between nature and behavior, with justice, the highest human standard, solely a property of nature. According to Strauss, there are only two ways to approach the pursuit of natural right: either through philosophy or divine revelation, Socrates or Moses. The irreconcilability of these two positions was for him the essence of the human condition and the fountainhead of civilization's vitality.

What greatly concerned Strauss was that the modern Enlightenment distorted this antagonism. By trying to exorcize religion from political life, and make philosophy more material, the Enlightenment had mistakenly rejected the fundamental questions raised by the classical tradition and natural right as mere symptoms of their time and place. The underlying inadequacy of the Enlightenment was for Strauss most evident in its continuing failure to solve the "Jewish question." Its most dire consequence was the nihilism that inevitably grew out of its very appeals to historicism because that historicism provided no real ground for value.

To illuminate this situation, Strauss often returned to Plato's story of the cave. But in Strauss's version of it, the Enlightenment philosophers had unknowingly moved not out of the shadows and into the light of day but rather into a second "unnatural" cave that could be typified by cultural relativism, historicism, and scientism. Strauss's effort can be described as an attempt at rehabilitation, an attempt to cut a path out from this second misleading cave and back to the life of philosophical inquiry that he identified with Socrates.

Norton observes that Strauss and the Straussians stand frequently accused of "secret teachings." She speculates that these secrets have mostly to do with the private elitism and bonding of men who feel they have a better understanding and grasp of difficult ancient texts than the rest of us. Second, she notes their conviction that "certain ideas are dangerous except to the well-educated and the wise." The secret teachings are nothing more than the belief, not uncommon among philosophers, that they are wiser than kings, priests, and the simple masses who are uninformed except by faith.

Ann Norton is able to keep an uneasy distance when she is alone in a room with Leo Strauss. But she lashes out at his disciples and devotees—spanking the Straussian monkeys. She can be playful and bounce the rubber mouse: "It used to be said that Chicago was a place where Jewish professors taught Catholic philosophy to Protestant students." Her overall approach, relying as it does on her own personal knowledge of familiar faces and whispered gossip, allows her to claim familiarity with the map of the Straussian labyrinth. But it is a claim to familiarity absolutely unencumbered by the need to document presented evidence with sources and times. She is an essayist who writes freely from memory, at times from what appears to be free association.

She is fond of the oral wisdom about the Straussian legacy. For instance, she states, "The political Straussians are less concerned with natural rights than with getting the natural right." She does not answer the question of whether this is the anomalous problem of a good tree giving off bad fruits, or disciples misunderstanding the master, or the logical extension of Straussian theory turned into policy. Some explanation by Norton of her own cryptic language here would go far to explain her argument to the uninitiated. But perhaps she is signaling her Straussian credentials.

Her critical claws extend when she gives a grandiose—and from a critical distance, stupid—quotation by Harry Jaffa, a rabidly partisan Straussian in California, who wrote, "The salvation of the West must come, if it is to come, from the United States. The salvation of the United States, if it is to come, must come from the Republican Party. The salvation of the Republican Party, if it is to come, must come from the conservative party within it." Because Norton does not cite the source of this quotation, one is dependent upon her own private fund of information for its veracity and context.

***

Allan Bloom became the most famous Straussian of them all. His 1987 bestseller, *The Closing of the American Mind*, lamented the decline of classical learning and traditional morality against the depredations of rock-and-roll music and popular culture. Bloom is made human in

Saul Bellow's roman à clef *Ravelstein* as a chain-smoking, spendthrift, aging homosexual of the queenly persuasion, whose sudden infusion of cash from the bestseller fuels his shopping sprees.

Norton will have none of this. Bloom, she says, is "hypocritical" for defending conservative values because of his homosexuality. Worse, for her, is the overall misogyny of the Straussians, "the determined joining of men and the exclusion of women." Her barbed caricature is hilarious. "Tiny little men with rounded shoulders would lean back in their chairs and declare that Nature had made men superior to women. Larger, softer men with soft white hands that never held a gun or changed a tire, delivered disquisitions on manliness." The personal tone here belies the hostile exchanges that have marked the gender wars for the better part of a couple of decades. We will recall that in the first salvo of that conflict, the unthinking male pronouncement was often to portray feminists as ugly, homely women.

The return fire by some women, Norton among them, is to claim that men advocating masculinity are either latently or actually homosexual and lacking in physical prowess. The ad hominem terms of the exchange say absolutely nothing about the quality of feminist or antifeminist arguments. In this case, we learn something of Norton's own sense of properly masculine behavior but precious little about what makes the Straussians tick.

Norton's book does contain interesting passages about a number of lesser individuals in the long Straussian retinue. One of them, Carnes Lord, once Dan Quayle's national security affairs adviser (doubtless a daunting pedagogical challenge) and now a professor of strategic study at the Naval War College, wrote *The Modern Prince: What Leaders Need to Know*. Machiavelli is his inspiration. He admires strong leaders such as Winston Churchill and Abraham Lincoln, but autocrats on the order of Pervez Musharraf of Pakistan and Lee Kuan Yew of Singapore are also held up as models of leadership. Norton contrasts the Straussian Lord with Strauss himself, who clearly wrote that Machiavelli was a "teacher of evil." Once again, this provocative observation leaves us wishing that Norton had developed her argument further than she does. We are left to puzzle the extent to which the Straussian students embody or distort the master, and because the content of the master's teachings can hide under the mantle of secrecy, resolution on this point is not forthcoming.

Paul Wolfowitz, Norton reports, was a student of Bloom and Strauss who left the halls of academe for the corridors of power, rising to deputy secretary of defense. He is widely regarded as the chief architect for the takeover of Iraq. If he is considered suspect by Straussian professors for his distance from the academy, he is also admired as a Straussian of power.

Because of his role in shaping U.S. foreign policy in Iraq, Wolfowitz has earned the attention of numerous commentators. James Mann, in *Rise of the Vulcans*, paints a far more complex portrait of Wolfowitz than Norton does. Mann places him in the shadow not simply of Bloom and Strauss but also of Cold Warriors such as Dean Acheson and Paul Nitze, nuclear strategists such as Albert Wohlstetter, and geopolitical game players like Henry Kissinger. In other words, Wolfowitz is another Master of the Big Idea, but the big ideas have not necessarily been the exclusive domain of the Straussians. Mann also points out that historical events tend to chip away at big ideas. Even Paul Wolfowitz stated, three months after the American takeover of Iraq, "Some important assumptions turned out to underestimate the problem."

Thus Mann's book provides a context and perspective on the Straussians that Norton's book, written in its noir-memoir style, does not deliver, in spite of her academic credentials. Her book is uneven, on one hand plying the shadowy technique of Lillian Hellman and on the other delivering a half-baked op-ed piece lambasting what she sees as the Iraq policy debacle. And a significant problem that Norton does not address is whether proximity to a significant teacher/guru/mentor forever keeps one in his shadow—or do other teachers and life experiences make Strauss merely one piece of a larger worldview?

Norton alludes to the secret teachings of the Straussians without naming them. Perhaps the secret teachings are in plain sight. Neither Strauss nor the Straussians are traditional Jews, Muslims, or Christians; they are far more Athens than Jerusalem in a world dominated today by religious struggle. They take their marching orders and find their first things in pagan philosophy. Their civil religion and patriotism are as much a front for abstract philosophy as heartfelt faith. This might not sit well with the hearth and home social conservatives who gave the president a second term in office.

NOTES ON MANLINESS

2007

Discussed in this essay: Harvey C. Mansfield, *Manliness*. Yale University Press, 2007.

"Girls are dumb," was once the playground taunt of small boys. Harvey Mansfield, a tenured professor of history at Harvard, has chosen to continue this playground tradition, but also to provide a rallying cry for men to buck up and be manly.

Manliness, he contends, is a virtue: the innate ability of men to be aggressive, command others, and act autonomously. Absent an external threat, the gentleman shows respect for others from a sense of noblesse oblige. As Mansfield sees it, John Wayne, Tarzan, and Margaret Thatcher are all positive examples of manliness. That the first two are fantasy figures and the third a strident lady with a large handbag is an unnoted irony. Other examples of manly men include Teddy Roosevelt, who killed wild animals, charged up San Juan Hill, and preserved our national parks, as well as Rudyard Kipling, who celebrated heroic male individualism and the White Man's Burden.

Mansfield's notion of manliness should not be confused with cultural criticism's historically relative term, "masculinity," something soft and socially constructed. Mansfield will have none of this, arguing that manliness is an innate and universal characteristic of the male gender arising from both a biological and social Darwinism: the survival of the largest and most aggressive male breeders for the overall advancement of the species.

Women, Mansfield contends, innately enjoy suckling infants, changing diapers, and being the household mistress. Nineteenth-century feminists taught them to value their feminine morality and bring it to the voting booth. (Mansfield is not so retro as to suggest the repeal of women's suffrage—or he is not sufficiently manly to advocate for this in print.) But, says the author, modern feminism with its claim of total gender equality betrays women and prevents them from using their superior (and innate) verbal and relational skills when it tells women instead to embrace a manly desire for authority and power. Mansfield concedes that for a few extraordinary women—notably, Margaret Thatcher and Queen Elizabeth I—manly ambition and forcefulness is possible. This book is only slightly more silly than those feminist meta-histories that show a sweeping panorama of a lost utopian Goddess era replaced by millennia of patriarchy which, in turn, is about to be shattered by women's polemics.

Both the 9/11 hijackers and the police and firemen who entered the World Trade Center are "manly men," according to Mansfield. If he is able to follow this insight to the unsurprising conclusion that the first were bad, and the second were good, his attempts to distinguish the ethical nuances of righteous violence are less clear and therefore less satisfactory. A manly man commands others—presumably both other men and women. Is the man who takes orders less of a man? Mansfield is enamored of the cavalry charge, the colonial outpost, and the hunting expedition—in which manly men provide authority and leadership. But he has far less to say about men as friends, peers, or even intimates.

Indeed, it is unclear whether, in his opinion, homosexual men are men at all. Too many stubborn facts refuse to fit Mansfield's narrative. Women entered the workforce in the past century for economic survival and not because of feminist theory. This fact is ignored by Mansfield (as well as by many feminist theoreticians). Men have greater upper torso strength, giving them an innate advantage over women at throwing a rock or a ball. In a high-tech world this is a skill of diminishing value. Fewer young men than women in America are getting college degrees. Has learning itself become less manly? Mansfield does not say. The task of advocating for men is legitimate. Thoughtful reflections on men are needed. Unfortunately, Mansfield, working from a perspective situated roughly in 1890, does more to bring discredit to this task than to advance it.

CHINESE WHOREHOUSE CASE NOTE, OR HOW I WAS TAKEN TO A CHINESE WHOREHOUSE IN GARY, INDIANA AND WHAT I LEARNED ON THE WAY BACK TO CHICAGO

2005

Let us call him Larry. Larry is forty-one, a white boy from the Canaryville neighborhood of Chicago, who found us through an

Employee Assistance Program (EAP) at the Chicago Transit Authority (CTA) after being suspended for excessive absences due to drinking. He is stocky, verging on fat, with thinning blonde hair. He wears a baseball cap turned backwards.

He lives with his parents, his father is a functional alcoholic, his mother a housewife in a very traditional Irish neighborhood next to Bridgeport. Never married, he has a ten-year-old son whose mother lives in Pilsen. The son spends nearly every weekend with his father, and the mother may not be functional.

Larry has worked dead-end jobs but recently passed the civil service exam for the CTA and swings a sledgehammer, pounding in railroad ties for the subway system. As a token white on the crew, he was subjected to serious racial harassment and has filed grievances prior to his suspension as a probationary employee.

Larry says he was in a special education program from sixth grade on. He reads at a second-grade level but excelled in sports and apparently finished high school with a special diploma.

He presents as anxious, with ongoing headaches and a sleep disorder. He states he does not trust women ("They are just out for your money") or men, other than select peers from childhood days. "I could never trust a male other than someone I jumped the fence with." It is a phrase I find unique.

He does attend AA reluctantly. For some reason he has decided that talking with me on a weekly basis is good. "You are like a friend."

He has made joking references to sex previously—showing an interest in pornography and getting oral sex from street prostitutes. I have let this pass without response. He has also made allusions to significant acts of violence in his past. He remains cryptic on these but hinted at parallel events when he described knowing a local fellow who hired a hit man recently to kill his wife. (This was a front-page story for several months in Chicago.) I suggested he share these sorts of details only when or if he felt comfortable doing so.

This week, he started a disjointed narrative. He said he had seen the Super Bowl game at an AA club, "My first sober game in fifteen years." He described, in minute detail, regular visits to an Asian brothel in Gary, Indiana. As a result, I learned all about the entrance, waiting room, the price of $200, the shower, massage, the oil, the feel of the woman's long hair on his back. He stated that he usually took a male friend along with him. There were clear hints that he would be happy to take me with him on a future visit.

Rather than set boundaries, I allowed him to continue what seemed to be a fantasy trip, and remained very quiet.

He described other male friends and plans for a trip to Michigan to see a friend now out of a twelve-year prison sentence. "I kept writing to him," Larry said. There was another friend who was gay, and recently back from a trip to Thailand.

Randomly he made mention of the computer on my desk. "Those things know everything about you," he said. I jokingly offered to Google his name. We did and of course a half-dozen persons with his name came up. He was fascinated.

"Can you get women on those things?" he asked.

I explained online dating.

"But I could not do that. I can't read or type," he said.

Out of the blue, he said, "Are there programs that would help me learn to read?"

Apparently both his driver's license and the civil service exam, traumatic events, had required months of coaching.

I agreed to research literacy programs for our next session. Maybe a tough guy needs to reveal vulnerability. I felt like a person taken into his private cave. I wonder if he would have let me past the entrance if I had set boundaries about the Chinese whorehouse.

THINKING ABOUT ANDREA DWORKIN AND JOHN STOLTENBERG

2005

These are observations and recollections on a Wednesday morning before going to work.

Andrea Dworkin, age 58, died this week. She leaves behind a grieving partner, John Stoltenberg. Her passing is a minor media event.

"Never heard of her."

"What an eccentric life."

"Thought she died a long time ago."

She was to feminism what the Reverend Fred Phelps is to the anti-gay movement today. She conveniently served as the straw man to give feminists the façade of moderation: "No, I am not Andrea Dworkin, and therefore I am a reasonable person."

For Dworkin, patriarchy was so malignant and pervasive that resistance by any means possible was justified. First, all heterosexual intercourse was an unequal power equation. (She denied saying all intercourse was rape, as is commonly believed.) Second, the portrayal of women as sexual beings was a key element of patriarchy. Thus, bans on pornography were justified at the expense of civil liberties. Her role in the Minneapolis, Indianapolis, and Canadian crusades against pornography are case studies in unholy, ironic alliances between feminists and right-wing moralists.

In her public years, Ms. Dworkin was a very large, unshaven, unkempt, and abrasive woman. Her memoirs indicate she was in a series of abusive male relationships and briefly turned tricks with men for income. (René Girard suggests that the youthful libertine often matures into the mature, prim puritan.)

Her adult lesbianism was ill defined. Her mission was to attack patriarchy, not to define an alternative. Her household was defined as being in a partnership with John Stoltenberg.

John Stoltenberg wrote *Refusing to be a Man* (1989). His tract on male resistance to patriarchy is still on the literature tables of pro-feminist men's conferences. By refusing to participate in militarism, aggression, sports, intercourse with women, pornography (very broadly defined), and a whole host of other things, according to Stoltenberg a male can say no to patriarchy.

Stoltenberg was coy about what the male should do with his free time after he had negated patriarchy. He dropped a broad hint that living with Andrea Dworkin was an appropriate lifestyle for the anti-patriarchal male. (But how many men could live with her, or how does one find other Andrea Dworkins as roommates?)

I was initially entranced when I first read *Refusing to Be a Man* some decades ago. Stoltenberg's attack on the aggressive, sports-based, "Let's-get-drunk-and-get-some-chicks" male culture resonated with me. But his conclusions were thin soup. All male bonding was suspect. Men must always seek permission from women to determine if their actions are oppressive. Even gay male culture could be oppressive because it excluded women. On the Andrea Dworkin website, Stoltenberg describes a household in which a lesbian and gay male lived together in harmony. Both focused their energies on scribbling furiously, he during the day and she during the night, with a sharing of notes during shift change.

I accept their choice of the scribbling lifestyle. I accept the decision of the Men's Studies association to always have women present at each session of their conferences to ensure that "patriarchy" does not raise its ugly, giggling head in any all-male environment. I accept the decision of some men not to watch porno because it oppresses women. (Gay porno does not oppress women—but generally women do not see it as a politically correct alternative.)

A young fellow named Funk wrote a book about rape culture. I ran into him at a men's conference and bought his book—partly because he was really cute and I hoped to discuss it with him over coffee. I scanned his book and, dang, it looked like I met most of the criteria for being a male rapist of women. Only the most subservient, humorless, non-sexual males fit his criteria of non-rapists. He acknowledged his debt to Stoltenberg. I decided he would not be a fun person to have coffee with.

It remains to be seen if the revolution in gender in the past fifty years will, in full maturity, evolve into nothing more than the grimness of the Puritans mixed with the primness of the Victorians with only the face of the fat white male diligent scribbler replaced by the face of the large, looming female scribbler in a sexless household.

ISLAMIC PROFILES

2008, The Common Review

Discussed in this essay: Paul M. Barrett, *American Islam: The Struggle for the Soul of a Religion*. Farrar, Straus and Giroux, 2006.

How might one speak of a "normative" Islamic faith and practice in America today? Paul M. Barrett, a veteran *Wall Street Journal* reporter now with *Business Week*, gets at this question by way of seven deftly selected biographical sketches depicting contemporary Muslim life in this country. His book also registers subtle insights about how

Islam is taking—and not taking—its place in American society; the resulting picture complicates efforts to find an Islamic "center" in this country. Barrett views his seven subjects from a longitudinal perspective, making each life story much more complex than the individuals' current positions might lead us to believe. Differences between the subjects, even internecine tensions, outweigh similarities that might constitute some kind of Islamic consensus.

On questions concerning the most basic facts and data, surprisingly little can be taken for granted. The total number of Muslims in America, Barrett writes, is itself a point of contention, with estimates ranging from two million to six million. It is further estimated that only about one-fourth of all Muslims in America are of Arab heritage, one-fifth are African-American, and a third are of South Asian ancestry. (Interestingly, Barrett notes, until the 1980s, most immigrants to the American Midwest from the Middle East were Christian, not Muslim.) About 85 percent of American Muslims are Sunni, and 15 percent are Shiite—roughly matching the ratio that exists worldwide.

Barrett notes one significant difference separating American and European Muslims: education. Nearly 60 percent of American Muslims have college degrees—double the rate of national matriculation—and their incomes are higher than the national median. This places them in stark contrast to European Muslims, who are far more marginalized.

The book opens with the story of Osami Siblani, a complex character who is more politician than pious Muslim. Born in Lebanon, Siblani came to America at the age of twenty, and became in short order a naturalized citizen, a successful salesman, and a vocally pro-business Republican. At the same time, he also retained loyalties to Hezbollah as a force defending his homeland against Israel. The author wryly says of Siblani: "His is a complicated sort of patriotism."

Siblani is the founder and editor of the *Arab American News*, published in Dearborn, Michigan. During a presidential debate in 2000, candidate George W. Bush denounced racial profiling of Arab-Americans in Dearborn, Michigan. He was incorporating a suggestion from Siblani, then a supporter of his candidacy. And the Republican effort to woo the Arab vote paid off, with large Arab-American voter turnouts in both Michigan and Florida. In the run-up to the election, the *Weekly Standard* declared that, if he won, Bush would have many people to thank—including Osama Siblani.

How a little time can change things. Three years later, Siblani's Dearborn paper ran an editorial headlined "The U.S., U.K. and Israel—the Real Axis of Evil" and compared George W. Bush to Osama bin Laden. In a testy post-9/11 meeting, then-attorney general John Ashcroft told Siblani he was fortunate that the administration did not do Japanese-style internment camps for Arab Americans. Rather predictably, the Arab American vote trended heavily Democratic in 2004.

Standing in sharp contrast to Siblani is the Egyptian-born intellectual and scholar, Khaled Abou El Fadl, who lives with his wife and two dogs in Southern California (many Muslims believe dogs are unclean—El Fadl has written a different theological perspective on dogs). After a brief teenage flirtation with Muslim fundamentalism, Abou El Fadl attended Yale and later earned a PhD in Islamic studies at Princeton.

Abou El Fadl might be characterized as a Muslim fluent in the language of the Enlightenment. "Muslims have lost their ethos of knowledge, as well as their moral and intellectual grounding," he contends. Rather than engaging in a debate over "Good Koran vs. Bad Koran," he pits the nuanced rationalism of the Usuli tradition against what he regards as the fundamentalism of Wahhabism. He uses without apology the modern tools of literary, textual, and historical criticism to see the Koran as a "layered discourse" with an essential core of mercy and compassion.

After 9/11, El Fadl raised his voice against what he saw as Islamist reactionary thought. In a commentary published in the *Los Angeles Times*, he denounced the "irresponsible and unethical rhetoric" heard in American Islamic centers and student organizations. Barrett notes how "Resistance to colonialism and secular Arab despots" had created, in the words of Abou El Fadl, "a dogmatic, puritanical and ethically oblivious form of Islam."

The mainstream American media fell in love with Abou El Fadl after 9/11. His was the voice of scholarly reason and detachment that fit well in the American intellectual tradition. But he enraged many Muslims, received death threats by e-mail, and, maybe most ominously, saw his monthly column dropped by the *Minaret*, the main Muslim newspaper in Los Angeles.

***

Many Americans can conjure an image of a Muslim from Palestine or Saudi Arabia, but it is important to note that not all American Muslims are of Arab descent. In 2005 the *Saudi Aramco World*—the public relations magazine of the Saudi-owned oil company—heaped praise upon one Siraj Wahhaj, the Imam of the Masjid At-Taqwa in Brooklyn. Wahhaj is a fascinating case study of the fluid shifts of African Americans who profess Islam. Over the course of 14 years Wahhaj has undergone four different religious transformations and two name-changes.

At the age of eighteen he was teaching Sunday school in a Baptist Church. In rapid succession he affiliated with the Nation of Islam, then later with Louis Farrakhan, then still later with the son of Elijah Mohammad. He eventually became part of an association of fifty African-Americans in Naperville, Illinois, at a school funded by Saudi Arabia to train American imams.

Wahhaj maintains good relationships with Christian clergy in his neighborhood. He has won acclaim for his battles with neighborhood crack dealers. He is fond of the Christian fundamentalist cliché in his denunciations of homosexuality: "God created Adam and Eve, not Adam and Steve." He has called for the stoning of adulterers and those having sex out of wedlock, and advocates cutting off the hands of thieves—in keeping with Sharia law literalists, and mimicking the most extreme forms of Christian theocratic restorationists. He also performs polygamous weddings in his mosque.

His mosque gained some notoriety for hosting Omar Abdel-Rahman, the blind Egyptian cleric who is now serving a life sentence for his involvement in the first World Trade Center bombing. Wahhaj expresses uncertainty as to whether Osama bin Laden is responsible for the attacks on 9/11. Despite these extreme views, Wahhaj serves as a bridge figure to more traditional Arab groups in the United States. He is a popular speaker with student groups, demonstrating all the classic rhetorical flourishes of African-American pulpit preaching: hyperbole, personal suffering, hope.

A second case study of an American-born convert to Islam is Victor Krambo, a Southern Methodist University graduate who became attracted to the mystical Sufi tradition. His journey is typical of many who have struggled through the gauzy chambers of New Age spirituality toward something more concrete. He now goes by the name of Abdul Kabir Krambo and is involved in the Islamic Center of Yuba City, California. Under the tutelage of Sheikh Kabbani—a Sufi leader who migrated to Burton, Michigan from Lebanon—he works as an electrician.

It must be made clear that the Sufi tradition is held in contempt by fundamentalists in the Muslim Brotherhood. Such Muslims sometimes characterize Sufism as the "crude religion of the uneducated" because of its syncretistic tendencies to absorb local customs. Barrett also notes that Sufis are sometimes accused by other Muslims of "fostering superstition and idol worship." Still, the Sufi tradition has appealed mostly to Americans for its inner-directed spiritual search. The twelfth-century poet and mystic Rumi is well known to Americans in the sentimental tradition, as is the poet Kahlil Gibran.

However marginal Sufism may be in America and Muslim countries, it does not prevent the *Washington Post* from calling Kabbani the spokesmen for "the silent majority of mainstream Muslims in the United States."

Even less traditional is the saga of Asra Nomani—a freelance journalist and a former colleague of Barrett's at the *Wall Street Journal*. Nomani's confrontation with the mosque of her university professor father in Morgantown, West Virginia, is a fascinating story in itself. Nomani has authored a book on tantric sex, and she is both divorced and the mother of an illegitimate child. She also found a supportive friendship with Daniel Pearl—the *Wall Street Journal* reporter beheaded in Pakistan while on assignment.

Nomani's struggle with Islam began with her concerns over her relegation to the women's section of the mosque and not being allowed to enter through the front door or to pray in the men's area. She didn't keep quiet; she went public with her dissatisfaction, and wrote a "Manifesto for Equal Participation by Women." Eventually, she founded a small group of like-minded Muslim women known as Daughters of Hajar.

When Nomani organized a public demonstration in Morgantown, the marchers were outnumbered by the press corps. When she attempted the unprecedented feat of having a Muslim woman lead a group of men and women in Friday prayers, only the Episcopal Cathedral of St. John the Divine in New York City offered to host the event. This time, Barrett notes, the eighty participants barely outnumbered the press corps.

Most ambivalent of all Barrett's profiles is the story of Sami Omar Al-Hussayen, a mild-mannered PhD candidate in computer science at the University of Idaho. While proud of his Muslim identity, Al-Hussayen seemed well assimilated to American culture. He enrolled his kids in public school and, like many other Americans, took them to Chuck E. Cheese's restaurant for special events.

He was arrested in 2003 by the FBI and charged with material support of terrorism. Al-Hussayen had allegedly provided technical assistance to websites advocating Islamic holy war and promoting a virulent hatred of Jews. After the jury deliberated for seven days, the judge pronounced Al-Hussayen "not guilty." But the INS deported him and his family back to Saudi Arabia. Barrett speculates that Al-Hussayen may have compartmentalized his integration into the American community—on a visible plane assimilating into the culture, while on an abstract and technical level perhaps giving support to jihad.

Muslims in America face challenges similar to those of other immigrant groups—particularly those viewed as alien by a Protestant culture. The price for Catholics and Jews seeking mainstream acceptance in America was adjusting to the transcendent civic values of tolerance, democracy, and patriotism. Virtually every ethnic and religious group in this country at one time or another has had to endure a gauntlet of suspicion, if not outright hostility. Eventually, it seems, the peculiarities of unique belief systems can be tolerated if they do not challenge the law or, perhaps more importantly, public opinion.

Thus it comes as no surprise that the scholarly Islam of Abou El Fadl, with his nuanced language of literary criticism and articulation of the highest good being "mercy and compassion," receives high praise from American media pundits. The feminist ideals of Asra Nomani, as well as Victor Krambo's search for an inner faith in Sufism, also meet the criteria.

Even the message of Wahhaj, the Brooklyn imam—with all its proscriptive sexuality and its rabid crusade to reform ex-cons and fight drugs—receives accolades. The doctoral students from Saudi Arabia in high-tech computer science and engineering are acceptable, but their conservative views on women and jihad are not.

It remains to be seen how Islam in America will adapt to this country's religious pluralism as well as its secular ideals of feminism, tolerance, and democratic process. Islam faces inevitable problems of accommodation in America. While many immigrant groups have adjusted public clothing styles to blend into mainstream culture, conflict will arise when the distinctive garb is a mark of piety and submission. If a religion stipulates that young initiates be genitally mutilated, will the American public—and the law—allow it to continue? Finally, American society ostensibly maintains a tolerance that subtly—and sometimes not so subtly—insists on a common fealty to religious and intellectual relativism and a primary loyalty to the nation-state. American Islam at times confronts and confounds this American consensus. Barrett suggests that neither wishful thinking nor blind intolerance will be the answer. He states the problem brilliantly but leaves solutions to the imagination of the reader.

WHY VIETNAM IS VACATION LOCATION

2008, *Hillsboro Free Press*

So why am I in Vietnam for a three-week vacation? I was there two years ago and had a fantastic time. Forty years ago, I was there and had an interesting time. But how do I justify or rationalize this third trip?

I can be cute and say that the American dollar still has some value in Vietnam. Many meals cost two dollars and the hotel room is fifteen dollars for two persons per night. (And this includes breakfast.)

Vietnam is a safe country. The nearest things to terrorists are aggressive street vendors selling fruits, books, and postcards. I thrive on the irony of being in a wildly capitalist country that flies the hammer and sickle over Fortune 500 industrial parks.

On a practical level, it is warm and humid in Vietnam and cold and damp in Chicago. Plus, I have enough frequent flyer miles from

United Airlines to make the flight free. It was not difficult to persuade Tim to leave behind his web-developing job and his wife with the promise of a guided tour of Vietnam. (He is going to probably kill me the first time I get lost and confused. No, he won't, he is a committed pacifist and will merely grumble.) Tim is a high-tech genius and fantastic photographer and can help me post blogs and take pictures. (Okay, compared to me, everybody is a high-tech genius.) From previous travels together he knows how to tune out my endless commentaries on life and my high anxiety about getting to airports and train stations on time.

This is a vacation. Our planned itinerary: explore the Mekong Delta, Ho Chi Minh City, the old imperial city of Hue, then Hanoi, with side trips to Ha Long Bay and native villages near the Chinese border. This is not dissimilar to trips taken by college students. And if we were willing to add a few lectures by local college teachers and government authorities, we could earn more than twelve hours of college credit.

If we spent a week in a local medical clinic and painted a few rooms under the auspices of some do-gooder organization, or listened to how folks suffered during the American war, or paid a friendly visit to Vietnamese church leaders, we could justify the trip as a short-term mission or affinity-group expedition. (I am not closed to the idea of spending longer periods of time in Vietnam when I retire and trying to make myself useful. I speak and write English fairly well and there is a demand for such persons in Vietnam.)

But this trip is tourism. I go, I see, I take pictures, and write a few notes; I eat exotic foods and sit in coffee shops watching the world go by. My intent is to do very little harm but also no good.

I could pretend I am a journalist. The *Hillsboro Free Press* needs an international correspondent writing from far-flung places in the style of Ernest Hemingway. I asked my editor, Don Ratzlaff, for a travel allowance after my last trip.

He chuckled. Leaned back in his chair. Said, "No." Cheap editor. I can imitate Hemingway but I can't access his expense account.

But seriously, why go back to Vietnam?

Maybe I am returning because I have a memory. Forty years ago, I saw naked, hungry kids sleeping outside on cold slabs of steel in the cold Saigon mornings when I returned from duty at the Port of Saigon.

Two years ago, my travel companion Adam and I played Frisbee on the beach at Hoi An. (He plays ultimate Frisbee; surprisingly, I did not make a complete fool of myself.)

I am going back to Vietnam to double check. "Are the kids okay?"

CYNICISM AS THERAPY: SEEING THE LOG IN OUR OWN EYE

2009

Today I am both a chastened pacifist and an equally chastened Vietnam veteran. But for this audience, my primary credential may be that my friend John Howard Yoder and I could often make each other laugh. I remember stumbling into the noted Mennonite theologian's class to take a final exam titled War, Peace, and Revolution—a year late. Several bright-eyed students, destined-for-doctorate types, challenged my right to sit for the test. Yoder growled, "Suderman has been in war, peace, and revolution longer than any of you." I sat for the test.

Much of the impetus for this assembly comes from a speech delivered in March of this year [2007] by Peter Dula, former Mennonite Central Committee director in Iraq. I have read that speech, and his despair and anguish are very moving as he recounts his experiences there.

The question before us today is what is to be done when the ideals of peace, justice, and truth are spoken and seemingly fall on deaf ears. The crisis of idealism is hardly new, nor is it insurmountable, but this is clearly a difficult time for individuals and movements. The problem, I believe, is not cynicism, but the need to reexamine our idealism.

Last night Ric Hudgens spoke about the ancient Cynics with some insight. I would simply add that being a cynic today is associated with being bitter and cold. But the original Cynics were a minor Greek philosophical school, often called "dog philosophers," whose thought stood parallel to the idealism of Plato. The Cynics mocked the pretenses of the emerging Athenian state, often violating public spaces—sometimes going naked and defecating and masturbating in public as a form of street theater calling for a return to more natural living.

When Alexander the Great came to see the wise Diogenes, a Cynic who was then living in a barrel in a public square, he asked if it was true that Diogenes had abandoned all desires. Diogenes replied that no, he did have one desire, and he requested: "Could you move a little over that way? You're standing in the light." This story may be apocryphal, but it remains illustrative: cynicism, what it is, is not nihilism, it is not bitterness, and it is not despair.

Plato and Aristotle rejected the cynical tradition and laid the foundation for our current Western idealism. The ideal exists both as a pure form in a heavenly sphere and can be fleshed out on earth. Plato's and Aristotle's concepts influenced Christian tradition—particularly the Johannine and Pauline concepts of Christ as the *logos*, broadly defined as the "truth" or the "word." In contemporary academic language we continue this with the academic disciplines known as psycho*logy*, theo*logy*, socio*logy*, and anthropo*logy*. The major exceptions among the truth disciplines in academia are history and literature. There is no historology or literology.

The pattern of peace activities moving from being historians to being theologians—from the messy historical world to the world of pure types—would be worth examining. Both history and fiction have their origins in earthy and primal storytelling around campfires rather than in the world of pure types.

I know there are other concepts of truth, and the noted philosopher Stephen Colbert has added a third dimension with the term "truthiness." But that is beyond the scope of this discussion. In the truth disciplines, the ideal is believed to exist—perhaps vaguely, but the ideal really is there—as first principle, best concept, highest good, best practice. And it if is discovered, it can be acted upon.

Now the idea that the ideal can be acted upon is not without controversy. Aristotle said that to merely know the good is to do it. The Apostle Paul admitted that he knew the good and was unable to do it.

For twenty years I have worked as a therapist, and as a therapist and as a human being, I deal daily with the problem of how individuals know the good and do the good on an individual basis. Contemporary Western psychology and therapy continue to wrestle with this dilemma: Is there an authentic ideal and true self? How is it to be discovered? One can go deep within oneself to spelunk in the Freudian subconscious of the id, the ego, and the superego. Or be content with the Myers-Briggs test and the Jungian world of discovering our true inner archetypes. But unless this quest to discover our inner self is somehow connected to the outside world, it can easily become simple narcissism.

Two Jesus stories illustrate this problem. The first is Jesus' teaching that before critiquing another person, before removing the speck from the other's eye, we must first remove the log from our own eye. Jesus' image of imperfect vision, myopia, leading to distorted vision of both oneself and others, is powerful. The second story is Jesus' dialogue with the Pharisees in which they contended that they would not kill the prophets as their fathers did. Jesus said that he would tell them a secret that had been hidden since the very foundation of the earth: You are precisely like your fathers.[1]

As a therapist I have spent years talking with alcoholics, drug addicts, criminals, and the mentally ill. That has been my exclusive caseload. A few of my clients meet all these criteria. As a rule, they are the most idealistic people I know. They can brilliantly spot hypocrisy, injustice, unfairness, and slights from others. It is impossible for me, in my role as a therapist, to live up to their high standards. But they can also justify their endless relapses and recidivism to criminal behaviors and chemical dependency because they see themselves as good persons who are doomed to live in an unfair world and who are entitled to find happiness in whatever way seems best for them. Their idealism is a core part of their problem.

One of my joking principles with clients is Rule Number 9: After age seventeen, you are not allowed to use the word *hypocrite* unless you are actually Jesus. (Children and adolescents either are in a state of sinlessness or lack the capacity to see the beam in their own eye. This is why they often require adult supervision.) Now a few of my clients do find the narrow path of humility and acceptance and do recover. Their struggle to do this reminds me so much of "normal" idealists—including peace activists.

It was perhaps the eighteenth-century Quakers who first used the phrase "Speak truth to power." But that strategy does not address the problem of what to do when power says, "I will not hear you. Now sit

---

1 See Girard, *Things Hidden*.

down and shut up." Marginalized people, be they criminals or Christian, peace-loving idealists, face the common problem of what to do when power will not listen. The response of gangs and criminals is to affirm that institutional powers are so corrupt and incapable of justice that they are justified in telling lies to power. Another alternative is to speak "power to power." Mass collective movements such as labor movements, the suffragettes' struggle, the civil rights movement, and Vietnam protests have effectively mobilized power to create change. But their efficacy has depended on coalition building and compromise—strategies that often seem cynical for pure-type idealists.

The purity of a witness against violence or injustice is often commensurate with its ineffectiveness in society. When we factor in additional principles such as our need for personal purity, our need to maintain our personal ideals in every situation, then a broad-based movement of speaking power to power seems impossible. The image that comes to mind is what happens when a vegan, antiracist, antisexist organizer seeks to build support against the Iraq war at a Teamsters barbecue. Which principle will be operative in that encounter?

Some Blanket Statements about Idealism

Whatever route we take when power refuses to listen, we usually have some explanation for the existence of injustice, war, racism, sexism, poverty, and environmental degradation—the opposite of peace and justice. But the alternatives are not often clearly articulated, and are even less so today because of the postmodern reluctance to make blanket statements about the human condition.

The problem with such blanket statements is that if they are true, then they are true also of us—because we ourselves are individually and collectively included in the human condition of original sin. This paradox is centuries old, and examples abound. As a rule of thumb, mainstream national identity operates on the principle of "Americans are good; the others are bad," while peace groups work on the principle of "Americans are bad; the others are misunderstood"—thus ensuring the peace activists' minority status in domestic society. But both thought systems deny original sin.

Despite the hazards of making blanket statements, I would like to make some blanket statements about idealism.

First, there is too much idealism in the world, and we are paying a terrible price for it. As the idealisms of Marxism and National Socialism have faded, they have been replaced by new demons of religious purity and orthodoxy—and even of "spreading democracy." The Middle East is now rife with overlapping and contradictory religious and political idealisms., and it is unclear how bringing more idealism will help a region already drowning in its own models of perfection. I recall John Howard Yoder offending both Muslims and Jews when he pointed out during an address at a conference that maintaining the ideal of the modern nation-state is in fundamental conflict with the peoplehood concept of space in the Middle East and therefore precludes the possibility of long-term peace in the region.

You see, idealism does not allow for compromise. If we are going to settle land claims and ancient grievances—some going back to the very dawn of history—we might learn a great deal about the history of injustice, but we are no closer to achieving peace.

Second, ideals are often highly fluid. This does not apply to anyone in this room, so you are off the hook here. But have you ever run into people who were evangelicals and then Marxists and then vegetarians and then vegans and then New Age and then into the simple life and then into radical pacifism and then got an inheritance and bought a condo? Each time they proselytize for their new ideal, but their intensity and commitment to the lifestyle of idealism may have—more than we realize—an economic foundation in our society of abundance. Philosopher René Girard points to a similar connection when he compares intellectual and political styles in France with seasonal shifts in French fashion industry. We highly subsidized North American young and retired people have the wherewithal to bring peace to the exotic climes that we visit in our affinity-group travels—and to attend conferences where we give witness to our idealisms.

In Edwardian England at the last turn of the century a new term was coined: *liberal guilt*. The affluence made possible by the colonial empire allowed people a sufficient surplus of time and money to lament the growing corruption of British society. Good things came from this: settlement houses, reform movements, missionary movements, and attempts at socialist communities. But very few people noticed the paradox that their attempts at reform were based on the economic surplus in which they were swimming.[2]

A libertarian historian recently observed that in our current age of abundance (as opposed to the mere affluence of the Eisenhower years) conservatives have learned to love the abundance resulting from a free-market system but hate the inevitable lifestyle diversity that it produces, while liberals love the diversity of lifestyles in modern society but hate the economic engine that produces them.[3] Cynical terms like *trustafarian* come to mind.

I know this fluidity of idealism is not consistently true and that these arguments apply to no one in this room, but I do claim the authority of old age, an ironic eye, and a historian's heart when I note certain changes in the idealisms of individuals over the past decades.

Third, frustrated idealism often becomes personally and collectively dangerous. When idealisms are frustrated, the fallback position is generally not cynicism. True cynicism is too ironic and detached for that. Rather, scapegoating takes over. We've got to find someone or something to blame for the failure of our ideals, whether or not that someone or something is actually the problem. Girard writes that in tribal communities the internal tensions of the community are assigned to a victim, who is killed in actuality or through a surrogate. Girard points out—and he writes as a devout Christian—that peace communities and other idealistic communities are no different from tribal communities in this. Witness the endless schisms, the debates, and even shunnings as we attempt to maintain purity by forcing out the heretic or the doubter, believing we would succeed if it were not for the doubters in our midst. This line of reasoning also produces the gulags of Marxism and the schisms in churches and families.

Scapegoating can also lead to conspiracy theories of bewildering complexity. Here the principle of *pharmacos* is operative. *Pharmacos* is a Greek word referring to an inordinately small object that is powerful enough to either kill or heal. It is the root of our word pharmacy: if you take a tiny pill it will make you well, or if you take another tiny pill it will kill you. So there is *pharmacos*—power in that very small substance. And so we have the witchcraft trials where we blame the

---

2. Born, *The Birth of Liberal Guilt in the English Novel*; Hartley, "Holiness Evangelical Urban Mission."

3. Lindsey, *Age of Abundance*.

capitalists or the socialists or the homosexuals or the heretics. Blaming the Jews has been an equal-opportunity heresy because anti-Semitism crosses right and left divides, class lines, and economic boundaries. All of these groups can serve as *pharmacos* for us. It is their fault.

When idealists are frustrated in achieving their goals, they too often ratchet up their idealisms into more complex, multilayered forms of personal purity, bitterness toward others, or greater zeal with even less insight.

Finally, idealism is often ahistorical. The subtitle of this conference is "Reclaiming Discipleship in a Postdemocratic Society." Stay with that phrase a minute: "a postdemocratic society." The assumption is that at some time in Western or American history we were once democratic! I am enough of an amateur historian to be curious when precisely this was. Maybe it was in Athens. I don't know! Historians are messy people. They note the complexity of change, often with irony and paradox, but they generally make poor activists. Don't annoy me by shouting out the names of two historians you marched with. Most historians just take notes and look on wryly and ironically.

For the most part, persons who have struggled for social change have contended that they were living in a predemocratic society. They were demanding that society and institutions live up to their potential for justice, equality, and fairness. If we are now working from the assumption that institutions are incapable of becoming fairer, more just, and more democratic, then we are living in a new historical epoch. But that assumption has got to be based on something more than just being frustrated because we are unable to achieve peace in the Middle East or some other goal that is important to us.

History is ironic. It is filled with unintended consequences. I remember speaking to a group of my fellow students at a Mennonite seminary in about 1972. I was speaking in support of the total withdrawal of U.S. forces from Vietnam, but I admitted that I suspected that this would mean great harm would come to specific South Vietnamese people with whom I had worked while I was in the military. My contention was that peace itself would not end the suffering. Fortunately, before I was peacefully lynched by a bunch of Mennonites for this heresy, a fellow panelist with decades of direct experience in tribal conflicts in Africa shared her experience of the death and suffering that can continue after peace settlements are achieved.

In 2006 I returned to Vietnam, where I visited the site of the My Lai massacre, my old billet in Ho Chi Minh City, and the imperial city of Hue. The massacres in both My Lai and Hue, one by American soldiers and one by the North Vietnamese army, are little remembered. In 2006 I saw a thriving country with a capitalist system that borrows more from Milton Friedman than Karl Marx.

My old mentor Delbert Wiens tells about an experience he had more than fifty years ago when he was the Mennonite Central Committee director in South Vietnam. When a street battle between warring militias broke out one afternoon, he and some Church World Service personnel heroically helped families cross a twenty-acre field to safety, with bullets whizzing overhead. At one point he took shelter behind some concrete blocks and realized he was hiding on the wrong side. In a telephone conversation just last week he told me, "Dale, I was too stubborn to admit that I was on the wrong side, so I just didn't move."

History, both immediate and long-term, is filled with such ironies and paradoxes. When madness is unleashed, there may be no simple solution. Peace in Iraq is what? More American troops? Fewer American troops? Partitioning of Iraq? All the options offer the risk of continued suffering. The madness has been unleashed.

Suffering is not new in human history, and neither is injustice. The church can witness against sin, but the task of the church is not to make history turn out as we would like. To believe that we can do that is to become part of the madness.

My friend Adam Schrag makes the observation that from a semiotics perspective even the term *nonviolence* is suspect because it leaves *violence* as the operative term. This brings to mind the image of a rowboat following a battleship. Despite the good intentions of the people in the rowboat, the battleship is still setting the itinerary.

Four Sources for My Personal Hope

My hope comes from different directions. First, the church is a source of hope. Today I am a convinced Episcopalian, even though I have a Mennonite ethnic heritage. I was long attracted to the church started by Henry VIII, which opposed the American Revolution, was once known as the Republican Party at prayer, and yet also provides sanctuary for racial, gender, and sexual minorities. Clearly such a faith community must have room for an ironic child like me. When I was confirmed along with other adults a decade ago, the bishop instructed us catechumens, "Do not add to the violence in word, thought, or deed." He did not tell us to stop the violence. He did not tell us to bring about world peace. He just said, "Don't make things worse."

A few blocks from here stands St. Luke's Episcopal Church. It is a lovely building. Walk over and see it sometime. It was built in post–World War I zeal, and it commemorates the war to end all wars. It has stones from the great European battlefields underneath the altar, and there are carved statues of World War I doughboys—American soldiers—lining the courtyard. The rector said to me, "There is no use trying to conceal this. First, this building reminds us of just how wrong we can be. And second, it also contains our yearning for a war to end all wars."

Tomorrow morning I will go to church and we will get on our knees and ask for forgiveness and admit that we have sinned in thought or deed because we are people who admit that sin exists both in us and around us. And we will affirm our hope as we do every Sunday: Christ has died, Christ has risen, Christ will come again. Though for the most part we are agnostic as to whether that is a pre-, post-, or amillennial event, this Christ-centered understanding of history is our hope. Our idealisms, ideologies, and social constructs are myopic: we see through a glass made darkly ironic and paradoxical by our inability to see our own eyeballs. We are certain that the church is eternal, but we are equally confident that it is made up of broken persons.

In a subtle way we will affirm the God of Abraham, Isaac, and Jacob, and the Father of our Lord. Platonic words like *truth*, *justice*, and *peace* are secondary to this pre-philosophical understanding of history.

The communion rail is ironic and moving in most services. From generals to peace activists, gay men to homophobes, the economic elite of the city to the dispossessed of the city, we will all leave our pews and genuflect and walk down the aisle to accept bread and wine at a common table. In doing this, we recognize that we are participating in a larger cosmic drama going beyond our personal lives and beyond historical events.

And then the benediction will be recited by a deacon, with one portion of the stole going across the deacon's front then tied at the side to symbolize moving freely on the streets as a servant of Christ. "Send us now into the world in peace," we will say, "and grant us strength and courage to love and serve you with gladness and singleness of heart, through Christ our Lord." Notice that this does not say "to save the world." We are just to move through it as servants, deacons, and emissaries.

For nearly a decade this benediction has been posted just beyond my computer where my clients cannot see it, because posting it more visibly would violate the religious neutrality policy. But I look at it nearly every hour as I speak to people. The church is my hope.

Second, an apocalyptic worldview is a source of hope. A turning point for my worldview was when I saw a stage production of *Angels in America* in Chicago. As we drank coffee after that production, my friend John Kampen, a biblical scholar of some renown, shared his understanding of the apocalyptic language in texts such as Daniel and Revelation. "It was not the end of the world that preoccupied" the writers of these books, he said. "It was their vision for a new order breaking through that cannot be expressed in normal language. And so they were forced to resort to these wild images. Their vision is for a new order so radically different from the present that we are unable to describe it, and it goes beyond our hope for incremental progress and gradual improvement."

And thus I understood *Angels* playwright Tony Kushner's subtle mocking of political correctness, right- and left-wing politics, and religious orthodoxies in his stage play. His is an apocalyptic vision of angels in America breaking through for something radically new. Apocalyptic vision is a source of hope if we are able to see radical change that is not of our making. It is a source of hope for me.

Third, friendship is a source of hope. In his final teaching to his disciples, Jesus oddly instructs them to be friends. This stands in contrast to the alternatives. He could have said to be mothers or fathers or sons or daughters or brothers and sisters. Instead, Jesus chose this most humble, yet strangely intimate relationship of friendship as his final model for his disciples.

Friendship trumps ideology. Friendships can trump the intellectual worlds of theology, politics, and peacemaking. Friendships can provide a sustaining sanctuary of storytelling, laughter, and tears—not merely about victories and accomplishments but also about doubts, failures, and pain.

I think we need to reexamine friendship because friendship is different from community and family. All three are valuable, but my own experience over the past decades has been that my friends—and they are a wildly diverse crew—are free to mock me, to critique me, to embrace my pretensions. And they are therefore a constant source of discipline and even discipleship for me. My daily hope is in friendships.

Finally, the scandal of the gospel is a source of hope. I want to end with a story about a man we should all know more about: the bourbon-drinking, straight-preaching Will Campbell from Mississippi. He is a good man, still living.[4] Campbell was born in Mississippi, was a bright fellow, and went to Yale, where he was embraced as a white Southerner who understood civil rights things. The National Council of Churches hired him as a civil rights worker.

One night Campbell was doing some late-night drinking with an agnostic small-town editor, P. D. East, who shared his hope for racial justice.

"In ten words or less, what's the Christian message?" the editor taunted him.

Campbell replied, "We're all bastards but God loves us anyway."

Years later Campbell learned from his brother Joe that a friend and seminarian, Jonathan Daniel, had been murdered by a special deputy in Alabama named Thomas Coleman. Jon had been registering Black citizens to vote in Lowndes County, and the deputy shot him. Now P. D. said to Campbell, "Brother, what about that definition of Christianity you gave me that time. Let's see if it can pass the test." And in the middle of their grieving for Jon, he confronted Campbell. "Which one of these two bastards do you think God loves the most?" P. D. leaned in close to whisper, "Does he love that little dead bastard Jonathan the most? Or does He love that living bastard Thomas the most?"

Eventually, under the pressure, Campbell broke down and had to confess that God loved them equally: both the Jon Daniels and the

---

4. Editor's note: Campbell died in 2013, six years after this presentation.

Thomas Colemans of this world. He was in tears. And he told P. D. that his agnostic taunting had pushed him to that scandalous recognition.[5]

It was the beginning of a change for Campbell. He resigned his job with the National Council of Churches and went freelance, hanging out with Pentecostals and attending baptisms at the creek, working with black militants and folks outside the mainstream.

He was also willing to have prayer meetings in the homes of Ku Klux Klan families when their fathers were being sent to prison for racial violence. Campbell would say, "Their children and wives cry, just like the black folks do." He was able to move freely in all of these circles and he does to this day, defying categories. I think there is a powerful message in Campbell being so consumed by the gospel that he refused to be part of any system or movement.

I know the scandal of the gospel can become an excuse for passivity or despair. But I think we can also see the scandal as a cause for hope, and therefore courage.

Our problem may not be cynicism so much as unfettered and unexamined idealisms, often the idealism of a naïve worldview. The world will be saved neither by the idealisms of peacemaking nor the idealisms of the craft of war. As an interim ethic or a least a viable strategy, the options of pragmatism, social realism, and even compromise may be needed in areas of conflict. These do not necessarily contradict the deeper hopes that Christians have.

Sources

Born, Daniel. *The Birth of Liberal Guilt in the English Novel: Charles Dickens to H. G. Wells*. University of North Carolina Press, 1995.
Campbell, Will D. *Brother to a Dragonfly*. 1977; University Press of Mississippi, 2018.
Girard, René. *Things Hidden Since the Foundation of the World*. Trans. Stephen Bann and Michael Metteer. Stanford University Press, 1987.
Hartley, Benjamin. "Holiness Evangelical Urban Mission and Identity in Boston, 1860–1910." ThD diss., Boston University, 2005.
Lindsey, Brink. *The Age of Abundance: How Prosperity Transformed America's Politics and Culture*. Collins, 2007.

---

5. Campbell, *Brother to a Dragonfly*, pp. 184–189.

THE GOD WHO PROVIDES PARKING PLACES

1999

On weekend trips to Lakeview neighborhood to visit restaurants and the Lucky Horseshoe, pious and rational friends are aghast at my claims that The God of Parking Places can provide street parking in Chicago's most densely populated neighborhood.

Lately I have been pondering my impious—or is it pious?—humor on the subject. My interest was heightened when during her sermon a youthful female preacher at St. Luke's told a similar story of circling the block with her mother and the escalating cry of a baby in the back seat. When a parking place miraculously appeared, the grandmother offered the Deity thanks. The daughter said, "Mother, liberal Episcopalians do not believe God offers us parking places, furthermore the person behind us doesn't have a parking place." I almost interrupted the service shouting, "He does so offer parking places!" On mature reflection I realized that after the service I should have suggested that either from the perspective of liberation theology or a sense of *noblesse oblige*—both equally present in her—she might have offered the newfound parking place to the man still circling the block.

My friend Pilgrim in Boston, with the logic of a schizoaffective, begs the question of The God of Parking Places by self-righteously intoning, "I ride a bicycle; not my problem." This merely proves that liberal Methodism lacks the crystalline purity of thought of High Church Anglicanism. Alas, both often do not adequately deal with The God Who Provides Parking Places.

The early Church focused on a simple essential message: "Christ has come, was crucified, and will come again." Said the local farmer, "This may be quite true, but in the meantime my cow is sick and there is no place to park the ox cart, so perhaps God could help out a little with this." His rustic concerns were dismissed as trivial and distractive from the great Cosmic Unfolding happening—with the result that he bought a lucky rabbit's foot from the local Pagan—and he found a place to park his ox cart and was happy. This happened so often for the rustic, and he was so vocally grateful, that the Church became unhappy and decided to offer him The Saint of Parking Places to keep him from running to the Pagans with every little problem. Saints multiplied nearly as rapidly as problems they could solve, as did special rituals and blessings.

This got entirely out of hand until the Reformation. At that time the Reformers said there was only one Deity, who heard all prayers and therefore no mediators were necessary. Now a Pious Child could pray for a puppy and a Righteous Man could pray to God for a place to park his wagon—if they had already prayed for their own Salvation. Thus our Pilgrim fathers and mothers thanked God for a safe journey and good place to park their boat.

Along comes the Enlightenment and difficult questions are raised about The God of Parking Places. Parking places are merely a matter of chance and fortune and random luck. Good urban design can provide more parking places, and good individual planning—resultant from good moral character—leads a rational person to arrive early before demand builds during the evening rush hour for parking places. And the good man said, "Ah, what good luck, I found a place to park my carriage!"

Now the Church was not pleased that good luck and logic were so highly praised. The theologians labored mightily and came up with many alternatives. They suggested there were some prayers which were suitable and answered, "Receive this baby we are about to baptize," and at the end of life, "Grant him eternal rest." In some cases, the prayer which shaped Bread and Wine into the Blood and Body of Christ was also answered. Lesser prayers in the hierarchy of human needs were more of a crapshoot. However, if these were answered and, often even when they were not, there were to be prayers of Gratitude for the results.

A second theological insight, by a theologian who later took up pastoral counseling and even later left the ministry altogether for a private practice in psychology, claimed that all prayers were valid to articulate because they made you feel better. "Now don't you feel better since you told God what you want, even though you know He won't do anything about it?"

The prayer business got very confusing. Some said you could and must pray for world peace—a good prayer—but not for parking places on Halsted—a bad, trivial prayer—though oddly that one was answered more often than petitions for world peace.

Some stopped praying altogether and just sat in silence for hours, listening for either some inner answer or external answer. (This may actually work. Ask for nothing, wait long enough, and you get something and that must have been what you wanted or needed in the first place—although I usually get leg cramps.)

Some tried to go all the way back to what they thought was the Early Church, where it seemed folks asked for all sorts of miraculous things and got them. These folks shouted and hollered a lot, some rolled on the floor, and they claimed to receive blessings, praying to a God who wears the ultimate Gimmie Cap.

Now Bob Dylan may not be a prophet or a seer but sometimes that boy is right on target. He sang, "You gotta serve somebody." And if you serve somebody, you pray to somebody.

In both the dark nights of our souls and the trivial nights of our souls, we all finally reach out and pray. We are often inarticulate. "Just give me a chance, a break, a drink, luck be a lady tonight." All we want sometimes is just a place to park the damn car and stop endlessly circling the block. We want our friends and families to be safe and secure and so we pray for them, a prayer far more complex in vector and logic than finding a place to put the Saturn. Oh, we say, "I wish you peace and joy," and tell them we love them but we know that won't do much good and so we pray because we love them passionately. Hell, we even pray they find parking places and travel in planes that don't crash.

Read the Psalms. Now that man prayed for just about anything he wanted to. "Smash my enemies and while you are at it, kill their boy babies too." "Hey, God, what have you done for me lately, I'm a little down today." Sometimes, "God, I am surrounded on all sides by Indians and even Tonto is smirking." Once he even prayed, "Hey, my lover and friend is gone." Didn't ask for anything, just reporting. And always gratitude, endless praise, to the point of arrogance: "Hey, I'm doing good. Look at me!"

David prayed to only one God about what was on his heart. Not as ritual, not to make himself feel good. He whined when the prayers weren't answered, rejoiced when they were, groveled when he screwed up, was thankful when he was forgiven. He would have had no problem riding with me on Halsted at nine on a Saturday night.

"Go for it, ask for a parking place. Ask Him. You are gonna pray to somebody anyway, so ask Him."

Interpretations

REMEMBERING DALE SUDERMAN

Keith Harder

Shortly before his stroke in 2008, Dale made a presentation titled "Cynicism as Therapy," which was later published in a collection of essays, *Cynicism and Hope: Reclaiming Discipleship in a Postdemocratic Society*, edited by Meg E. Cox (Wipf and Stock, 2009). In the essay Dale called himself a cynic. This word may have some negative connotations, but Dale clarified that he thought of himself as someone who was grounded in the realities of life as it is and not in idealism, or how life should be.

He recalled that when he was confirmed in the Episcopal church, the presiding bishop instructed him and the other catechumens "not to add to the violence in the world in word, thought or deed." Dale noted that the bishop did not tell them to stop the violence. He said, "Don't make things worse."

This rather modest charge stood in contrast to idealists across the political spectrum who would seek to end violence, poverty, or discrimination, or whatever evil that was at hand, and in the process impose their ideals on others and thereby justify all manner of oppression and hate. From this stance Dale critiqued doctrinaire Marxists and the crusading Christians in the moral majority.

I hear echoes of the bishop's word in Ecclesiastes chapter three which describes life as it is, and of Jesus welcoming Cornelius without telling him to leave the Roman army, or Jesus saying that the poor would be with us always. Be careful about trying to eliminate war or poverty. Just don't make things worse; don't add to the violence and poverty that are all around us. So Dale could say that he was a chastened pacifist (rather than an idealistic pacifist), a war veteran who never fired his weapon in combat. He wanted not to add to the violence that threatened to engulf the world.

These are wise words for idealists of all stripes, be they conservative or liberal.

At Parkside Homes where Dale lived his last eleven years, someone put a floor-to-ceiling poster on one wall where Dale took his meals. The words we heard earlier from John chapter eleven were on that poster. "I am the resurrection and the life. Those who believe in me will live even though they die."

One day Dale asked a friend of his to take his picture kneeling in front of that poster. When his friend asked him why, Dale made it clear that this was the promise for which he was preparing. He was ready to die, and these words from John were the focus of his hope. This may be the closest we have to Dale's last testament and testimony: his hope and belief that he would live even though he would die, through the resurrection of Jesus.

In a similar vein Dale's sister Elva said he had recently asked her what she thought heaven was like. She said she was confident it would be a lot better than what they were experiencing now, and he said in a loud voice that he wanted to go there.

I have thought a lot about these two themes in Dale's life—his calling himself a cynic and his faith in resurrection. One might think they were in conflict. What could a cynic say about resurrection? Would a cynic believe in resurrection? This is another example perhaps of Dale holding disparate ideas together, letting one inform the other.

Those who knew Dale recognized that resurrection informed Dale's life, not just his death. Heaven was more than a destination; resurrection hope was more than fuzzy idealism. At the end it was the hope by which he lived.

We hear more of Dale's testimony in his own words from "Cynicism as Therapy":

> Tomorrow morning I will go to church and we will get on our knees and ask for forgiveness and admit that we have sinned in thought or deed because we are people who admit that sin exists both in us and around us. And we will affirm our hope as we do every Sunday: Christ has died, Christ has

risen, Christ will come again. . . . this Christ-centered understanding of history is our hope. Our idealisms, ideologies, and social constructs are myopic: we see through a glass made darkly ironic and paradoxical by our inability to see our own eyeballs. We are certain that the church is eternal, but we are equally certain that it is made up of broken persons (p. 49).

Dale continues:

> The communion rail is ironic and moving in most services. From generals to peace activists, gay men to homophobes, the economic elite of the city to the dispossessed of the city, we will all leave our pews and genuflect and walk down the aisle to accept bread and wine at a common table. In doing this, we recognize that we are participating in a larger cosmic drama going beyond our personal lives and beyond historical events. (p. 49)

Dale had an uncommon sense of that "cosmic drama," an uncommon capacity to see beyond immediate needs, desires or causes. In his conclusion, he recites the actions and words of the deacon and the people in the communion service:

> And then the benediction will be recited by a deacon, with one portion of the stole going across the deacon's front then tied at the side to symbolize moving freely on the streets as a servant of Christ. "Send us now into the world in peace," we will say, "and grant us strength and courage to love and serve you with gladness and singleness of heart, through Christ our Lord." Notice that this does not say "to save the world." We are just to move through it as servants, deacons, and emissaries.
>
> For nearly a decade this benediction has been posted just beyond my computer where my clients cannot see it . . . . But I look at it nearly every hour as I speak to people. The church is my hope. (pp. 49–50)

Dale's last years were more difficult than any of us can imagine—cut off as he was from the work he loved, from lively conversation, from the city of Chicago that he loved, from friends he loved deeply. He would sometimes cry out in pain and frustration, especially when he couldn't say what he was thinking, but through it all, he seemed to maintain a kind of graceful equanimity, a contentment that always amazed me. I suspect that it was a sense of this cosmic drama that sustained him. It provided a frame for his loss and suffering that kept it from being overwhelming.

While expressing love and respect for Dale, people who knew the man are sometimes quick to note that he was not a saint. By this we mean that Dale was not perfect; he had faults which he would be the first to acknowledge. He lived a large life on a big canvas, fearlessly and sometimes recklessly. But I believe that actually he was a saint, as are all who profess their confidence in the love of God expressed in the resurrection of Jesus.

"LITTLE BROTHER" COMES HOME SOONER THAN ANYONE PLANNED

Elva Suderman

[Hillsboro Free Press editor's note: Dale Suderman, a Marion County native who made his home in Chicago, wrote a popular column called "View from Afar" in the Free Press from 2001 until April 2008, when he suffered a severe stroke. With our encouragement, Dale's sister wrote this essay on the seasons of their close relationship.]

Dale, you have finally achieved one of your goals when you moved to Hillsboro from Chicago recently. Our thanks to Dan, Tim, Doug, and Ben for bringing you back.

You were getting excited about coming to town to retire in two more years and constantly checked the *Free Press* realty ads to find your dream home.

However, things did not go as planned. You never expected that your dream home would be a room at Parkside Homes and not a home with a deck where you planned on drinking many cups of coffee.

On your last visit to Hillsboro, you said that on this trip you were going to see if you could really retire in Hillsboro. After checking the Tabor College Library for current newspapers to visiting with the local men's coffee drinkers, you said that you could make this transition.

Your massive stroke on April 19 changed many of your future plans. After numerous brain surgeries your life was spared and you started to relearn many of the skills that we take for granted.

I am your older sister, and we have shared sixty-four years together. Sorry, but I did not always appreciate you and got very tired of reading the same stories to you and brother Ron time after time when you were young. Then I was expected to babysit you and Ron while our parents went to town. This was totally unfair as my friends always went with their parents when they went to town.

As you attended Hillsboro High School and Tabor College, I would get phone calls from you stating that I was your favorite (and only) sister. My comment would always be, "What favor do you want this time?" I have typed many of your school assignments, but let's face it, nobody else could read your writing.

You like to tell the story about Dad when he said you were never going to be a farmer and that he would have to send you to college. Perhaps daydreaming and trying to read while driving the tractor were good clues.

When you and Ron both left for military service in Vietnam, we corresponded from time to time. I will never forget the day when you were finally discharged and I drove you out to the field where Ron was working. When you saw each other after almost two years, you both ran as fast as you could and gave each other a big hug. To this day you and Ron have had a special bond.

In the following years we saw each other when you came to Hillsboro twice a year, and occasionally we talked by phone. In the almost twenty-five years that you have spent part of your vacation days at my place, I estimate that it adds up to more than ten months of time.

Our parents got married during the Depression and placed value on material assets. You, however, placed value on friendships and traveling.

Your love of people is evident in the many close friends you have from near and far. Your home was often open to them on weekends and you loved to entertain.

These friends are worth more than any monetary assets. Your friend John stated this very well in a recent e-mail when he wrote, "What has been most amazing during this experience has been to recognize how many good friends Dale has who are very devoted and committed to his welfare. I can think of no other person who could marshal such a number and array of persons to his bedside and to assist with his care."

Gradually our roles changed and you became my encourager. I will never forget visiting you in Chicago when I started using a folding cane for walking longer distances.

I certainly was not going to embarrass you by using it when meeting your friends. You got very stern with me and said I had proved to everyone that "I could do it" and it was time to make some changes.

Little did I know that you would need to help me through many more stages of adjustment from retiring fourteen years ago due to post-polio syndrome to using a scooter and now for many years using a powerchair. You gave me confidence to speak and write about post-polio syndrome and thus help other polio survivors.

I have been reading your scrapbook of "View from Afar" articles. Your column started in 1985 when you wrote for the *Hillsboro-Star Journal* for about two years. In 2001 you started writing for the *Hillsboro Free Press* and you have written more than one hundred columns. When your column was due, I knew I would get a phone call from you asking me to proofread it.

About three years ago I came to the realization that you made a commitment to phone me every day in addition to many e-mails. You always said "Hey, it's Dale," and I could often tell if you were having a good or bad day according to how you said this.

Sometimes we talked just for a minute to check if I was all right but on weekends we discussed issues from politics, books, news about family or what was happening in Hillsboro.

This is something that I miss so much now as you were my rock for many years. Now your words "I love you" mean so much to me.

Our roles have changed and I am once more your encourager. Shortly after your stroke I purchased a bracelet with the following inscription: "God grant me the serenity to accept the things I cannot change, the courage to change the things I can, and the wisdom to know the difference" with the word "courage" in large letters.

I wear this bracelet 24/7 as a reminder that there are some things I cannot change and that God will provide both you and me serenity for the days ahead.

DALE SUDERMAN: THE SEER OF FRIENDSHIP

John Kampen

I have been talking with Dale Suderman since 1969. I have never had a boring conversation. We first met when students at the Associated Mennonite Biblical Seminaries (now Anabaptist Mennonite Biblical Seminary) in Elkhart, Indiana. He had enrolled on the GI Bill, a source of some pride and wonderful distinction for him. I have to confess it was always difficult to envision Dale in basic training. I was living downtown at the time above the Partly Dave Coffeehouse on Main Street in Elkhart and we immediately became good friends. The coffeehouse closed at midnight, we were cleaned up by 12:30, and I never got to bed before two a.m., as Dale and I decoded the events of the day, the week, the nation, the church, the times. With Dale such a conversation was always a unique blend of the social, the political, the religious, and the personal.

In the meantime we listened to a wonderful array of hitchhikers; a variety of people associated with the drug scene; people who routinely went around town in Beatles uniforms and other forms of unconventional dress; hippies in crash pads evicted by landlords who simply didn't like them; teenage runaways from town and off the interstate; Vietnam veterans who could not readjust to the local scene; pregnant women who needed abortions in a state where it was still illegal; folk singers; rock bands; community organizers; and artists, some very good, others very bad. The list goes on. Dale and I shared our own ongoing sagas in the midst of this incredible diversity of stories and experiences that entered our lives on a daily basis. Today in seminary education we talk a lot about formation. Dale and I engaged in a mutual formation process from midnight to two a.m., three to four nights a week, that changed and in part determined the course of each of our lives. I used to joke that I wouldn't blame him for how I turned out if he was willing to reciprocate.

It was already in those two intense years we shared in Elkhart that I became aware of certain events and situations in Dale's life that would arise and which I did not understand. He was anxious about and threatened by things that made no sense to me. It was only after he told me during that time that he was gay that I could put these events into some perspective. That was the beginning of my education about the life of a gay person in our society. Since we had gay persons involved with different activities at the coffeehouse, this did not cause a crisis or create particular problems. I think it safe to say that the walls against the participation of gay persons in religious life had not yet risen as high as they would in the next decade or so.

With the completion of his degree at Elkhart, Dale became associate director of the coffeehouse and then moved on to the position of associate director of Mennonite Voluntary Service for the General Conference Mennonite Church. We recognize that this was a time in which he worked with, among others, Gene Stoltzfus of blessed memory, founder of Synapses, Christian Peacemaker Teams, and various other projects that erupted out of that creative and scheming mind. The two of them were a great team. Mennonite Voluntary Service was an interesting and creative organization in the hands of Dale and Gene.

In 1979 Dale moved to Chicago and took over the Logos Bookstore on Clark Street just north of Fullerton. For ten years he managed and eventually owned it and its successor, Dale's Bookstore. We can engage in debates about the viability of the business models he employed but there was no doubt that this store had an impact on young Mennonites and evangelicals new to the city, on academics who relied on Dale's expertise about all of the ancillary literature they should be reading, on the lives and careers of all kinds of persons moving into the urban professional and creative worlds. Urban planning, community development, and the city of Chicago were the topics of both books and conversation. This bookstore, the embodiment of Dale, was a source of both support and of an unqualified push to experience and take advantage of all the new opportunities. Nobody seemed to mind paying full price for a book that already had a coffee stain.

This also was a time of severe alcoholism and then redemption, through AA and then through the Episcopal Church. Dale, who embodied a highly complex intersection of incredible vulnerability and unbelievable strength, survived both the closing of the bookstore and his alcoholism, and he began a new career in addictions counseling. In this way he redefined himself, finding a new home and level of success. He first worked in the hospital setting and then in the facilities of the Salvation Army, where he saw hundreds of clients until the stroke ended that career.

In Chicago for the first time Dale began to live as an openly gay man. It was a joy to watch and experience his development in that environment. Visiting him was an entrée into the restaurants and other institutions of the gay community of North Side Chicago, and meant visits to the other MCC, Metropolitan Community Church, the denomination founded as a church for gay people. By this time, I was in graduate school where I developed friendships with more gay friends. As a result of that experience, I can highlight the uniqueness of Dale's response to gay culture and the direction of the remainder of his work on gender. For the most part, educated gay men with intellectual interests focused their attention on issues of gay identity, later known as queer theory. This is the kind of question our gay seminary students write about today. Not so, Dale. Instead, he began talking about men and their identity. And in a remarkable manner. I remember breakfast with him and Jon-Henri Damski, an influential Chicago journalist, poet, and activist in the gay community. Even in those conversations, Dale advanced arguments not for a strict division of gay and straight culture, but rather called for a discussion about what it means to be a man. Dale was somebody who had consistent trouble with the status quo, and in this case, he challenged the accepted premises of the gay community of which he was a part.

From my perspective, Dale was always the outsider and the bridge builder. The fact that he was gay placed him outside from a rather young age. From that position, he was able to develop an astute intellectual perspective as observer of the edges. He watched not simply how institutions worked, he noticed who was left out, and he was willing to comment on what that meant for both the health and welfare of the institution as well as for those who had been excluded. That vantage point, combined with an acute intellect, permitted him to see and write about things that most people overlooked or would prefer to ignore. This stance also permitted him to be a bridge builder because he had the ability to point out who was being left out, why, and what it meant both for those shut out and those holding power. With a stubborn refusal to get caught in any hardened ideological positions, either left or right, Dale was one of those rare persons able to actually see things and from that vantage point carry out his role in speaking truth to power.

I have in my files the outline of a book proposal Dale wrote and never developed for submission to a publisher. Those of us who knew Dale have folders of material written by Dale but never published. We saved all of it. Here are my notes from Dale's book proposal:

Introduction:

1. Males in modern America, particularly straight white males, are tired, angry, alienated, confused, and lonely.
2. This is the result of the incongruity between changing cultural expectations for them, their inner life, daily experiences, and changing place in American society.
3. Women, gays, and minorities have been forced to and have already begun to address the changes in their situation.
4. Males will be more happy and more peaceful when they understand themselves better, see the incongruities, and build a new foundation for relating to other males and to women.

This book proposal was written in 1991. In the *Chronicle of Higher Education*, which might be called the *New York Times* for college administrators, the problems of underachievement among white males only began to receive significant attention about a decade after this. Dale had already focused upon this question in the 1980s. How did he know about it already at that time?

He knew it because of his ability to listen, to develop meaningful connections and relationships, and to bring his creative intellect to bear on the question. From 1979 until the conclusion of his sojourn in Chicago I do not think that any one of us can fully appreciate the number of men that came to Dale for support and advice. This intelligent and astute observer of the American political scene who had spent a good deal of his career working for or with church structures and who intuitively understood the connection between the political and the personal for both church and world was consulted by the homeless, the disoriented college student, the alcoholic, as well as many church leaders and intellectuals. Regardless of your social station, when your personal life was in shambles, Dale was the person you went to see.

He accomplished this through his deep commitment to friendship, with the circle of people represented by the contributors to this volume and many others. What was most remarkable is the range of the friendships he entertained. Sociologists document the narrow circles in which the majority of us develop close relationships. We tend to become friends with people like us. But there seemed to be no limits to Dale's friendship circles. When you walked down the streets of the Belmont area of Chicago, Dale knew the panhandlers and the shop owners. And he could tell you the life story of each. When he moved to Huron Street on the Near West side, there was a different vibe. There were always new territories for exploration, and Dale was ready to light out for them. There are few experiences that match being on the streets with Dale and listening to his running commentary. Or to spend time at his all-night coffee spots. Notice I said "his." He didn't hold the deed, but they were "his." He knew the people, the history, and the gossip. I always thought my greatest failure as a friend to Dale was my lack of interest in excessive gossip. Dale loved it. Even after he was at Parkside Homes in Hillsboro, his final home for his last remaining years after the stroke, I can recall phone calls in which his question was, "What's the gossip?" The intrigue, the personal conflicts, the secret lives of the powerful, a number of whom he knew—this was the real stuff of human life that Dale relished. That desire to understand and establish a connection with another's deepest humanity is what made friendship with Dale so irresistible and valuable, and, ultimately, so important in the course of our own lives.

Why did so many men want to talk with Dale and share their stories with him? Why did so many of us seek out Dale's counsel? I think there were several basic elements at work. If you said things were in shambles, Dale offered no counternarrative. He didn't sugarcoat the situation, he didn't pretend to fix it, he didn't even always give you hope, certainly no false hope. But there was no judgment. And at the end of the day, you knew you could live. That's friendship. The list of people that relied upon him is extensive. The breadth and scope of those relationships is even more remarkable. Waiters, bartenders, corporate executives, community organizers, academics, street hustlers, pastors, church leaders, alcoholics, druggies, artists, Black, Latino, white, gay, straight, nurses, social workers, the welfare dependent, janitors, administrative assistants, all came within the purview of Dale's friendship. In the vast scope of this list, we see the moral and social power of friendship, the power of deep commitment to the life and welfare of another.

And so he learned about the lives of men. And as he listened, he also read prolifically. And what was at the heart of his thinking and teaching? For Dale, the key to male identity was to be found by defining male relationships. How do men relate to other men? How do men relate to women? What is the connection between sexuality and our relationships? Dale asked all of these questions more honestly and probed them at greater depth than any of my academic colleagues have been willing to consider. In the exploration of these questions of relationship, Dale was also asking about and looking for redemption. Aren't we all?

Recognizing the depth of his knowledge and the innovative nature of his perspectives, he was invited to teach at Garrett Evangelical Seminary in Chicago and to lecture at North Park University, Goshen College, Bethel College, Marietta College, and the University Church in Chicago, to name only a few.

The many conversations that Dale and I carried on for more than fifty years have stayed with me. Shortly before his death, I asked Dale what he wanted included in his obituary. His response was, "That I was gay." He was quite willing to leave the rest of the agenda up to others. Then he asked me, "What will you talk about at my service?" After a few moments I replied, "Friendship. I would want people to know what I learned from you about friendship." I continue to reflect on Dale's prescience on this. The importance of friendship has gained greater prominence in recent years, perhaps because of the contentious times in which we live. Some people regard it as the center of Christian ethics. The discussion of it as a virtue by Aristotle receives regular mention, as does Augustine's consideration of it as a central practice of the Christian life.

I have spent the majority of my professional life in academe. We identify issues that need attention: racism, sexism, homophobia, income disparity, the decline of rural communities and the family farm, urban decline and gentrification, the opioid epidemic. We identify issues, we study them, and we often maintain the illusion that we could solve them if people would only listen to us. The punch line is that we start with problems, issues. From Dale I had learned already by 1970 that there is a different way. There are people and they are wondrous, the source of endless fascination if you give them a chance and get to know them. All people have obstacles that stand in the way of their well-being. These are both individual and social. The social obstacles can be organized according to the groups of people affected by them.

But they are not issues; they are problems that people face in their daily lives and we develop some understanding when we actually get to know the people affected. No ivory tower solutions here. We develop an understanding of the problems of our society and our communities through friendship, and it is also through the bonds and connections of friendship that they are solved.

Dale tackled society's problems, and his own, through friendship, and his many friendships began and evolved through his mastery and understanding of the formative power of conversation. A very remarkable man is no longer with us and I grieve. I will admit I've been grieving for a while because I couldn't hold the conversations with him I was accustomed to from an earlier time. But even after his stroke some of us had glimpses of those conversations, the one-sentence insights that still had the capacity to astound, the short, pithy questions that would set us back on our heels. That talk now continues only in our own heads and in the voices of others who were also the products of those earlier sustained conversations. It is hard to imagine a world without Dale's voice in it. And yet Dale's words, those conversations conducted till two in the morning half a century ago, still rumble through my head at the unexpected hour.

THE ARC OF A RESTLESS MIND

Benjamin L. Hartley

Our friendship began in 1992 in the sparsely furnished and unofficial staff smoking room at University Hospital, across the street from Humboldt Park on Chicago's West Side. It was a struggling psychiatric hospital with no real university affiliation. The name was a desperate ploy for respectability it never had. No pictures hung on the walls in the room; just four steel chairs around a white plastic table designated the space for conversation.

I had recently graduated from Wheaton College in the Chicago suburbs and was a few weeks into my first job. I was twenty-three years old. Then in his mid-forties, Dale stood just over six feet tall (like me), wore brown-rimmed glasses, and had coffee-and-cigarette tinted teeth. Conversation unfurled between us like waves rolling in steadily on a beach. Dale grew up Mennonite in a small town in Kansas. I grew up sort-of Methodist in an even smaller town in Minnesota and knew just enough about Mennonites to think well of them. In one email to me years later, he noted that his rural heritage—"I be a country boy from Kansas"— helped him stay humble and sober.

The sobriety was hard-fought. Years before we met, Dale was forced to close the bookstore he managed at 2423 North Clark Avenue in the Lincoln Park neighborhood. At that time, he was deep in the throes of alcoholism. The address of his store now fronts a southern food restaurant with an extensive whiskey selection. Dale would have relished the irony of people whiskey-tasting in his old space. Bourbon whiskey had almost killed him in December 1980. The following month he began his life as a recovering alcoholic which for him also meant becoming an addictions therapist.

I will never forget the conversation that began on the corner of Kedzie Avenue and Division Street as I walked with Dale to his bus stop after work. I asked him why he was working for $12.50 an hour as a 45-year-old addictions counselor in a two-bit psychiatric hospital. He took a long drag of his cigarette before he spoke. "God saved me from bourbon, and I want to give the rest of my life to helping out people like me. It is that simple." From my vantage point, working at that hospital was part of my young adult struggle to figure things out while making enough money to get by. For Dale it was a calling.

Our friendship continued for years after that smoking-room conversation in 1992. I got married, and after a year as Dale's co-worker at University Hospital, left for graduate school in Michigan and Boston and then went on to academic jobs in Philadelphia and Oregon as a historian of Christianity. Dale left University Hospital shortly after I did for a position a dozen blocks away as a therapist at a Salvation Army addictions treatment center. There he had clients for longer spans of time and he honed his gifts. Until Dale's stroke in 2008, we corresponded weekly by email, sometimes more—and spoke frequently by phone.

As the essays in this volume illustrate, Dale's range of interests sometimes seemed limitless and his curiosity in the presence of a person or a book was palpable. But Dale was no academic. The life of an academic would have required him to focus on a smaller set of ideas and a much narrower range of books in one or two fields of study. Dale could not do that, and I am glad. But there were a few academic practices and touchstones in Dale's thinking that animated his life as a friend and his work as a therapist and writer.

Dale had the sensibilities of a historian. Listen to these words from Dale about historians printed in the *Hillsboro Free Press* a few years before his stroke:

> Historians are dangerous and subversive. While often soft-spoken and mild mannered they quietly undermine our conventional wisdom. How often do we hear folks say, "But this is the way we have always done it" and "This is what we have always believed"? Sometimes we are taken down the opposite road, "Here is a wonderful new idea or insight that will change everything." Historians are messy people. They subvert both our certainty of eternal truth and our discovery of what we believe to be new by digging through old books and archives and emerging with data that challenge both our past and our future. If a school is given a choice between hiring a Marxist or a religious fanatic versus the option of hiring a good history teacher, schools are safer with the former two rather than the latter. Historians don't picket, preach or shout; they just quietly assemble enough evidence to challenge and confuse everybody's thinking.

Dale doesn't describe himself as a historian in this essay, but as I read over his many journal entries about clients (always with identities concealed), it is clear that Dale's work with men in recovery began with his ability to listen. He listened carefully to men's stories and searched for clues and connections and things that didn't fit to explore later, like a meticulous historian searches through an archive. As he processed his work with clients through journaling and conversations, he rarely referred to psychological theories. He was convinced of the validity of the disease-model for addictions and found many of Carl Jung's insights compelling. However, he thought that theories of psychotherapy often hid as much as they revealed if one applied them too heavy-handedly. Instead, Dale understood people's histories, and in his own way tried to help his clients see their connection to a wider story in which they could perhaps find healing.

Dale was also an anthropologist. His interest in anthropology began in classes he took at Tabor College in the 1960s with Jacob

Loewen, but toward the end of his life he was most drawn to the work of René Girard, a Stanford-based literary critic who developed an expansive theory of culture derived from his study of ancient and modern literature. What fascinated Girard and Dale alike was the mystery of violence in human societies and how repeating spasms of violence—what Girard called the "scapegoating mechanism"—persisted. For Girard, Judaism and Christianity as reflected in the biblical record both point to a concern for the victim. Even more, in Girard's reading, the scriptures expose the scapegoating process and they hold the clue as to how the spiral of violence can be stopped. A Roman Catholic scholar, Girard drew attention to the problem of violence and provided a way for Dale to access his Mennonite commitment to nonviolence but to do so within a framework of traditional Christian liturgy that Dale found so meaningful.

Dale experimented with Girard's theories of culture in his work as an addictions counselor. He paid close attention to the people his clients implicitly and explicitly modeled their lives after. These "model mediators" (a Girardian term which Dale used frequently) revealed for Dale how his clients experienced desire and what they desired. Girard's ideas about desire helped Dale understand addictions in a deeper way. He once told me that both in his work as a therapist and also his personal life, Girard's ideas had become more prominent than anyone else's—including those of Carl Jung—as a map for understanding the complexities of the lives he encountered.

On a dreary day in early January, I heard the news that Dale had died. I was in a Chapters bookstore and coffeeshop in Newberg, Oregon when I received the phone call from Dale's cousin Keith. In light of Dale's love for books and coffee, it was a fitting place to receive the news that our friendship had come to its end. A couple days later I came back to this shop to speak with the only other person in my town who knew Dale. Ed Springer held court at the coffee shop almost every morning. I only needed to show up and wait. Ed had moved to Newberg, Oregon in retirement, but years earlier he had pastored Mennonite churches in Hillsboro and Illinois and knew Dale from his time with Mennonite Voluntary Service. Ed repeated stories of his encounters with Dale that I had heard from him at least twice before, but I did not stop him. I found solace in the stories.

A few days later I sent an email to Dale's first therapist, informing him of Dale's passing. Dale had reconnected with Chris Schlauch, now a professor at Boston University, just a few years before, at my graduation from that school. Chris wrote back to me expressing his grief. He had known Dale as a client nearly forty years earlier. He asked to see a recent picture, so I sent one I had taken of Dale in front of a plaque marking the spot of the 1969 Stonewall uprising in Greenwich Village, New York City. Dale's slight smirk in the photograph reveals his own sense of the absurd as a tourist at the site.

For the funeral, an inner circle of friends from across the country converged at Ebenfeld Mennonite Brethren Church on the Kansas prairie a few miles south of Hillsboro. It was the church of Dale's childhood and early youth. A couple of these friends are professor-types like me, but the cast of characters that comprised Dale's circle of friends was always a more diverse lot than my own. At the funeral I imagined into presence the many friends and co-workers who would have liked to have been there but weren't, for one reason or another. One of those present would be Matt, a young man Dale had given a spare room to for a few months in 1992. Dale's place was safe and away from the drugs and alcohol that haunted Matt. I remember sitting next to Matt watching the election returns come in at a party at Dale's house when Bill Clinton won the presidency. In my imagination, social workers, therapists, and psychiatrists Dale knew would be at his funeral as well. A jaded psychiatrist named Dr. Tilken would show up dispensing witticisms and packing almost as strong a verbal punch as Dale himself. Former clients whose lives Dale saved (we will never know the exact numbers) would also be at my imaginary Ebenfeld Mennonite congregation to see Dale off. Oscar was there, an older African-American gentleman and recovering heroin addict whom Dale continued to see "off the books." He and Dale enjoyed one another's company. (The line between therapist and friend was always, in Dale's words, "thin but critical.")

At the funeral the congregation sang, "What a Friend We Have in Jesus," a fitting tribute to someone who prized friendship so strongly—and who had asked that these words be inscribed on his headstone. After the funeral, a smaller group of a dozen friends gathered at a historic hotel in the neighboring town of Marion. We told stories, did impressions of the man, laughed, and cried together. The following morning, I woke up early to drive a few miles east to the Tallgrass Prairie National Preserve in the Flint Hills. This was a place Dale loved. He once told me that on his frequent trips between Chicago and Hillsboro, driving through the Flint Hills signaled for him that he had "come home." A couple hours later I prepared to leave Hillsboro for the airport in Wichita.

I drove out of town but on the way, I had a final stop to make. It was Sunday morning, and when I pulled into the gravel parking lot at Ebenfeld, I could hear the congregation gathering in the church next to the cemetery. I thought about what kind of liturgy Dale might appreciate. Twenty years before, he had become Episcopalian, but at the end of his life his connection to this church of his ancestors grew stronger.

So I walked to Dale's gravesite under a tree, close to the edge of the cemetery, and looked out over wheat fields and pasture. A quotation from Elie Wiesel came to mind that years earlier had resonated for both of us. "Friendship marks a life even more deeply than love. Love risks degenerating into obsession, friendship is never anything but sharing." I lit a single Winston cigarette, and when it burned down, I buried it under the raw, cold Kansas soil, and then I drove away.

DALE SUDERMAN, EDGE WORKER

By Tim Nafziger

My friend Dale Suderman died quietly on January 5, 2020 in his recliner in Hillsboro, Kansas. Dale is not the kind of person often celebrated by the mainstream Mennonite community. Though he grew up Mennonite, he chose to fight in the Vietnam War. For part of his life, he was a closeted gay man involved in leading Mennonite organizations. He hung out with radicals, conservatives, and sinners, and didn't judge them. He was an alcoholic all his life and always open about his commitment to Alcoholics Anonymous. He was deeply committed to Eucharist at whatever Episcopal church would have him. He actively subverted propriety whenever he could get away with it and sometimes when he couldn't. Some of us in his close circle of friends called him a shaman. In short, he queered the bejesus out of the Mennonite box. That's why I loved him so much.

I first met Dale in the fall of 2002 during my senior year at Goshen College in Indiana when he came to speak to a short-lived, somewhat tongue-in-cheek group calling itself the Goshen College Men's Association (GSMA). I am still indebted to the administrator who invited him, who knew a lot of the baggage Dale proudly carried.

It was shortly after my second hospitalization for a major mental health crisis and my world was in fragments. I was struggling to juggle my commitments as a student and activist, as well as maintain friendships. Family and friends were concerned that the healing and recovery process was not going as well as I thought. A few months after getting out of the hospital, I was back in the full swing of multiple activities: holding down a part-time job, doing an internship at the local paper, and serving as page editor for the *Goshen College Record*, the student newspaper. It was a lot for anyone, let alone someone who had just had a full-blown psychological episode.

I was the student assigned to escort Dale around campus between events and locations. We walked down to the dam in the neighborhood west of the college. I told him about what it was like to experience two manic episodes. "Whiskey will really take those over the top," he said.

I was gobsmacked. On the surface it seemed a wildly irresponsible thing for him, a trained addictions counselor, to say. But he had been doing the work long enough to know when to break the rules with a higher goal. He was open about his experience as an alcoholic in recovery, and his response was a tremendous breath of fresh air that let me know others had been through what I had, or worse, and put their lives back together. His matter-of-fact response to my story of mental health crisis was a critical part of my healing journey, at a time when my experiences were far outside normal, acceptable behavior in my small community.

Dale became my friend and mentor for the rest of his life. He even grudgingly agreed to be one of the groomsmen at my wedding, after grumbling to me years earlier that he didn't do weddings anymore. And in the strange poetic vocabulary of the universe, he died the same weekend my wife packed all her things on the porch and left.

I wrote most this piece on January 6, 2020 the first day of my new life on my own. One more time, Dale was there for me at one of the most painful moments as I sat for hours trying to tell the story of a man I had spent twelve years saying goodbye to. As a writer, Dale knew well that making meaning in one part of one's life can be a life raft when the whole ship is going down. In his life at the edge, I know the short essays that he often banged out in the wee hours of the morning were his lifeline. The writing process itself probably saved his life any number of times. Now I knew how that felt.

ii

Dale grew up in Hillsboro, Kansas, on a farm in a Mennonite Brethren community. He told enough stories from that period to know that he never fit in, like many queer Mennonites growing up amidst miles and miles of winter wheat and corn. Dale's reasons for joining the military were complex and his reasons for going to Vietnam even more so. But fundamentally, it was a way out. His plane landed in Hanoi just as the Tet offensive was in full swing. He had a desk job, but it was also clear that at that point in the war, everywhere was a front line.

After returning from Vietnam, Dale became part of the peace movement. He took a class on "War, Peace, and Revolution" with John Howard Yoder at Anabaptist Mennonite Biblical Seminary. Dale told the story more than once about how he showed up a year late to the final test. When some young whippersnappers in the class complained that Dale hadn't even attended (he had taken it the year before), Yoder said, "Dale has seen more war, peace and revolution than you ever will."

Dale's wide travels and wider reading led him to an expansive cosmopolitanism. He appreciated the finer things in the world with the affectionate eye of a cynic. In a November 2007 talk, "Cynicism and Therapy: Seeing the Log in our Own Eye" (*Cynicism and Hope: Reclaiming Discipleship in a Postdemocratic Society*, ed. Meg. E. Cox, Cascade Books, 2009, pp. 41–51), Dale identified as having the "heart of a historian." He was clear that one of his remaining goals in life was to be a "big dog hanging its tongue out the window of the car as it drives down the highway." This was a subtle nod to the dog philosophers who Dale enthusiastically reclaimed from bitterness and despair. Dale, Walt Whitman, and the author of Ecclesiastes would have enjoyed a good smoke and a cup of coffee together.

In that same presentation, Dale made it clear that his hope was rooted in a "pre-philosophical" commitment to the Jesus who calls us to see the log in our own eye first before turning to righteousness. Dale loved the Jesus who pointed out that the Pharisees were just like their fathers (p. 43). There is nothing new under the sun. Dale found deep hope in this ancient wisdom, made manifest at the communion rail and the rituals and garb of the Episcopal deacon who also welcome him as a gay man (p. 49).

Dale had spent forty years embracing beauty in both extravagance and simple gestures in his own queer way. As a self-described "old faggot," he had no illusions about possessing any of these things. He was just along for the ride. My friendship with him gave me a sense of the vastness of human experience, which had a big impact for me as a Mennonite kid with more than a little insularity and wariness of the worldly world. Dale taught me, as the writer of Ecclesiastes said first, there are times to scrimp and save and times to enjoy life. Frugality, to my surprise, was not the only valid choice in life. During our travels together, Dale was the person who helped me understand that sometimes I needed "cave time" after being around people. He said: Tim, sometimes you disappear, but when you come back, you are more present and more fun to be around.

Dale believed in the power of male friendship rooted in deep vulnerability, honesty, and playfulness. He reflected back to me my gifts as a conversationalist because it takes one to know one. He also taught me that I could be a masculine man while throwing many of the traditional tropes of masculinity out the window. In the language of today's LGBTQ community, he had queered his masculinity, although the term "queer" was too domesticated for him by the time I met him and he was focused on reclaiming the term "faggot."

Dale modeled this vulnerability as a writer in emails to his friends. In October 2006 he wrote:

> Once again, all the demons came out last night as I went to sleep. The deep fear of abandonment and my financial foolishness combined with the ongoing stomach ache of the past few days produce despair.
>
> So I fight back this morning by "scribbling," drinking coffee, smoking cigarettes, and looking out the window. There are changes in a quarter century of doing this. Now I scribble in the morning, use a computer, and write at home. But I still

have boxes of incoherent journals scribbled in pen or pencil while sitting alone in all-night coffee shops. The site and technology change. The principle that I swat demons, my pesky psychic flies, using a pen and paper, remains consistent.

Dale was an edge worker, adapting to change and embracing the blurry lines of a world that self-righteous peace and justice activists like me often see as all or nothing. He generously tolerated my young idealism, but also challenged me with the gritty realities of political organizing as well as the failures of the Left. He spent his life dancing on the margins of many different communities and weaving relationships with stories and wit wherever he went. When he talked about vegans trying to organize Teamsters against the Iraq War (p. 44), it came out of hanging out with both of these crowds. In the 1980s he ran Logos Bookstore in Chicago, a gathering place for all sorts of nerdy misfits, or so I imagine from all the stories I heard about it. Dale taught me to see nuance and complexity in life and to learn to love even old white men like him. After all, every day I am in the process of becoming one of those myself.

Dale was an inveterate smoker. I had been raised to disdain smoking by my health-conscious, simple-living Mennonite parents. I didn't realize the extent of my prejudices toward smokers until I became friends with Dale. I won't say he completely cured me of my anti-tobacco prejudice, but he certainly taught me to love the sinner. His only concession to my snobbery was that we'd sit outside on the open-air rooftop deck behind his second-floor apartment while he smoked and talked. I listened.

In the spring of 2008, Dale had a massive stroke that would eventually shut down most of the functions on the right side of his body. While both my grandfathers had been dealt this hand, this was the first time that it had happened to a friend. Dale moved into The Imperial, an assisted living facility in Lincoln Park. Twice a week I would stop on my bike home from work to visit him. For the first few months he was still trying to figure out how to catch a smoke on the balcony of the Imperial when I would push him out there in his wheelchair.

In the ensuing years, Dale taught me a lot about grief. I missed my friend deeply even as I sat with him while he struggled to put a complete sentence together. One time he wanted to tell me something with such urgency that we spent half an hour with a staff member trying to decipher it. He would stretch for a sentence arc like a brittle rubber band that kept on snapping before he could finish. He was making progress through May and June, but after a subdural hematoma in July, it was clear that he would never live independently again.

In the fall of 2008, four friends—Douglas Bermudez, Ben Hartley, Daniel Born, and I—rented a Winnebago RV and drove Dale from Chicago to Hillsboro, Kansas, where he moved into Parkside Homes. He lived there until early January 2020. Seeing the genuine compassion and care the staff showed Dale brought home the difference between the realities of a big city where you are an anonymous one among millions compared to a small town where you grew up. It was clear that even though Dale had been gone from his hometown for more than four decades, he was still welcome there. It probably helped that he had written a widely-read column, "View from Afar," that ran in the *Hillsboro Free Press* for many years.

iii

In his early adulthood through his mid-thirties, Dale was in the closet. His friend community always knew, but he told stories of working with Mennonite Voluntary Service in the late 1970s and always having a resignation letter ready in his drawer. He came out fully and publicly to his home town on Friday, November 9, 2012, four years after his stroke. His close friends were there among the crowd at a Tabor College library reception in which he was honored. He had donated his vast collection of books on addictions to the library and invited his circle of friends to be there for his coming-out moment. John Kampen and Ben Hartley read reflections on their friendship with Dale that included, at his request, some remarks about his sexuality. Dale sat in his wheelchair, listened, and nodded as if to say, "This is who I am." It was a powerful moment witnessed by the Tabor community.

When I visited Dale last summer, he told me he was ready to die. Given the state of his health, for a decade I'd assumed that any visit to Dale might be my last. But this time felt different. Dale was in his mid-seventies, after twelve years living with the devastating impact of a stroke.

He shared similar things with other friends who visited him in 2019. Dale asked me to take a photo of him kneeling in front of a poster that said, "I am the resurrection and the life. The one who believes in me will live, even though they die." He said, "Tim, that's me. I'm ready." I felt some tension with the old cynic I loved and the deeply religious Episcopalian sitting in front of me, but I accepted that Dale was defying my expectations one last time.

SHOCK AND AWE

Ruth Harder

At the risk of making Dale Suderman out to be some villain or antagonist upon his death (which he was not, in my experience), I can't help but see striking similarities, if only physical, between these two cigarette smoking men—one being a character named C. G. B. Spender (perhaps just one of hundreds of aliases) in *The X-Files* television series, and the other a relative of mine whose life, at least to me, always seemed stranger than fiction.

What started as a minor role in *The X-Files*, the Smoking Man turned into a memorable performance, due in part to increasing fan interest. My guess is that Dale will also continue to live on and his story will continue to captivate new audiences. There is still much to uncover and know about Dale's life. Like C. G. B. Spender, Dale was full of surprises and remained somewhat mysterious to the very end.

One didn't always know the motivations of these smoking men, which kept them both interesting and, at times, not always easy to understand or appreciate in the moment. Fans loved—and still love—to speculate about what long game Smoking Man might have been playing. The actor has said of his character: "Underneath it, there's a human being that has suffered enormously, but I don't know if the audience picks up on that." I certainly did. That was true for Dale too. Behind both of these handsome faces, there are hints of struggle and pain, but also fierce intelligence and keen observational skills. These smoking men both stood afar—at a distance observing, making notes, not speaking a lot, following their own course—going where the smoke took them. Dale, of course, also knew how to connect in meaningful ways. His friendships were deep and real. He was loyal even to those he didn't necessarily like, even hated.

It's interesting to note that C. G. B. Spender was the only one, along with Mulder and Scully, to appear in the first and last episodes of *X-Files*. And while the actor William B. Davis wasn't nominated for any of his work alone on the series, he and several other cast members were nominated in the category "Outstanding Performance by an Ensemble in a Drama Series." I want to nominate Dale for something like that too, along with his fiercely intelligent community of friends. Dale loved them and they loved him back. There was a long stretch after Season Five when fans of *The X-Files* debated whether the Smoking Man was dead or alive. In June and July 2019, I received two messages from people in Chicago who knew Dale. "Was he still alive?" they both wondered.

> Hi, I'm trying to get in touch with any relatives of Dale. I worked with him when he was in Chicago. I'd love to get some updates.

> Hello, I'm attempting to reach Dale Suderman who I knew from Chicago, Illinois. Hillsboro native, Vietnam veteran, former bookstore owner, worked at Salvation Army, gay, former counselor at Swedish Covenant Hospital (Dr. Tilken) who was instrumental to my professional life. Please contact me.

I won't be surprised if I continue receiving these messages. His life touched many, just as his life was touched by so many. A complex cast of characters, both living and dead, accompanied his life. These saints and sinners, past and present, were always close in his mind, especially during those days cooped up at Parkside when he couldn't do all the things he still wanted to do. He lit up (those days without a cigarette) whenever he would hear from a friend or when a friend's name was mentioned. In those days when I recorded conversations with him, with hopes of helping him record his life story, he thought "Shock and Awe" would be a good title, and I agreed, along with the tag line: One man's story of being a Mennonite war veteran, gay, alcoholic, Christian bookstore owner, war protestor, stroke victim, friend of Roger Ebert and Philip Yancey.

He wanted Chapter 1 to start with him waking up at Parkside Homes in his hometown of Hillsboro asking, "What the hell am I doing here?"

I think he asked that question his whole life, wherever he was. Perhaps it was his exploration of that question that kept him so interesting. We never talked much about death or the process of dying. He never admitted to being scared.

Perhaps it's just another chapter of shock and awe.

Rest in peace, Smoking Man.

LETTER TO DALE SUDERMAN

Clint Stucky

The pen in my hand feels about as cold as your Ebenfeld Cemetery gravestone must feel on this chilly day in January. Thinking of your big, wide grin warms me, though—as did the many "bottomless" cups of coffee held in my hands over the years as I sat in rapt attention.

Initially, that was when you held court most every night at Leonida's Santa Fe train station restaurant in Newton, Kansas. Then later, during Mennonite Voluntary Service, at perhaps one of Seattle's dirty Skid Road cafes. And still later, Charlie's Restaurant at the Newell Truck Plaza outside Newton, where we would meet to talk during your trips home to Hillsboro. Always a newspaper in your hand when I arrived—sometimes several more stacked beside you.

No longer am I regaled by your tales of the absurd, the ironic, the surprising, your analysis of current events, the latest theories about human behavior, some comment on church or theological matters, the wise words of a man or woman you particularly admired, your new love interest. And then there was your outrageous sense of humor...

Remember the time when I was publicly accused of being "a practicing homosexual"?

"Practicing? I'm darn near perfect!" was the response you suggested.

Considering that you were gay, the amount of time and energy you expended worrying about straight men and their changing roles in society always puzzled me. I tried to seem interested, but couldn't match your fascination with the subject.

Physical grace, I'm sure you'd admit, was not one of your "gifts." I can't for a moment visualize you as a U.S. infantryman. Nor were you known for your cooking skills. Sometimes I wondered whether you subsisted on cigarettes, pie, and coffee. However, that casserole you prepared and served to me and a few others at your shotgun apartment in Chicago some years back was pretty good. You were so proud and excited at your achievement. "Beaming like a teenager," I thought to myself.

I miss you. I've missed you for a year now. And I've missed your stories for more like a decade. After the stroke stole your tongue, it was up to *me* to tell the stories, the jokes, to share observations about human behavior, to comment on the latest news. But I couldn't do it as well. Who could?

Not that you didn't talk at all, of course. "Yes!" "No!" "You bet!" One or two or three-word imperatives, mainly. I remember that first Christmas after you arrived in Hillsboro. I offered to send out a Christmas email in your name and asked what you wanted to say to your many friends and acquaintances—none of whom had received any correspondence from you since your cerebrovascular accident.

Do you remember what words you chose? "Don't give up!" I asked several times if that was really the Christmas message you wanted to send, and you adamantly indicated it was. "Would it be okay if we added 'Merry Christmas'?" I asked. And it was.

Of course, you had ways to communicate other than speech. Nods and winks and smiles. Do you remember that bigger-than-life picture of Obama we hung on the wall of your room after Barack was elected? You loved having it there, didn't you? Take that, you Hillsboro Republicans! And then there were all those anti-Trump T-shirts I had Amazon send—which you proudly wore. And the coffee mug which read "I Hate When I Wake Up In The Morning and Donald Trump Is President."

"What a friend we have in Jesus," your tombstone reads. It was all about friends, about being a friend, wasn't it? "I don't have any friends in Newton," you were fond of complaining, "because I've sent them all off to Voluntary Service!" Then you sent me off, too. But we remained friends during and after that life-changing event.

There were long, late-night phone conversations, however, when you would excuse yourself intermittently. The clink of ice cubes against glass was heard in the distance, and your words got more and more slurred.

You and Alcoholic Anonymous were a perfect fit though. You'd describe those meetings to me with all the joy and fascination one might expect of someone who had just returned from a trip to a foreign country. Percolators and people. What more could one want? People to spend the evening with every night of the week. And you did. People to talk to—and just as importantly, listen to. There were public confessions of human frailty and proud reports of small victories. A place for friendships of the "anonymous" sort, one might say. And lots of them.

Friendships, you once wrote, "provide a sustaining sanctuary of storytelling, laughter, and tears—not merely about victories and accomplishments but also about doubts, failures, and pain. My daily hope is in friendships."

Science, medicine, politics, even religion will all fail us, you told me. It's friendships that buoy us up when the seas of life get rough. And it's Jesus that saves us. When you departed from this world, Dale, the countryside was left littered with your "best friends forever"—folks who counted you as one of their best, closest, most trusted friends.

I am one of those. I will treasure, especially, those memorable occasions when you saved my butt and/or my soul with your sage advice—after listening to me long and carefully . . . in dead silence.

Actually, "Pastor at Large," is how I mainly thought of you. Street Pastor. Coffee Shop Pastor. A veritable savior, at times. You could drop in on a troubled Mennonite Voluntary Service Unit, and—in the space of twenty-four hours—gingerly untangle the interpersonal mess we had gotten ourselves into over the space of six months. And then ascend into the clouds just like your friend Jesus, to leave us wondering, "How did he do that?"

Peace was a big deal with you. Am I correct? That's how you always signed off your letters to me—"Peace, Dale." You have your peace now, but the friends you left behind have not had much peace this past year. God, how I wish we could avail ourselves of what might have been your commentary on the anti-maskers, racial disparities, the presidential race, election, the attempted insurrection.

What a friend we had in you, Dale. A lot of us could use a friend like you right now.

INSATIABLE DRIVE, PROFOUND PASSION

Delbert Wiens

"Wiens, I've figured out why we put up with you always trying to crowd us back into the boat. It's because we know you're also telling our parents it's time for them to get out of it."

It was Dale, grinning broadly as we passed on the Tabor College campus. I had preached at Ebenfeld Church the preceding Sunday about a time when Jesus told the apostles to take their boat to the other side. Boats, I explained, symbolized "ships of state." The sea imaged the chaos that destroys order, the very house and haunt of demons. When Jesus, who was not in the disciples' particular ark of salvation, appeared out of the storm, they screamed, "It is a phantasm." Peter had to learn that his Lord was the Master of Chaos *and* of fallible earthly vessels. Peter also learned that those called to captain earthly arks had to step outside of them on occasion—and by doing so could relate them to their larger natural and human contexts and their dependence on God.

I admired Dale's insatiable drive to discover what is real, to reject hypocrisy, and to avoid going out of his way to offend others, at least most of the time. But I also feared his willingness to take risks, as when he and another student dared to edge into extremist groups, some of whom were creating their own militias. About the time he graduated, someone at a gathering of right-wing clans slipped up to him and said, "We know who you are; you're Suderman from Hillsboro. We're onto you." He took the hint. The extensive materials that Dale and his colleague gathered for this project are now housed at the Bethel College archives in North Newton, Kansas.

While in college he began to write brief obituary notices in the *Christian Leader*. He tried hard to smuggle a few words into them that evoked their subjects' legacy. Another of his "multiple contraries" was that he left his Ebenfeld boat to step into the chaos of Vietnam, where he continued to experiment with life and to question the truths of established orders. Whatever ecstasy and terror he had known while walking on water here and in later life, he returned from Vietnam with an addiction. He also grasped the hand of Jesus, joined Alcoholics Anonymous, and shared sacramental grace with Christians. And, as before, he read much and thought hard about the storms both males and females face. In letters and emails, occasional visits, and in this collection of his selected essays and writings, Dale becomes my mentor.

Here I speak briefly about some of the "storms" he helped me better understand:

He writes about retreats and marches to help men recover order and meaning in their lives. Like the evangelical "Promise Keepers" who were organized by a Colorado football coach and convened in stadiums, the non-Christian movements he describes told males they needed to begin their recovery with repentance and apologies for their inability to relate with integrity to a changing world. The different varieties of the "men's movement" were alike insofar as they offered places and rituals for males to bond with each other in a spiritual sense.

Dale knew that loss of male status and meaning is the result of underlying social and economic changes. Most of the greatly reduced percentage of males who still earn enough to maintain a household on their own are aging. In fact, many of them are older than sixty-five. Upper torso strength has diminishing importance these days. The gender gap in college graduation rates between males and females skews increasingly toward women. More and more women earn the diplomas that better-paid jobs and professions require.

Since deeper causes are not the conscious fault of individual males, the apologies and repentances by men in the movement have often sounded sociologically uninformed and at times deeply confused. While appreciating the impulses that drove the men's movement, Dale also recognized that healing required more than brief retreats and makeshift bonding rituals. Dale understood that he needed to recover the older wisdom of his father, the disciplines of primary communities, and spiritual rituals rooted in daily life.

To become extraordinary and to experience ecstasy, one has to take risks. Dale knew this terrain. Those who choose chemicals to experience euphoria risk the addictions that can lead to poverty, domestic violence, and homelessness. As Dale puts it, "The chemical quest for euphoria is the ultimate banality," and those times when one is "surprised by joy" within a blessed life must be found within a prosaic and disciplined life.

Addictions counselors have limited theoretical options that guide their art and science, and many Christian therapists and leaders in the men's movements have made Carl Jung their guru. Dale recognized this and felt the attraction. His essay on Richard Noll's book, *The Aryan Christ: The Secret Life of Carl Jung*, published in this book for the first time, has special significance for anyone seeking to comprehend the shape of Dale's thinking, which sometimes proceeded not in a straight line but by way of zigs and zags.

Dale argues that Jung's scholarly writings deployed abstractions that could be entertained rationally. For a small inner circle Jung revealed a terrifying encounter with heavenly "powers" (the *archetypes*) from a transcendent reality (the *collective unconscious*). To true believers in his inner circle, he promoted a pagan, Germanic (*Aryan*) mythos and a religion which he borrowed from Pietism and from German nationalism. He conducted séances, said that Wotan was "the true god of the German people," and argued that "evil" Nazis and Lucifer (Satan) were necessary to prepare the way for light and healing. Dale notes that Noll did not write about Jung's later life. I agree with Dale that "principalities and powers" are "dangerous shadows" that lurk behind all civilizations, including "liberal democracy."

Dale addresses another current storm in a review of two books analyzing Leo Strauss, a political scientist who came to America in 1932. Strauss's books are so difficult to read that some suspect they were written to be understood only by "initiates" such as Paul Wolfowitz, George W. Bush's Deputy Secretary of Defense, and others who held important positions in the White House, the Pentagon, and the State Department in the last Republican administration preceding Trump's.

A less-paranoid perspective holds that Strauss was a mild-mannered Jewish philosopher who made justice a property of *nature* that should be the highest human standard. One has to choose between "Socrates" (natural reason) and "Moses" (revelation), and, according to this understanding, Strauss chose Socrates. In short, true philosophers are wiser than kings, priests, and ignorant masses who live by faith. This is Thomas Mann's view of Strauss in *Rise of the Vulcans: The History of Bush's War Cabinet* (Penguin Books, 2004).

A different approach to Strauss is taken by Anne Norton in *Leo Strauss and the Politics of American Empire* (Yale University Press,

2004). Norton focuses on the personal lives and character of Strauss and his devoted disciples, and she takes special issue with their hatred of women. Dale agrees in principle with her challenge to Straussian misogyny, though he chides her for not clarifying whether students of Strauss distorted what he taught.

Dale suggests that it might be helpful to put Straussian thinking into the "larger landscape" of a long American narrative that ranges from Manifest Destiny to the muscular patriotism of Theodore Roosevelt. This is one of Dale's characteristic intellectual moves: trace the history of the idea comprehensively over time. In this sense, Thomas Mann's book resonates in Dale's critical outlook, because it paints a nuanced picture that adds the influence of Cold Warriors like Dean Acheson, Paul Nitze, and many others to the Straussian worldview.

Those who read this revelatory collection of Dale's writings will recognize that his "insatiable drive" to understand himself and the worlds he dared to explore expresses only one aspect of his complex identity. We must ponder also that his frequent returns to his family and to Ebenfeld and Hillsboro were motivated by something deeper than nostalgia.

I joined the Ebenfeld congregation when coming to Tabor College to write and teach after one year of teaching at Corn, Oklahoma. In my experience, I learned that Ebenfeld, like Corn, was still marked by tensions from comprising different strands of the European Mennonite tradition. From earlier generations, Ebenfeld had developed leaders that helped found Tabor College and supplied some of its best teachers. And I remember sitting in the upstairs balcony and noticing those below me whose experience of foreign missions and of Mennonite Central Committee assignments had added "worldly" sophistication to the proverbial wisdom of a long tradition of primary rural communities. Dale's admiration of his father reflects a larger context for sanctification than that of a modern "nuclear family" or contemporary evangelical congregation.

A good number of students at Tabor College and Bethel College in the early and mid-1960s were stimulated by that era's experience of hippie culture that featured a radical critique of American values, early lessons of the failure of Cold War policies, and the celebration of love by a generation losing the important lessons of "prosaic and disciplined" primary communities. Because many of them came from rural and Mennonite pieties and disciplines, they had often retained the common sense to fit the compartmentalized insights of educated specialists into their own quest to recreate "primary communities" that went deeper than conducting brief "crusades" in typical evangelical style.

Dale and others have mentored many of us. In one of his numerous emails, he noted that both tears and sobs were more often heard coming from the addicted he counseled than from those in other rooms. Dale was a no-nonsense counselor who dared to share himself and dared to confront clients who might become friends. He once mentioned to me a very tough client who started to give a Freudian explanation of having suffered a mother's assault on his ego. Dale told him that if he wanted to avoid taking responsibility for his failures, he would immediately help to arrange his transfer to a counselor who would welcome these evasions.

In a January email from 2001, Dale wrote of one particular "family myth." After his first night in Marion County, Kansas, Dale's great-grandfather was found weeping beside a haystack. He lamented coming to "this forsaken country" and having "abandoned the good life in Russia." Dale imagined a line of ancestors uttering the same laments over three hundred years for having left Holland for Germany, Germany for Poland, and Poland for Russia. He concluded, "We are all homesick in either space or time."

Four days at home, apparently for the holidays, was enough for Dale to "get his prairie fix" and then it was time to return to Chicago—"to people cursing in four languages . . . daily screaming newspaper headlines of local death, destruction, and scandal. I am going from infinite prairie to infinite grit."

Dale ended this epistle with a quotation from a friend: "We are all born a little distance from where we should live our lives. And finding that place is why life is a journey." Those of us who want to be mentored by Dale must also take up his profound passion to recover a wisdom that surpassed traditional *status quos* and his equally profound instinct to rebuild, within a modern and postmodern city, elements of a primary village and community with disciplines and spiritual rituals rooted in daily life.

Contributors

Daniel Born is a writer and editor based in Chicago. He has taught literature and writing at various institutions including Northwestern University's School of Professional Studies, Dominican University, Marietta College, Queens College (CUNY), and the University of Kansas. A former vice president at the Great Books Foundation, he is author of *The Birth of Liberal Guilt in the English Novel: Charles Dickens to H. G. Wells* (University of North Carolina Press, 1995), and co-author with Dale Suderman of *Unpardonable Sins* (Wipf and Stock, 2021), a hardboiled crime novel published under their shared pen name, David Saul Bergman. His essays have appeared in publications including *Novel, Literature & Theology*, the *New York Times*, and the *Chronicle of Higher Education*.

Keith Harder is a retired Mennonite pastor and denominational minister for Mennonite Church USA. He lives in North Newton, Kansas. Dale Suderman's mother and Keith Harder's father were siblings, making Dale and Keith first cousins with many shared experiences.

John Kampen is Distinguished Research Professor at Methodist Theological School in Ohio. He has published widely on the Dead Sea Scrolls and the New Testament, as well as Jewish history and literature of the Greco-Roman era. His most recent book is *Matthew within Sectarian Judaism* (Yale University Press, 2019).

Benjamin L. Hartley is a church historian. He was Associate Professor of Mission and World Christianity at Seattle Pacific University, and previously, Associate Professor at Palmer Theological Seminary for eleven years and at George Fox University for four years. His publications include *Evangelicals at a Crossroads: Revivalism and Social Reform in Boston, 1860–1910* (University of New Hampshire Press, 2011).

Tim Nafziger is a Mennonite with a degree from Goshen College who lives in the Ventura River watershed on the traditional lands of the Chumash people in southern California. He works as a digital consultant, web developer, writer, photographer, and organizer.

Ruth Harder was educated at Bethel College in Kansas and Anabaptist Mennonite Biblical Seminary in Elkhart, Indiana. A former youth and communications coordinator at LaSalle Street Church in Chicago, and associate pastor at Bethel College Mennonite Church, she began her current position as senior pastor at Rainbow Mennonite Church in Kansas City, Kansas in 2013.

Clint Stucky grew up on a Mennonite dairy farm southwest of Moundridge, Kansas. After a brief stint at Bethel College in Kansas, he was recruited by Dale Suderman into Mennonite Voluntary Service, serving two years at Seattle Mental Health Institute. He is now retired from an occupational therapy teaching career at Newman University and lives in Wichita.

Elva Suderman is the sister of Dale Suderman. She worked at the Mennonite Brethren Publishing House (later Multi Business Press) in Hillsboro, Kansas for forty years, first as secretary and bookkeeper, and later, as one of the partners, as office manager and accountant. A charter member of the Hutchinson Post-Polio Support Group, she edited the Post-Polio Syndrome newsletter for the state of Kansas from 1999 until 2006. She is currently retired and living at Parkside Homes in Hillsboro.

Delbert Wiens, Professor Emeritus at Fresno Pacific University, was the first field staff worker for Mennonite Central Committee in Vietnam, beginning in 1954. Educated at Yale and the University of Chicago, he is author of the essays "From the Village to the City: A Grammar for the Languages We Are" and "New Wineskins for Old Wine," as well as *Stephen's Sermon and the Structure of Luke-Acts* (D & F Scott Publishing, 1995). Wiens's life and intellectual influence are examined in *A Dangerous Mind: The Ideas and Influence of Delbert L. Wiens*, ed. W. Marshall Johnston and Daniel J. Crosby (Wipf & Stock, 2015).

www.ingramcontent.com/pod-product-compliance
Lightning Source LLC
Chambersburg PA
CBHW060600230426
43670CB00011B/1899